D0323917

Independent Schoolmaster

BY CLAUDE M. FUESS

THE LIFE OF CALEB CUSHING

RUFUS CHOATE, THE WIZARD OF THE LAW

DANIEL WEBSTER (2 vols.)

CARL SCHURZ, REFORMER (1829–1906)

AMHERST: THE STORY OF A NEW ENGLAND COLLEGE

CREED OF A SCHOOLMASTER

CALVIN COOLIDGE: THE MAN FROM VERMONT

JOSEPH B. EASTMAN: SERVANT OF THE PEOPLE

INDEPENDENT SCHOOLMASTER

Photo by George H. Davis Studio

Claude Moore Fuess

From a painting by R. S. Meryman

Independent Schoolmaster

by CLAUDE M. FUESS

An Atlantic Monthly Press Book

Little, Brown and Company · Boston

LIBRARY OF CONGRESS CATALOG CARD NO. 52-9092

FIRST EDITION

ATLANTIC-LITTLE, BROWN BOOKS
ARE PUBLISHED BY
LITTLE, BROWN AND COMPANY
IN ASSOCIATION WITH
THE ATLANTIC MONTHLY PRESS

Published simultaneously
in Canada by McClelland and Stewart Limited

PRINTED IN THE UNITED STATES OF AMERICA

To
LULIE

Uneasy lie the heads of all that rule,
He most of all whose kingdom is a school.

"The School-Boy,"
OLIVER WENDELL HOLMES

Now, there is no one more easy to trace than a schoolmaster.

Sherlock Holmes,
The Hound of the Baskervilles,
A. CONAN DOYLE

Foreword

ASIDE from the ingrained propensity of all men to talk about themselves, the best excuse for this excursion into autobiography is that for more than forty years I was close to the center of things in the evolution of American secondary education. Because of my position at Phillips Academy and of my connection with the Headmasters Association, the New England Association of Colleges and Secondary Schools, and the College Entrance Examination Board, as well as other educational groups, I was acquainted with what was going on and in many instances helped to make the decisions — *Pars Minima Fui*. The period covered was one of startling change and changes, not merely in the everyday details of living but in basic philosophy. Not only the *mores* but even the fundamental concepts of adult men and women were altered, and it was inevitable that boys and girls should also modify their views and conduct. This development was due in part to the impact of two global wars, with consequent shifts in American political, economic, and cultural theory. But whatever the causes, the process of education at Andover in 1948 was very different from what it was when I went there in 1908. Indeed it may be asserted that the changes of the last half century in education as well as in scientific discovery have been more far-reaching than those of the preceding thousand years. And the movement is not yet finished!

If this is true, the comments, however casual, of one who

saw and participated in these developments may be interesting not only to my fellow teachers but even to those citizens who watch education with a blending of fear and hope. This volume should reflect the growth — if I may call it that! — of a schoolmaster who started in the conservative tradition and is ending with a passion for experimentation in the light of new knowledge. The longer I remained active as a teacher, the more convinced I became that all of us in the profession have much to learn and that the future of our confused communities depends largely on the capacity of our schools for adjustment to changed conditions. The powers which control education in this country must decide whether to remain resistant to progressive ideas or to work with new media and perhaps towards different objectives. Just what steps we should take to meet emergencies is not always clear, but from my viewpoint we have only one sound choice. Lowell's observation, "New occasions teach new duties," applies to education as well as to political crises. The inexcusable crime is to remain static.

Something of this gradually deepening conviction will doubtless come out unconsciously in what I have to say. I am not rash enough to predict what will happen in the next quarter century, but education for American young men will not be the same in 1977 as it is now. Daniel Webster once declaimed, "The past at least is secure," and at any rate we can do nothing about it. What we can do is to look forward with our minds open, our opinions flexible, and our faith unshaken. In this mood we can face the future with some confidence, realizing the inevitable fluctuations of human history.

I am very grateful to the people and the circumstances which have enabled me to pursue an occupation so important in our society. The schoolmaster, if he functions properly, should literally mold the characters of the young and thus determine the reactions of the middle-aged and the old. We should choose him, — or her, — carefully, give him the freedom under which he flourishes, reward him adequately, and encourage him with our confidence. Thus treated, he will be a primary factor in the creation of that Brave New World which we all in our heart of hearts desire.

C. M. F.

Chestnut Hill, Massachusetts

Contents

Independent Schoolmaster

I

Background

AS I think back, it seems to me that all my life I have been either the victim or the instrument of education. Yet I should probably never have become a schoolmaster if a huge, rather arrogant-looking Amherst College professor named George Bosworth Churchill, on a gloomy afternoon in November 1904, had not read to his English class in his deep-throated voice a poem beginning:

Five years have past; five summers, with the length
Of five long winters! And again I hear
These waters, rolling from their mountain springs
With a soft inland murmur.

I had come to Amherst in the autumn of 1901, a callow youth of sixteen, from a little village in the Mohawk Valley, intending rather vaguely to enter the law and succeed my father in his office. My scholastic career up to that point might well have been described as aimless; and when the imposing Churchill began to recite from "Tintern Abbey," I was in just the right mood to be susceptible to his own emotion and the magic of Wordsworth's verses. Then and there I underwent a conversion — on a lower level like that which transformed Saul of Tarsus or John Bunyan. Suddenly, but irrevocably, I resolved that I must study English literature — that I must dedicate myself to the pursuit of learning. In later life, I often listened to Robert Frost as he read his own lines:

Two roads diverged in a wood, and I—
I took the one less traveled by,
And that has made all the difference.

At precisely that point in my undergraduate days the choice between two professions was made. The road which I took was one seldom traversed by my family, but it has indeed made "all the difference."

My education in Americanism began long before I came into the world, and the story will show how readily "foreigners" were assimilated in the United States in the mid-nineteenth century. My grandfather, Jacob Fuess, was born in Annweiler, a small and ancient village located in the picturesque, semimountainous district of the Rheinpfalz, or Bavarian Palatinate, perhaps fifty miles north of Strassburg. When I paid it a visit in 1906, I approached by railroad from Speyer, twenty-five miles to the east across the Rhine Valley. It was then a provincial, hospitable, gossipy place, removed from the main currents of modern thought, in which at festivals the peasants still wore unashamed the quaint, traditional costumes handed down from their ancestors. The French border at Nancy was not far off, and many of the residents, like my own cousins, traced their lineage back to Huguenots expelled from France by Louis, the Sun King, in 1685, through the tragic revocation of the Edict of Nantes.

In 1906, however, the Fuesses still in Annweiler seemed thoroughly Teutonic in speech and appearance, with no traces of their French origin. But they were Bavarians, not Prussians, and were careful to explain to me the difference. Their private inclinations were clearly not militaristic. Rather they acted like a peace-loving folk, unambitious for themselves and with no desire for further *Lebensraum*. Like the Yankees of rural Vermont, they were happiest when left alone.

My grandfather might have dwelt there all his life if he

had not been unexpectedly caught up in the whirlwind of a European popular revolt. Like many thoughtful Bavarian youths, he had a dream of a United Germany, with a constitutional government; and when a German parliament assembled on May 18, 1848, at Frankfort on the Main, he attended as a member, although he was only nineteen. Unfortunately this body, which had hoped to bring together all the German states, had no strong leader. Finally when in sheer futility it elected Frederick William IV, King of Prussia, as hereditary Kaiser, that timid and obstinate monarch, under pressure from jealous Austria, perversely declined the leadership of the new empire. Young Carl Schurz, at the University of Bonn, whose biography I was to publish in 1932, helped to organize a protest, and King Frederick William soon had on his hands the necessity of suppressing some other minor rebellions.

My grandfather died in 1891, when I was only six years old, and I cannot recall many of the stories which he told of his hazardous boyhood. His father, John, remained royalist in his views, as did the oldest son, my grandfather's brother, Philip; but Jacob and his younger brother, John, joined the revolutionists. Once when the old gentleman, my great-grandfather, was captured and condemned to death by a party of guerrilla insurrectionists, he was saved by the unexpected arrival of a troop in which his two rebel sons, Jacob and John, were soldiers. As the war turned inevitably against the poorly equipped rebels, the Rheinpfalz became less and less salubrious for Jacob, who fled across the border and ultimately made his way to America, disembarking at New Orleans and proceeding to New York City. As far as I am aware, he was the first member of my family and the first citizen of Annweiler to come to the United States from Germany. How he earned a living in those early days I do not know, but he did send for his sweetheart, Johanna Valeria Woerner, who came to join him, and they were married in New York City on September 14, 1854. Two years younger than he, she belonged to a wealthy and distinguished family which had lost its money when she was a girl of twelve.

After his marriage, my grandfather continued to live for some years in New York City, where his two oldest children, Jacob and Louis (my father) were born. He had neither the ability nor the inclination to enter political life, like his friend, Carl Schurz, nor did he join the Northern army, like so many of his compatriots. By that time he had his sons to care for, and he could not be spared. He was by every instinct a country man. His family for generations had been brickmakers and tilers in Annweiler, and he was unhappy in the bustle of a large city. About 1870, he purchased a farm just outside of Waterville, in Oneida County, New York, about twenty miles south of Utica, and there introduced the cultivation of hops, which he had seen in the Rhine Valley. Within a few years Waterville became, with Oregon and Kent, one of the world's great hop centers. Indeed the prosperity of that countryside was shortly to depend largely on the annual income from hops, and when in one golden year the price reached a dollar a pound, every farmer thought himself a prospective millionaire. As Jacob Fuess wrote back to Germany about his modest prosperity, other members of the family emigrated, and by the close of the century I had many second and third cousins in that locality.

My grandfather certainly did not become wealthy, but he soon was making an adequate income. His farm at Conger's Corners stood at the top of a moderately high hill, overlooking what was then called the Nine Mile Swamp, which filled the valley to the east with almost impossible underbrush and marshland and was the hiding place of the notorious Loomis Gang of horse thieves. The view, although attractive, was not as noble as that at Annweiler, where the pine-girt Trifels, sixteen hundred feet high, dominated the landscape. The soil, moreover, was not rich, and hard labor was required from each male child as he became physically strong enough to work. But Jacob Fuess was his own master — a fact to him of immense importance — and even as a child I learned from him the value of *Freiheit.*

Even when other Fuesses arrived with their families, they did not, like their fellow immigrants in Wisconsin and Missouri, keep up their *Turnvereins* and rural celebrations. The melting pot in their case very quickly transmuted them into Americans. They had found what they wanted. Their faces were turned towards the future, not backward towards the past. As soon as possible both my grandparents became American citizens. Jacob Fuess was known locally as "that Dutchman," as Schurz was among his Washington friends, but he himself had no doubt where his allegiance belonged.

As I recall him dimly, my grandfather was a tall erect man, of dignified bearing, and a rather unusual type of beard once known as an imperial. His eyes were those of a visionary, sunk rather deep in their sockets, and I was later told that in practical matters he was as guileless as a baby. Because he learned English so late in life, he always retained a foreign accent, and his speech was punctuated with interjections which sounded in English much more profane than they were intended to be in German. He died of pneumonia, when he was only sixty-two years old. He had never returned to Germany, and apparently had few regrets at having been exiled. My grandmother, who survived him twelve years, presents a much clearer picture to my mind. Although I was often told that in her girlhood she was the belle of Annweiler, I remember her as much wrinkled, with a white ruff around her neck and a lace cap on her head, looking very much like one of Rembrandt's portraits. To the end she still spoke German with some of her children and other relatives, and she taught me to say *Gute Nacht* and *Guten Morgen.* At Christmas she always prepared a gorgeous tree, decorated with ornaments brought from the Fatherland. In the kitchen were baked the well-known kuchen, filled with caraway seeds and cut into the shapes of animals. Holly and mistletoe were all over the home, and on Christmas Eve we sang carols very lustily. My first recollection of "O Tannenbaum!" is from my grandmother's gentle soprano. As she grew older, her thoughts turned more and more to the past, and she talked with nostalgic sentimentality of the Trifels and the impressive mansion which had been her home. Actually she never really wished to go back. Her children, when she would weep a little over her girlhood, accepted it as an elderly lady's transient weakness. They were happy enough where they were. So was she!

Jacob Fuess had naturally some problems connected with anglicization of his name. Originally spelled Füsz, it presented difficulties in both lettering and pronunciation, and finally he resolved to substitute *ue* for the unfamiliar umlaut. As for the pronunciation, it was certain that no American could reproduce the correct German sounds. The family seem to have wavered between *Fease* and *Feece,* with a preference for the former. My friends tell me that the two are equally bad. I have become accustomed to answering to *Fuss, Few-ess, Fuse, Feis,* and *Foos.* In fact, no pronunciation of the name has ever startled me very much. The following bit of doggerel, published when my *Daniel Webster* came out, will illustrate the difficulties in pronunciation:

FUESS PLEASE

He'll exclaim, "Oh, what's the use!"
When he hears you utter "Fuess."
And he'll like it even less
If you say it's Mr. Fuess.

If you want to hear him cuss
Just be sure to call him Fuess.
All his wonted calm he'll lose
If perchance you murmur "Fuess";
But he'll thank you on his knees
If you will but call him "Fuess."

My father, when he was enrolled in Columbia Law School, was tempted to alter the spelling, but finally through what he described as "sheer inertia" continued the accepted form. During World War I, when the feeling against Germans ran high, several of my well-meaning associates advised me to simplify my name, but by that date I was identified, for good or ill, with it as it stood. Furthermore the legal difficulties involved were considerable, and I had developed a strong sense of clan loyalty. After all, the name had been honorably held in Bavaria, and I did not wish to abandon what it represented there as well as here. It is interesting that although I was for several months in the army, nobody at any time commented on my conspicuously German name. Actually I was no more of a foreigner at heart than a Saltonstall or a Bradford or a Phillips, with their heritage of continuity.

As I have said, neither my grandfather nor my father kept in close touch with Germany. Of my seven Fuess uncles and aunts, not one as an adult had the faintest trace of an accent. My father, growing up in a household where German was habitually spoken by his parents, carried small acquaintance with the language into later life, while he employed English as if his ancestors had been in this country for nine generations. The rapidity with which the children adjusted themselves to the talk of their schoolmates was remarkable. Their French forebears had become Germans; now they themselves were becoming Americans. I cannot recall in my home as a child any pictures of German scenes, any books in the German language, any memorabilia of my grandfather's revolutionary days. Everything was "made in the U.S.A."

None of the children of Jacob and Johanna Fuess had any interest in agriculture, and they all escaped from it as soon as they could, not forgetting to tell "tall stories" of their struggles and privations. My father, Louis Philip Fuess, is an interesting example of what happened to the second generation. As a small boy he attended intermittently the local "district school." Then he persuaded his father to allow him to enroll in the Waterville High School, two miles off, and walked back and forth each weekday, carrying his lunch with him. He did well there in his studies, but when he was graduated, further doors of learning seemed closed. There was no reason why he should not have settled down on some neighboring farm, like other boys whom he knew — no reason but his driving ambition. When he reached the age of twenty-one, he quietly but firmly told my grandfather that he would stay at Conger's Corners no longer. Going to Waterville, the only metropolis in the vicinity, he studied law in the old-fashioned Websterian way in the office of "Squire Lamb"; and it was through the wise influence of this elder attorney that my father took the astonishing step of going to New York City to enter a law school. So it was that, at the age of twenty-six, after being admitted to the bar, this son of a German immigrant hung out his shingle in Waterville and waited for clients.

Meanwhile he had become engaged to my mother, Helen Augusta Moore, whose genealogical tree is rooted in New England magistrates and clergymen, so that I now belong to the Society of Colonial Wars. It was a strange whim of fate which brought together a man and a woman of such different origins — one all German, the other all Welsh and English. My mother was supposed to have married slightly beneath her in taking a husband with a name and family so clearly alien. Indeed her two sisters occasionally indulged in mild banter at the expense of her new "in-laws." But she had too much common sense and individuality to be sensitive to the critical comments of her own people. Lou Fuess may have been a "Dutchman," but he was also a promising young attorney, and she loved him. That was enough for her. My father used to enjoy the story of the inquisitive snob who once asked a man with a name much like my own, "Did your ancestors come over on the *Mayflower?*" "No," was the reply, "they arrived when the immigration laws were more stringent!"

My younger brother and I were brought up as American boys in the democratic atmosphere of a country village, and it never occurred to me that there was anything to be ashamed of about my name or antecedents. It is true that my playmates promptly nicknamed me "Dutch," in spite of my protests and my readiness to use my fists in warding off the inevitable. When I went to Amherst College, it was with the hope that I was at last rid of the obnoxious nickname; but my closest friend, who accompanied me there, saw to it that it was not forgotten. So it was that I was Dutch all through college — indeed still am to my classmates when we assemble at reunions.

Once when Amy Lowell had been dining at my house after a lecture, with her companion, Ada Russell — whom she commonly called "Peter" — she turned to me suddenly and inquired, "What's your first name?" Just a little ashamed I answered, "Claude." Then Miss Lowell cried, "Peter, come here!"; and putting one arm around my shoulder and the other around Miss Russell she exclaimed gleefully, "Here we are — the three worst names in the world — Ada, Amy, and Claude!"

My first wife early in our acquaintance indicated a similar

aversion to my Christian name and asked whether I would not choose a suitable nickname for her benefit. We shortly agreed that Jack was a name with good connotations, and almost from that moment I was "Jack" Fuess to everybody in Andover — like "Peter" Higginson and "Dono" Minot and other Harvard celebrities who were rechristened. So it developed that I now, in different environments, respond to three names: Claude back in my home town; Dutch at Amherst reunions; and Jack with all my friends of post-collegiate days.

Not until I reached graduate school and had begun to spend my summers in travel did I develop any sentiment about Germany. In 1906, I deviated from the conventional tourists' route down the Rhine and spent three days with my relatives in Annweiler. Their hospitality was unbounded. They walked me at dawn to the summit of the Trifels, regaled me with the delicious *vin du pays,* and shouted German melodies to the accompaniment of the zither. From their conversation it was clear that the United States was to them a land of promise and that I myself, for the first and only time, was regarded as a man of wealth. They were simple people, with good taste in music and a cheerful attitude towards life; but I was even then conscious that the young men had always to be ready for war, like puppets waiting for the master hand. My male cousins showed me their orders in case of mobilization and talked as if conquests were in the air, and I didn't like it. They seemed bewildered when I pressed them as to what was impending, but they were resigned to whatever might happen. I enjoyed the beauty of the Rhine and the rustic charm of the Bavarian countryside. I could appreciate Bach and Mozart and Beethoven, Schiller and Goethe, Hauptmann and Sudermann, but my heart was not with the Bismarckian philosophy. I could feel no strong bond with a country so different from the one in which I had been born and of which I felt myself a part. Within ten years, many of those unbelligerent German youths had been killed in a war for which they could have had no desire.

With the outbreak of the First World War, I heard and read much of "hyphenated Americans" — but there were none in the Fuess family. To them the Germany of Bismarck and Kaiser Wilhelm II was not the Germany of Luther or of Goethe. I had rather feared that my father, only one generation removed, might lean towards the Germans against the British. But not at all! His letters to me indicated that as soon as the German troops entered Belgium, his moral sense was outraged, and he would hear no more talk about the "Fatherland." He knew as well as I that millions of Germans were naturally peace-loving people, but he was equally convinced that they were misguided. If the Berlin government, even in those days, hoped that the descendants of German immigrants in the United States would be sympathetic with the Kaiser's policies, it was soon disillusioned.

I early reached the conclusion that the doctrine of a Master Race was sheer nonsense. In this connection I must relate a hitherto unpublished story. In my biography of Carl Schurz I referred more than once, in passing, to Schurz's marriage with Margarethe Meyer, daughter of a "well-to-do Jewish manufacturer of Hamburg." That Mrs. Schurz had Jewish ancestry was well-known in her family, and Schurz himself mentioned it frankly in his letters. In 1935, when Hitler had come to power, a letter arrived for me from the Carl Schurz Foundation in Berlin stating categorically that Mrs. Schurz was of pure Aryan stock — *dass Frau Schurz, geb. Meyer, rein arischer Herkunft ist.* Evidently I was regarded as impertinent for having disclosed the facts. Even in dealing with the dead it was thought necessary to keep the legend of Aryan supremacy unsullied.

In my blood, I am sure, was a belief in the rights and privileges of all men, and a conception of the United States as a land of opportunity. These concepts were talked about in my home and perhaps account for my responsiveness when Professor Churchill read from "Tintern Abbey." I knew that because my grandfather had sought liberty in America, I could with freedom choose my own way of living.

II

Small-Town Boyhood

AS I have explained, part of my education happened painlessly, before I was born. Even more of it came to me as a child in a small country village, where I formed my first conceptions of the universe. Waterville was on the D.L. & W. Railroad (known locally, and unjustly, as the "Delay, Linger, and Wait"), and trains rushed through it on a direct route to New York; nevertheless in preautomobile days it was isolated and had to provide its own industries and diversions. Why it was named Waterville I cannot explain, for it has no stream except what is euphemistically called Big Creek and no lakes except Dead Pond and Tower's Pond, two infinitesimal and by no means pellucid bodies of water. One mile to the south lies the hamlet of Sangerfield, on the Cherry Valley Turnpike, now a crowded cross-state motor highway, and Waterville is today within easy access of urban centers like Utica and Syracuse. In the 1890's when I was growing up it was in the midst of an agricultural community, and retired farmers moved to it in their old age to find solace and society.

My father was a country lawyer who worked hard and was in his later life a leading citizen. His wedding bells had hardly ceased to ring before he was beset by two misfortunes: he was sued for a note which he had endorsed for a friend to the amount of $1500 — much more money than he had in the world — and he came down with typhoid fever. While he was convalescing, his first son, named Claude Moore, was born. Having passed through these ordeals, he prospered and by careful living became well to do. His acquaintance with the financial difficulties, the marital differences, the pleasant vices of his neighbors was profound. He knew what farms were held on mortgages, what accounts at the bank were overdrawn, what the local minister had to pay to keep his brother out of jail, why one farmer committed suicide and another vanished into the unknown. He was the repository of countless secrets and kept them all to himself.

I should like, if possible, to present an accurate picture of that village as I remember it. It was a perfect democracy, with virtually no social distinctions, except for the "summer folks" who came for July and August; and even these notabilities put on no airs as they drove or walked about. At dancing school and church festivals and Grange Hall we were on the same level — although my mother, who did not like what she called the "shanty Irish," frequently looked dismayed when she saw me dancing with a pretty girl of Celtic extraction. Senator Coggeshall's boys and the sons of the saloon-keepers were equally acceptable as waltz partners. Whatever some of the more opulent residents may have felt in their hearts, there was no recognized aristocracy.

The population was extraordinarily homogeneous, composed chiefly of Anglo-Saxon elements, descended from settlers who had migrated in the late eighteenth century from Connecticut. Among my boyhood friends were Wilsons, Terrys, Congers, Kings, Joneses, Bissells, Mayers, Westcotts, Emmonses, Bennetts, Jewetts, and Brainards, with a few Ryans and Murphys; indeed my name was almost the only one with any exotic connotations.

The village was so democratic that everybody, old or young, was called by his first name, or a nickname. As a mere fledgling I used to speak thus intimately to "Lon" King, a veteran of the Battle of Gettysburg, and "Dan" Hill, a blithe spirit of not less than seventy. The Town Supervisor, "Mert" Felton, was at one time sent to Sing Sing Prison because of a slight error in his accounts. When he returned from his incarceration, he resumed his familiar seat on the front porch, living by the money which his faithful wife earned through dressmaking. Every morning he strolled to the post office to get the circulars which comprised his mail. Once as I was striding along sturdily by his side down Madison Street, I asked, "Mert, how did you like being in jail?" Quite unembarrassed, he replied, "Young fella, when I first came back I worried about it a lot — couldn't sleep at night — didn't want to see any of my old friends; but then I thought it over, and now I don't give a damn!"

Although the scale of living was not high, there was no dire poverty, and everybody could find work of some kind. In our community there were only a few servants, and we boys felt proud when mother engaged our first "hired girl," named Maggie, at the wages of two dollars a week. Even after that my mother, unwilling to let any one else take over, did most of the cooking, leaving it to Maggie to make the beds, sweep the rooms, and watch out for us children. Each housewife was locally famous for some special dish, like chocolate cake or doughnuts, and regularly made that her contribution to church suppers and Grange parties. My mother's was Saratoga Chips, and when these were being prepared, they took precedence over everything else in the home economy. There were no dinners, formal or informal, although we often had guests for Sunday luncheon. In the Fuess household, as in nearly every other, alcoholic beverages were taboo. Nobody would ever have thought of serving cocktails or wine at a meal. The saloon was the horrible place where that craving was satisfied. In the Fuess family one of the worst charges against a neighbor was, "He drinks!" Some experiments which I carried on with California Port — twenty-five cents a bottle — had to be planned surreptitiously, and the results were disastrous.

My father stopped smoking after his two sons were born, in order to set us a good example. The consequence of this sacrifice was that I smoked almost everything, beginning with tea and "doc" seed and corn silk, and continuing through old horsewhip (made of rattan), dried leaves, cubebs, Sweet Caporals, and Cycles — twenty for five cents — the last unquestionably the rankest form of alleged tobacco ever placed on sale. But all our smoking was done stealthily, usually in the woods. Not until I returned from college as a freshman did I venture to light a cigarette in my father's presence. He then calmly but happily resumed the habit which he had abandoned fifteen years before.

It sounds like a dull community, but the members did not find it so. The Pickwick Club, for men only, offered relaxation to my father, who punctually returned to his office after supper to be available for business with farmers driving in for the evening. About eight o'clock, if clients were lacking or had left, he would stroll up the street to the club and there play pool, billiards, or hearts until just before ten. He was a first-class left-handed billiard player, and more than once a stranger, warned that Lou Fuess could beat him left-handed, would find himself after the game minus two or three cigars — the stakes being small. My mother in the meantime, after the dishes had been cleaned up, would seek a table of hearts or whist with her women neighbors — of course not for money. Occasionally in those days before the movies, a troupe would visit the Opera House and present *Uncle Tom's Cabin* or *Ten Nights in a Barroom* or *Fritz in a Madhouse*. Less frequently local talent would stage a show for the benefit of some charity and the theater would be packed with parents eager to hear their children perform.

Through the winter the Grange, with its spacious hall, was the center of social activity, and we had card parties, dances, and other entertainments to our hearts' content. The popular dances were the Money Musk, the lancers, and the quadrille, but the returning college boys brought back with them the two-step and the waltz, which were regarded as very lively.

My father, perhaps as a result of his farm experience, had a very annoying conception of "the dignity of labor" for his children, and I was commissioned at the appropriate seasons of the year to spade the garden, mow the lawn, cut the asparagus, dig the potatoes, rake the leaves, and shovel snow. I began this as a small boy of six or seven, and always I had to complete my chores before I was allowed to play — unless my merciful mother intervened when she thought her sons were tired. In Waterville the great period of the year was "hop picking" during the first two weeks of September, when virtually everybody except the housewives went into the fields for a few days to earn spending money. I started as a boy of perhaps seven or eight to pick hops, at the rate of forty cents a box. When I reached fifteen, I was promoted to box-tender, with the duty of pulling poles and supplying the pickers with vines for stripping. For this ten-hour-a-day job I received $1.75 a day, and earned it. We wore white canvas gloves to protect our hands from the rough vines and the almost ineradicable dark stain which the hop juices produced. There was a good deal of fun about it all — some harmless kissing of the pretty girls and plenty of rough-and-ready repartee.

During the hop-picking season hundreds of people, mostly Italians and Poles, came to the little village for what might be called a "working vacation" from Syracuse, Rome, and Utica, and the evenings saw the saloons doing a rushing business. Those who had picked hops all day tested the brew of the hops at night. Fakirs, patent medicine sellers, evangelists, and vendors had their stands set up along Main Street, and sometimes the crowds would pack the square. How proud I felt when my mother permitted my brother and me to stay out after eight o'clock and watch what was going on! Sometimes a mouth organ or an accordion would start up, the ranks would part, and two or three "foreigners" would undertake a native dance, to the delight of the spectators. Most of the visitors spent in recreation what they had earned during a hard day's work: but the whole experience was to them a holiday, a relief from city pavements, a return to their peasant festivals, and they liked it! For them, and for us girls and boys, it had all the elements of romance, with its flaming torches, its color, its vibrant music, and its flirtations in the park under the stars.

One spectacle particularly absorbed my attention. A traveling preacher stood with a pointer in his hand, explaining a large strip of canvas divided into two sections, one depicting the successive steps in a modern "Rake's Progress," the other showing "Virtue Rewarded." On the left half at the top was a fine fresh-faced youngster following down the "primrose path of dalliance," being seduced into smoking his first cigarette; and below were crude drawings of him as he sank lower and lower, drinking his first glass of beer, then being enticed by a damsel clearly no better than she should be, stealthily robbing his employer's till, and finally in an ecstasy of viciousness slaying his employer, like Lizzie Borden, "with an axe." The last scene ending this "strange eventful history" revealed the sinner as roasting in what anybody could see was a well-heated environment, as a punishment for his wrong-doing. On the other side another equally attractive boy began by refusing to smoke a cubeb. Then he moved upward, declining to listen to profanity, rejecting an invitation to play poker, and resisting even the temptation to go swimming on Sunday. Eventually, as he drew near the top, he married the boss's blonde daughter and at last was disclosed in a place of pearly gates, playing an instrument of at least ten strings, and magnificently crowned. The lessons for us boys should have been obvious, but I regret to say that we were moved only to ridicule. At the end of an impassioned discourse, when the preacher called upon his audience to testify, more than one of us would have loved to step forward, but we did not quite dare. Some fear of being eternally damned held us back. Perhaps Hell might be a very real place!

These religious ideas were not remote to me and my childhood companions. From an early age I was accustomed to Sunday school and church; and as I approached adolescence the lure of girls drew me also to Christian Endeavor and evening service in the Presbyterian Church. I was received into the fold at the age of eight, following a recital of the Shorter Catechism. My father, slightly on the skeptical side, approved of the church as an institution and accordingly allowed himself to be made an elder, an office which did not require membership. He was a regular attendant and, with considerable dignity, passed the collection plate. He also disagreed almost audibly with those ministers who relied on orthodoxy to get them by. The visiting speakers from Hamilton College and Colgate University were much more to father's liking, probably because they were more ethical than theological.

On Sunday afternoons we were walked on a pious pilgrimage to the cemetery, my brother and I in front, wearing identical velvet suits and white Eton collars, both feeling uncomfortable and very much annoyed. In a photograph taken when we were about five and seven respectively we looked like two innocent cherubs, with our heads placed lovingly together; but I distinctly recall in my exasperation whispering to him at the moment, "Wait till we get out of this and I'll knock your block off!" Remember, he was younger than I! As we grew up, our parents weakened to the extent of hiring a surrey and going for a drive into the country. It was less gruesome than the procession to the cemetery and soon became, by common consent, our accepted pastime for Sunday afternoon. In the evening we gathered around the organ in the parlor to sing "Moody and Sankey" hymns, such as "Shall we gather at the river?"; "I am so glad that Jesus loves me!"; "God be with you till we meet again"; "Pull for the shore, sailor, pull for the shore!"; "Let a little sunshine in"; and "Jesus, Saviour, pilot me." Later on at Andover, when the school organist, Dr. Pfatteicher, a virtuoso and musical critic of eminence, would comment sorrowfully on my taste in hymns, I could only take refuge in sentimentality and nostalgia.

School for me was, of course, the public grammar and high school, preparing for the so-called New York State Regents' Examinations. Five of us, one girl and four boys, were the last pupils in the Waterville High School to take Greek. It is true that our teacher completely ignored the accents and the breathings, so that my indifference to them caused vigorous comment when I arrived in Amherst and had to compete with graduates of Andover and Exeter; but he did catch the spirit of Xenophon and Homer, even though our translations left much to be desired. As for Virgil, we accepted it frankly as a romantic adventure and, without paying too much attention to grammar, drove our way through book after book, reading entirely for pleasure. I hardly knew a caesura from an antepenult, but I loved the sound of the lines! We had mathematics, very badly taught, through plane geometry, but no science. Because I was a wide reader, with a quick, flexible mind and an excellent memory, I did well on examinations, with the result that I acquired a larger number of Regents' credits than any one had ever secured in the state up to that time and was in grave danger of being regarded as a prodigy. Fortunately I was enough of a hell-raiser to escape that fate; and when I arrived in college, my instructors soon discovered — and told me — how little I knew.

At an unbelievably early age I was an indiscriminate and omnivorous reader, and that passion has not yet abated. *The Count of Monte Cristo* was my first and best-loved romance. I liked everything — Horatio Alger and Oliver Optic, Louisa M. Alcott, and H. Rider Haggard, *St. Nicholas, The Youth's Companion, Golden Days* and (when I could find a copy!) the *Police Gazette.* I read all the volumes in the Sunday school library, from *Raftmates* to *Queechy,* until the librarian insisted that I could not possibly have gone through them so fast. Once — it must have been about 1895 — I came home from the village library with a new novel called *Jude, the Obscure.* My Aunt Jennie Watson, who had been a schoolteacher, picked it up one evening and read the first three or four chapters. She then turned to my mother and asked, "Do you know what Claude has taken out of the library?" There was a family conference, at which I pleaded my innocence of wrong; but the book was confiscated and I never read it again until I reached college. I can to this day recall the circumstances under which I read for the first time *David Copperfield, The Man Who Would Be King, Nostromo, Far from the Madding Crowd,* and *The Hound of the Baskervilles.* I told my mother at the age of nine or ten that my main ambition was to write a book which somebody would buy — although I never dreamed that such a desire could be realized.

In certain respects my early education was notably deficient. I took piano lessons as a child and acquired just enough proficiency to annoy the neighbors and not enough to please myself. I never heard a symphony concert until I went for the first time to Boston at the age of eighteen. I was never in an art gallery until I came to live in New York. And I knew nothing of poetry beyond Longfellow and Whittier.

The life which the Waterville boys enjoyed led them, without realizing it, to depend on themselves for their diversions. Not being regimented or guided, they developed an amazing degree of ingenuity and initiative. We made our own plans for our athletic teams, asking one of the two male teachers to coach us if he could, but carrying out the arrangements ourselves without their help. We created the first football eleven ever to represent the Waterville High School, managing to wangle enough money from our parents to buy a pigskin and some cheap uniforms. Our first game, against the nearby mill village of Oriskany Falls, was a victory by a score of 11 to 6, thanks to my picking up by sheer luck a fumbled punt and running the length of the field for a touchdown. After that our heads swelled to enormous size, and we began to dream of ourselves as the greatest schoolboy team east of the Alleghenies. Our next contest was with Colgate Academy, a preparatory school fourteen miles away. We drove there in a hay wagon, singing as we went and absolutely confident. The Colgate boys appeared with nose guards and shin guards, the first we had ever seen. When we kicked off, a massive Colgate backfielder caught the ball and started down the field, dodging, changing pace, and slipping through our players as if he had no opposition. Finally he had passed everybody except me, and I was directly in his path. The hour was ripe for heroism, and I prepared to stop him in his tracks. But almost before I knew what had happened, he had pushed me aside with a stiff arm, and I was lying, flat and ashamed, while he dashed on for a touchdown. The same thing occurred again and again and again, and the final score was 87–0. We returned home that evening, chastened and unmusical. It was only one of many times when my hope of becoming a Frank Merriwell was shattered. That defeat was definitely part of my education.

In one other form of athletics I was slightly more successful. We organized the first track team ever formed in the village, and some of us spent all one summer vaulting with bean poles over the clothesline, manufacturing hurdles, and earning enough money by odd jobs to buy a twelve-pound shot and a hammer. The bicycle races were my events, and I practiced diligently on the old dirt half-mile track, where the county fair was regularly held. I got into condition by making what were called "century runs" — a ride, with several companions, of one hundred miles on a cinder path, laid out by the side of the customary dirt roads of those preautomotive days. In the triangular meet with Oriskany Falls and Clayville, I won the half-mile and the mile bicycle races, thus getting two prizes: a standing lamp, considerably the worse for the wear, and an umbrella discarded by a local store as too ancient to be sold. Encouraged by this success I entered in bicycle races at fairs in adjoining counties, and now and then was fortunate enough to win. When I entered Amherst, my reputation as a champion had preceded me, and I trained all through the fall to make the track team in the spring. In February, however, the New England Committee met and abolished the bicycle race as one of the regular events. Once again I had been balked of my athletic ambitions and having met with disappointment, had taken another step in my education.

It seems to me now that we carried normal boyish activities to abnormal lengths. There was a slack period in the winter when, debarred from many outdoor sports, we developed forensic ambitions. I asked some advice from my father, who as a lawyer naturally had practiced public speaking, and then we resurrected some antiquated oil lamps, cleaned and filled them, and begged from the principal permission to use a room in the school basement where we could carry on debates. For weeks I memorized long passages from Daniel Webster and Robert G. Ingersoll and Wendell Phillips, some of which I can still recite, and we carried on discussions with a fervor which astonished our parents. The light from the lamps was dim and the smell from the furnace pipes unaromatic, but our ardor did not wane. Then and there an interest was aroused which has lasted all my life. My biographies of Rufus Choate and Daniel Webster were largely the result of that early passion for oratory.

Not everything was joy during those hard Mohawk Valley winters when the earth was literally "a universe of sky and snow." Usually after Christmas I would pick up an ear infection and come home from school with an earache, spending agonizing hours until the abscess broke and I had relief. Everybody has his vulnerable physical spot, and there could be no doubt that the ears were mine. My mother used a "hop bag" to allay the inflammation; the local doctor, T. Z. Jones, commonly known as T.Z., tried modern methods of shrinking my tonsils and blistering my head to avert mastoiditis, but nothing worked as a preventative. It seemed to me that earache was an ordeal to which I was doomed by the nature of things. The wonder is that I was able to keep up with my classes in school when such long interruptions occurred; but even when I was suffering most I could still read. It was a great comfort.

Of all the older men that I knew, my father excepted, the outstanding figure was Senator Henry J. Coggeshall — the Coggy of New York State politics, known as the "Tall Sycamore of Oneida County." That section had already produced Roscoe Conkling, Grover Cleveland, and James S. Sherman — Sunny Jim — not to mention other minor personages, but no one of these was more richly endowed by the gods than

Coggy. More than six feet in height, slender and graceful in bearing, with a melodious voice which had about it a wooing, glamorous quality, he could move men as few speakers I have ever heard. He exuded charm. But Coggy was also easygoing, and in an era when "influence" was very widespread, he did not resist temptation. It was easy for him in those days to secure passes for his constituents on the New York Central Railroad, and I blush to admit that on my trips back and forth from Amherst I usually traveled on a pass signed by Chauncey M. Depew, and thought nothing of it.

Those were the days of torchlight processions and uniformed political clubs, and I well remember marching in a McKinley parade in 1896, when I was only eleven years old, absolutely certain that somebody called Bryan was as dangerous as the Devil himself. My father was a Gold Standard Democrat, who voted in 1896 for Palmer and Buckner, but evidently was not disturbed by my joining the Republicans. In the 1900's, Senator Coggeshall was a candidate for the gubernatorial nomination and was escorted to a special train from the Waterville station by virtually the entire population. But something happened at the Republican convention. His indiscretions may have caught up with him, or his money may have given out. At any rate, his followers came home bitterly disappointed, and he himself was never quite the same again. A little later he was repudiated by his Republican adherents, who gave another aspirant the nomination for state Senator; whereupon Coggeshall, with magnificent audacity, presented himself to the Democratic convention, was nominated, and elected. It is true that some damage was done to the slogan of his earlier days, " 'Coggy' never wobbles!" but the Tall Sycamore did not mind that. He was in financial straits, and he wanted to keep on being Senator. For a year or two more he did retain his office. Then came the era of the "muckrakers" and reform movements and investigations, and Coggy's career was over. He was the product of his generation, attractive, tolerant, generous, not unlike Warren G. Harding, who found it impossible to say "No." For me no political candidate can ever have quite his magnetism.

Waterville was no Spoon River or Winesburg, Ohio, permeated by degeneracy and inhabited by frustrated spinsters and unedifying failures. It did, however, have its "crusted characters," its quaint personalities, whom everybody recognized as such; Ben Cady, the fat man, who always seemed kind and jovial but who one day drowned himself in a well back of his house; "Birdie" Mason, who had been jilted by one of the village beaux and after that went around languid and melancholy, like some modern Ophelia; "Toe" Casey, who was said, under our breath, to be a gambler and certainly looked like the romantic hero of *Show Boat;* Sheriff Filkins, who had years before rounded up the Loomis Gang and who was to me as fascinating as Superman and Joe Palooka have been to my grandchildren.

Of the several local inebriates, viewed always with charity by the more sedate citizens, Frank Thompson was perhaps the most engaging. Through the week he managed to keep relatively sober and to accumulate a small financial surplus, which on Saturday evening he dissipated royally. Close to midnight he would stagger by our house, yodeling his favorite ditty, "Roll on, silver moon!" on his way to a convenient haymow, where he would "sleep it off." He was the authentic originator of a story which I have often told — and listened to from other after-dinner speakers. We all knew Frank, and both liked and pitied him. One morning my father met him on the street, lent him the dollar for which he asked, and then said in his friendly way, "Frank, why don't you cut out the booze? You're getting to be nothing but a bum, and before long nobody will even speak to you." Then Frank, who was by no means unintelligent, answered, "Well, Lou, sometimes I do get to feelin' mighty mean, an' my stomach goes back on me, and I decide to swear off. I go for two or three days without touchin' a drop, and then one morning I wake up, and the sky is blue and the birds are singin' and the sun is all bright and warm — and then, by God, Lou, I rally!"

Poor Frank! He was a lonely soul, and found companionship in the bottle. But Lynn Perkins (this is not his real name) had a wife and attractive children and a comfortable home — yet he couldn't stay sober more than a week. He, too, was a "Saturday night drunk." But on Sunday morning some of the deacons of the Presbyterian Church would call on him, see that he had a bath, dress him in clean linen, and then lead him to the choir, where in a melodiously plaintive tenor he would sing solos: "Nearer, my God, to Thee!"; "Oh, Calvary!"; and "Lead, kindly Light." His features were strangely like those of Edgar Allan Poe, and his temperament was much the same, except that he found relief in singing, not in poetry.

Down the street on the corner lived Reuben Tower, an eccentric bachelor who resembled Mr. Pickwick, with a completely bald head and rimmed spectacles fitted to a rubicund and benevolent countenance. His home was a shapeless structure crowned by a bell tower in which he had installed a set of Westminster chimes striking the quarters and the hour, which could play tunes on festive occasions. His huge living room, with a gigantic fireplace at the end, must have been thirty by twenty feet. He once bought in New York City a magnificent rug for the floor, but it proved to be too long; whereupon, instead of cutting it off, he had an addition designed and built to meet the demands of the rug. Although he had inherited a fortune, he lived a hermit's existence, seldom appearing in public, but once in a while as I was passing he would call me in and give me oranges as big as my head. The tower is today a Masonic Temple — a use for which it is perfectly adapted — and the bells still ring out, a foreign touch in a Mohawk Valley village. Later at Fiesole I was reminded of Waterville when I heard the tinkling of the bells from Florence in the valley.

In those days Waterville was regarded as something of a summer resort, to which each June would come the "rusticators" from the outside world: Charlemagne Tower, of the resounding name, Ambassador to Austria-Hungary and Russia, and later to Germany, who once when I was home from college invited me to lunch, recounted some of his diplomatic experiences, and said as I left, "Young man, get all the education you can — it's the most valuable asset any ambitious fellow can have!"; William Cary Sanger, later Assistant Secretary of War under President Theodore Roosevelt and, like Tower, a Harvard graduate; and Earl B. Putnam, of Philadelphia, a very polished gentleman of the Old School, who occasionally invited me to dinner on a hot July or August evening. These and other summer visitors, most of them relatives of the Towers, took us out of our provincialism and made us feel that Waterville was something more than just another Mohawk Valley village. The big houses of the Towers and the Putnams and the Sangers were so massively opulent in appearance that I felt proud to be associated with them. After all, didn't my father do their law work when they were in town?

I did not feel unsophisticated. I had spent two or three weeks each summer in the Adirondacks — at Cranberry Lake and Fulton Chain and the Adirondack League Club, and knew a good deal about what we called the North Woods. My longest trip away from home had been to the Buffalo Fair in 1901, just before going to college. The adventure was packed with romance and sensation, especially since President McKinley was assassinated there on September 6. I was staying with my family at a house in a Buffalo suburb, and the daughter of the family had, for some reason, a pass which admitted us to all the entertainments on the Midway — the "Hoochy-koochy," the camel farm, the cyclorama of the Johnston flood, the Scenic Railway in all its primitive and spine-shaking allurement — and we used to spend our days in sampling what was offered. When our week was over, Bessie Potter and I knew more about the *danse du ventre* and other even less refined diversions than anybody of our age on the grounds; but as I was only sixteen I regarded them as purely anatomical phenomena. Of the educational features of the fair I was almost entirely ignorant, for Bessie's pass was too seductive, and I was there for fun.

For the "lad I used to be" I have very little admiration, and I am sure that I was a poor example to others. At the other end of the village lived a classmate whom I shall call Ralph West — a thoroughly good boy, not unlike the omniscient Little Rollo, who walked with his mother to church every Sunday morning, like Little Lord Fauntleroy and "Dearest." How I hated him, especially because my own mother was constantly drawing my attention to his virtues! One day a friend and I caught Ralph unaccompanied behind the high school outhouse. He was neatly dressed, looking quite angelic with his hair nicely parted and his shoes more than adequately shined. By incessant taunts we finally succeeded in getting him to "put up his dukes"; and then, with an occasional jab of assistance from my companion, I massacred the "sissy." The next day my mother had a call from Mrs. West, who described me as a fiend incarnate; and that evening I had a notable session with my father, who had Mr. West for one of his most lucrative clients. I was sore for a week — but it was worth it! The incident illustrates my lack of even a fundamental sense of sportsmanship. Ralph West was smaller than I, and we were two to one against him. The fight was too easy, but I had proved that he was not altogether superior.

In June 1901, I had graduated from Waterville High School, delivering the Valedictory Address in a cutaway coat with striped trousers and winning a prize of twenty-five dollars for my oration. My parents had long before decided to make the financial sacrifices necessary to send me to college. They were tempted, naturally enough, by both Hamilton and Colgate, but I secretly thought them too close to home. Moreover my father's former fellow law student, Frank L. Babbott, had been an Amherst man, as had his friend, Dr. Claude Wilson. The literature from Amherst seemed all right to me, and my high school classmate, Harold Coggeshall — the son of the Senator — decided that he would go also. There was little difficulty in securing admission, for we both had studied Greek and Latin, and our records as indicated by Regents' Examinations were good. So it was that in mid-September we took the train for Utica, Harold Coggeshall leading his white bull terrier, Euripides — Rip for short — on a chain.

My mother's able mind kept her sentimentality tempered by humor. She did not dare go to the depot with me for fear of breaking down; but as I stepped into the "bus," she kissed me good-by with her eyes brimming with tears, and then said, "Well, Claude, you are homely, but you may do well." It was a peculiar benediction, covering her very deep emotion, and even now it seems entirely characteristic of her thinking.

I was some months from seventeen when I set off for college, and of course very immature. Life in Waterville, however, had been healthful and normal. I knew nothing of phobias or inhibitions or sublimations. During those impressionable years, moreover, some ideas derived from my surroundings had sunk into my consciousness: the importance of self-reliance; the lesson — learned from my father — that hard work may be an acceptable substitute for genius; the feeling that discrimination because of race, color, or religion does not fit with our Declaration of Independence; and the conviction, absorbed from my parents and two or three inspiring teachers, that every human being has a moral obligation to become as intelligent as it is possible for him to be. I was blessed with a love of books, which has never left me. Although I was in many respects appallingly ignorant, I behaved at times like a smart aleck or a show-off. At the moment I was aimless, with no goal set for myself beyond the immediate desire to graduate from college. I was undoubtedly irritating and had been refractory. In after years, when I had become a headmaster and had to deal with students who were in trouble because of indiscretions, I remembered what I had been, and tried to deal with them patiently.

More than to any course pursued in high school I am grateful for my typewriter. When I was a lad of ten, my father was about to discard an ancient Smith Premier machine; but I begged him for it, carried it off to my room, and began practicing on it. Soon it had become almost as much a part of my body as my eyeglasses or my hands. Without it I should be hardly able to think, and I now have three: a gorgeous Smith-Corona, the Rolls-Royce of typewriters, presented to me by the faculty when I retired as headmaster; a portable Remington; and what is described as a "noiseless *de luxe* Corona." One of the two latter goes with me wherever I travel, and I should be lost without it. My handwriting, distorted by the so-called Spencerian system, is almost illegible, even to myself; and ideas transferred to the typed page seem to gain in clarity and logic. I am still a "peck-and-punch" operator, but my expert secretary once confessed that I could go along as fast with two fingers as she could go with ten. Every child should be given a typewriter as he is given a bicycle. The dividends will mount with the years.

My most recent visit to the village was about three years ago. My wife had never visited it, and as a Southerner had an intense curiosity about Central New York; so we motored down from the Au Sable Club, in the Adirondacks, to see "the spots which my infancy knew." The automobile has effected an amazing transformation by bringing the village into touch with the outside world. The tiny house where I was born was still standing on Tower Avenue. The larger residence where I spent my boyhood was still there also, its lawn decorated by an enormous doghouse. My wife constantly exclaimed at the beauty of the symmetrical maples, the broad lawns, and the rolling hills. But to me the memory was of people. Many of them, of course, have gone the way of all flesh, but here and there I met a boyhood crony, who hailed me as "Dutch" and let me understand that, although I had become a schoolmaster, that was no great distinction. My brother now holds the position of leading citizen, as my father had done, and is associated with many good works. My wife now understands, I think, my pride at having been born in the Empire State — first in wealth, population, manufactures, and commerce. Long ago, of course, I was converted to New Englandism; but however much I may have become like the Late George Apley, deep in my heart is a love for the Mohawk Valley which can never be eradicated.

III

"The Fairest College"

I AM still many months short of that decisive and dramatic moment when Professor Churchill's recital of "Tintern Abbey" accomplished my conversion. Into a college community which harbored graduates of Andover, Exeter, and other exacting private schools descended two very green and untrained freshmen from the public high school in a tiny Central New York village. In those days students arriving from the West changed trains at Springfield for Northampton, and there again for Amherst. When we stepped off at the Amherst railroad station, with Rip in the lead, we were greeted by pained, discordant cries from waiting sophomores, who clearly did not expect any such figures as we presented. "Fresh" we were dubbed, and "fresh" we were; and we were hazed properly for our presumption. Fortunately within a few days Rip met and engaged the Psi U bulldog in the lobby of the Amherst House, and won a noteworthy victory. By that date Cog and I were pledged to Alpha Delta Phi, and the triumph over the enemy mascot won us prestige on the campus.

In the undergraduate life at Amherst, fraternities played a dominant part. During Rushing Week at the opening of the collegiate year the various chapters competed with one another to entice the more desirable freshmen. Cog and I had agreed that we would accept our bids together, and when several crowds pressed their importunities upon us, we had to retire for consultation. After an all-night conference in our room at Dr. Paige's we yielded to Jim Nelson's solicitations and allowed ourselves to be decorated with the "Alpha Delt" pledge pin. Up to that moment we had been treated by the upperclassmen like visiting royalty. But the minute that button was inserted in our lapels, we became, like other pledgees, the lowest of the low. Our former charm seemed to have vanished, and we were just common, or garden, freshmen. It was time, for the flattery had gone to our heads, and we had begun to think that the college could not get along without us.

What had actually been a casual and rather ignorant choice turned out to be a very good one. Alpha Delta Phi, the oldest of the Amherst fraternities, still maintained the literary and intellectual traditions which were the basis for its reputation. As freshmen, we found ourselves under the guidance of upperclassmen, who took their functions as our monitors very seriously. Seniors, who themselves had undistinguished records, urged us to do well in our studies and to conform to the regulations of the college and the chapter. After the dignified initiation ceremony, we found ourselves going on every Tuesday evening to what was colloquially called "Goat" — the weekly meeting of the brothers. In the 1900's this was an impressive occasion, when all the members dressed up in dark suits with stiff white collars and went solemnly to the "Goat Room." The under classmen were obliged to participate early in "literary exercises" which were by no means perfunctory, and in which our attempt at essays and debates received an unaffectionate and often ferocious scrutiny. I do not exaggerate when I declare that I profited more by some of these criticisms than I did by many of the comments of my English professors in the college. The memory of the caustic adjectives of "Shorty" Ells (now a distinguished judge in Connecticut) and of "Colonel" Atwood (later the well-known free-lance writer) survives to this day.

Fraternities have been condemned for their alleged snobbery and absurd exclusiveness, and I have done my share of the censuring. But Alpha Delta Phi as I knew it was for me a very real spiritual force. It encouraged discussion, but it also reached deep into the heart, stirring latent loyalties and demanding devotion to its ideals. The members, varied in their backgrounds and sensitivities and ambitions, achieved almost in spite of themselves a kind of unity. They might wrangle over trivialities on their vacations, or even outside on the campus, but within the walls of the house these divergences were subdued, as communicants lower their voices in a church. Somehow it was easy around the wood fire to speculate on the universe, even to voice noble aspirations without being ashamed. It was an indirect method of education, difficult to measure at the moment, but as it turned out lasting far beyond the labored memorizations of the classroom. Even a Philistine yielded to the fascination of the ritual and could be heard mouthing some of the phrases, like a child repeating a psalm that he does not fully understand. Nowadays, in the late afternoon of life, I find myself returning to the familiar scenes in a mood which is supernostalgic. It is belated gratitude for all that I learned without knowing it at the time.

In the lecture rooms, meanwhile, I was confused and groping, too immature to appreciate the fare set before me. From my courses I derived very little during my first two years. Looking at a transcript of my record, I am amazed to note that my grades were all B's and C's, with the exception of German, in which I received a disgraceful D. The Bright Boy from Waterville had turned out to be a dullard. The fact was that I had acquired a new and wrong sense of values. Thrown among classmates with more money than I, who laughed at pluggers and bookworms, I longed to appear like a man of the world and foolishly took as my models more sophisticated campus figures who liked to sit up till dawn playing poker or spend their Saturday nights at Dick Rahar's Inn, in Northampton, drinking more beer than was good for them. It was a harmless form of dissipation, but expensive for a boy on a modest allowance and incompatible with industrious habits.

One manifestation of this change of heart was a desire to be a campus Beau Brummel, and this had amusing consequences. As winter turned to spring, I ordered a tailor-made suit from William K. Staab, of Northampton — Calvin Coolidge's tailor, even after he entered the White House. The suit arrived in May, in time for the end-of-the-year festivities, and I wore it with satisfaction, even though it was not paid for. Shortly after I returned home in June, my father said to me, "Claude, I wish you would drop in at the office sometime during the day." That afternoon I stopped to see him, wondering what was up and fearful that he would comment adversely on my scholastic record. After some amiable preliminaries, he took up an envelope on his desk and handed it to me. It was, as I could detect at a glance, the excellent Staab's bill for $45. When it is recalled that I had always, like my father, worn ready-made clothes purchased in Utica, the situation can be imagined. "Is the bill all right?" asked my father, without a trace of irritation. "Yes, I guess so," I responded, "it is a good suit." "Of that I have no doubt," continued my father in an even voice, "but how are you going to pay for it?" "Well," said I in a nonchalant tone, "I thought you might make me a present of it." "No," responded my father, rather pensively, "I don't think your record quite justifies that. As a matter of fact, I've made arrangements with Fred Terry for you to begin work tomorrow on his farm. You'll ride three miles on your bicycle, getting there sharp at seven o'clock. You'll have an hour off for your lunch, which your mother will put up for you, and you'll be through at six. You'll be paid $1.25 for the ten-hour day. Maybe before the summer is over you'll have saved enough to settle Mr. Staab's account."

My father's decision, though offered calmly, was obviously final, and the next morning I was off at dawn for the Terry farm. The story of how I toiled pitching hay under the scorching July sun or unloaded from the fork up in the sweltering haymow until the sweat rolled in torrents down my face needs no amplification here, especially for my contemporaries whose boyhood was spent in the country. No forty-hour week for me! I worked exactly fifty-five hours each week, including half of each Saturday, at twelve and a half cents an hour, which gave me precisely $6.87 each Saturday noon, when I was paid off. It needs no Einstein to compute that it took me just about eight weeks to earn enough to pay Mr. Staab. I still had the suit, but at the loss of my summer vacation at Lake Woodhull.

That was a very important step in my education. I was rapidly discovering that not all knowledge was contained in the books which I so much enjoyed reading. I had heard that Cyrus, the Persian king, was taught in his childhood to ride, to shoot, and to speak the truth, which seems to have been sufficient for a monarch in those far-off times. The suit episode showed me the folly of extravagance. It made me realize how hard money was to earn. Furthermore it set my father up for me as a model of tolerance and wisdom. He handled me in my "salad days" exactly right, and I have always been grateful to him.

I wish I could honestly say that this summer experience turned me at once into a model of the Benjamin Franklin virtues. But although I had learned one lesson, I was still a candidate for improvement. As a sophomore I drifted along, never failing a course, and securing A's in German and history, but content with comparative mediocrity. Towards the spring I did show enough interest in public speaking to attract the attention of my instructor; and in the course in Biblical literature under the learned Professor Henry Preserved Smith (known to the undergraduates inevitably as "Pickles"), which I had chosen because it looked easy, I actually won two prizes of ten dollars each — the first for an essay on "The Religious Ideas of Isaiah, 55–59" and the second for "A Comparison of the Theology of Paul and James." It is not true, as some of my friends alleged, that I was the only competitor. The fact was that Professor Smith, a patriarch with a long white beard, had interested me in spite of myself, and I responded with something resembling scholarly ambition. I was discovering for myself the tremendous power of motivation.

The upperclassmen in my fraternity were by this time frankly disgusted with me. I had been heralded before I entered Amherst as a brilliant scholar, likely to win the Porter Admissions Prize and thus to reflect credit on the chapter. Actually I was only superficially clever and badly grounded in the subjects which counted, like Latin and mathematics. Unfortunately also I did not seem to be trying. More than once during my sophomore year a senior would take me aside and chide me for leaving undone the things I ought to have done. When Bob Maynard described me as "footless," he was using just the right adjective.

Matters came to a climax rather unexpectedly. During the winter we were supposed to perform physical exercise in the gymnasium four times a week; but for some reason I had obstinately decided that attendance was not necessary and had accordingly accumulated a rare collection of "cuts." When the spring term examinations were over, Dean Edward Hitchcock, the "Old Doc" of Amherst tradition, summoned me to his office and in his high-pitched voice told me what he thought of my behavior. His language was direct, uncompromising, and emphatic. He said, in substance, that I had ignored the regulations of the college and would not be allowed to return. He then proceeded to add in his kindly manner, that he was greatly disappointed with me. "The trouble with you, Fuess," he declared, "is that you're in with the wrong gang and haven't guts enough to break loose." If he had added that my aims were low, my ambitions vague, and my attitude perverse, he would not have exaggerated.

Back in Waterville that summer I said nothing about this interview, not even to my father, knowing that his heart would be broken. Fortunately no letter arrived from the college, and my marks, although far from distinguished, did not indicate failure. As a demonstration of contrition, I found a job in a canning factory, where I worked during speed-up periods sixteen or eighteen hours a day in the room where peas were steamed. I was earning very high wages but getting more and more bleached out. In early August I came home one night exhausted and was unable to rise from bed the next morning. Dr. T.Z. was called, took my temperature and diagnosed typhoid fever — in those days a frightful scourge. For the next two weeks I was seriously, even critically, ill, with my mother as my nurse. Once the physician put me into our zinc-lined bathtub filled with ice to lower my temperature and nearly lowered me into my grave. But I did recover, and while I was convalescing, lying in a hammock on the lawn, had plenty of leisure in which to meditate. That meditation was my first significant approach to a stage resembling maturity.

Meanwhile I had received no official communication from "Old Doc" or, indeed, from any one at the college, and my family of course assumed that when I was strong enough I would resume my studies there. Each morning I awaited anxiously the fatal letter, but it never arrived; and at the opening of the fall term of my junior year, very pale and thin, I appeared in the dean's office at Amherst. The kindly old man greeted me as if nothing untoward had happened, and then I explained that I had been ill. "You do look peaked," he said, "You'd better go slow for a while." "But, Dr. Hitchcock," I replied, "you told me I couldn't come back." "Did I? Did I?" he growled. "Let's look at your record." The report, which he had evidently forgotten, was brought to him, and he scanned it, whistling softly through his whiskers. "Pretty bad, pretty bad," I could hear him muttering. Then he looked up at me and asked, "Fuess, did that sickness do you any good?" "Plenty," said I, "I've made up my mind that I'm going to do a better job — if you'll give me a chance."

So I was allowed to continue at the college, on condition that I make up each of my accumulated gym cuts by bowling in the basement of the gymnasium, at the price of twenty-five cents a string. It was expensive, but the mild exercise was beneficial at that point in my convalescence and I was soon back in excellent health. I did not reform my habits overnight, but from that date my record was almost straight A's, and I was elected to Phi Beta Kappa at the close of my senior year. There is no moral to this tale. The combination of Dr. Hitchcock's forgetfulness and a typhoid fever germ had given me the reprieve that I needed. Not every sinner can count on such good luck.

Of the Amherst which I attended from 1901 to 1905 I have written much.* It was a period of transition, when many of the distinguished professors of an earlier era were growing old and a brilliant younger group had either not yet appeared or had not reached their prime. The irresponsible President Merrill E. Gates of the 1890's had been followed by the urbane George Harris, who, rather easygoing and inclined to

* *Amherst, the Story of a New England College* (1935), and my *Joseph B. Eastman, Servant of the People* (1951).

avoid trouble, symbolized the mood of the college. Professor William P. Bigelow, a vigorous critic of his faculty contemporaries, declared unreservedly that under Harris all emphasis on scholarship was lacking and that "any approach to an intellectual life was impossible." This is, in my judgment, too extreme a view. Nevertheless it is unquestionable that social and athletic interests did dominate undergraduate life and that outside activities absorbed the energies of some of the ablest students. Talking blibly of the importance of "all-round men," they made this an excuse for neglecting their courses. Their attitude was to some extent justified by the indifferent instruction in some of the important fields. On the other hand, a vigorous minority, among both faculty and undergraduates, looked upon the current trend with profound and unalterable disapproval.

The great Charles E. Garman, one of the most dynamic teachers of philosophy of his generation, was, when I sat under him, struggling constantly against physical weakness. He was still a mysterious figure in his black frock coat, with coal black hair, deep-set eyes, and gleaming white teeth, speaking with carefully articulated precision as if every word must count. I was affected, I think, more by his legendary reputation than by his living personality. Although, like Joe Eastman, I found myself resisting his efforts to guide us "willy-nilly" into the port of orthodoxy, I could not help admiring him. Towards the end of my course he sent me a little note inviting me to call at his house. It was a sultry afternoon in May, but he sat in his study with a muffler around his sensitive throat. Then and there in measured phrases he commented on my resistance, but also uttered words of commendation which I have never forgotten. I was so much disarmed that I became almost a convert.

Two upperclassmen whom I greatly admired — although from a lower level — were Stanley King, who was destined to become one of Amherst's ablest presidents, and Joseph B. Eastman, afterward Interstate Commerce Commissioner and Director of Defense Transportation. Stanley King, even in college, was the brilliant "white-headed boy" whose future seemed assured. Nobody was astonished when he graduated from Amherst in three years and from the Harvard Law School in two, and moved on to his fine record of public service. Eastman was slower in mind, more phlegmatic, and advanced less rapidly towards success. I debated with both of them and profited by the contact with very different but equally stimulating personalities who were throughout their lives intimate friends.

Garman was gone by 1907, and Professor Henry B. Richardson (Richie), a stimulating interpreter of Goethe's *Faust,* died a year earlier. Esty, in mathematics, and Morse, in history, were to retire in 1906. Not one of these professors was in good health or at his best when I was an undergraduate. Because I did not lean towards science, I missed some of the ablest men on the faculty: Emerson in geology, Harris in chemistry, and Kimball in physics. Fortunate I was to have come into contact with such teachers as John M. Tyler (Tip), in biology, with his radiant red whiskers and his bald skull of unusual shape and dimensions which, according to undergraduate legend, he had sold to a German museum; the urbane and fastidious William L. Cowles (Billie), who made Catullus seem very modern; John F. Genung (Nungie), stout of body and soul, a productive scholar who was a remarkable combination of epicurean and saint; and George D. Olds (Georgie), who lured me for a brief period into the mysterious world of logarithms and graphs.

There was, as in every college, some indifferent instruction, and certain courses were notorious among the undergraduates as "guts" or "soft snaps." It is my impression that it was relatively easy to secure passing marks without much cerebration. But the teachers and the material were there if a student had genuine intellectual interests. When I began to put time on my work, I found no lack of encouragement from the faculty. In most respects the standards were as high as those of other New England colleges of that period. My failures, such as they were, were not due to the professors or to the curriculum, but to myself.

As I entered my junior year, I happened to select by sheer good luck Professor William P. Bigelow (Biggie), in German. He was tough-minded and hard-boiled, contemptuous of idlers, and he discerned in me qualities of which I myself was unaware. The result was that I found myself so eager to win his approbation that I worked as I had never worked before. In the winter he assigned me the leading part in a five-act German play, which claimed all my energies for weeks and indeed brought me to the verge of collapse. The highest compliment he ever paid me was after the performance was all over, when he said quietly, "Fuess, you have never been as big a loafer as you pretended to be!" For me at that moment it was the equivalent of being decorated with the *Croix de guerre.*

I must also mention John Erskine, who came to Amherst in 1903 fresh from Columbia and gave a delightful course in seventeenth-century poetry, which introduced me to Herrick and Suckling and Carew. In his book, *My Life as a Teacher,* Erskine commented caustically on President Harris and the Amherst faculty as he knew them. He found the unproductive attitude of many of the professors unbelievable, and he described them as leading "a pleasant but lazy life," spending their evenings playing bridge and making excursions to neighboring taverns for jolly dinner parties. A scholar by temperament and training, he could not understand how or why so many of his colleagues appeared to have lost their ambition.

I am sure that I was much happier during that junior year when I first began dimly to realize the difference between ephemeral and durable satisfactions. I had never been a reprobate, but I had been wasting my father's hard-earned money. Now at last I was on the right track. I took an active interest in the public speaking and debating courses and practiced using my voice walking along country roads. Some modest successes gave me encouragement. But I really think that what cheered me most was my altogether unexpected election in the spring as president of my fraternity for the first half of the next year. There were nine men in my delegation, including Harold Coggeshall, who had become one of the outstanding athletes and, because of his magnetic personality, a leader in the class, and Edwin J. Van Etten, one of our most brilliant students. When I was chosen over these two, my morale received a tremendous boost. I was to profit on a small scale from the education which comes from responsibility.

After a long vacation in the Adirondacks, I came back to the college in a new mood, resolved to set an example for the younger brothers in the fraternity. It was obvious that I could not tell a freshman what to do without showing him the way. One result was that I received straight A's through the year in all my courses — economics, history, English, philosophy, public speaking, and modern government. I was improving but was still uncertain about my plans for the future. At precisely the right moment, when I was developing high but unchanneled ambitions, along came Professor Churchill to set me right.

George Bosworth Churchill was decidedly a man of parts. I came across him first in his courses in public speaking, in which he showed himself to be an orator of the Websterian school. When he announced his course on the romantic movement, I could not resist enrolling. To those interested in the educational process, the influence which an older personality can under the right conditions exert on a younger and malleable one is almost terrifying. Churchill, of course, had no idea of what he was doing to me — that he was literally restoring my soul. Not altogether popular on the campus, he was thought by many to be cold and pompous and egotistical. But his brusque manner veiled a warm and sympathetic heart. In 1904, he was only fifteen years out of college and still under forty, but he seemed much older to a youth of nineteen.

Many years afterwards, when I had become an inveterate though not too skillful dry fly fisherman, I discovered that Churchill had written some delightful fishing yarns, especially a story entitled "Miramichi Days," published in *Field and Stream* for August 1924. He was also drawn into politics, serving his apprenticeship as moderator of the Amherst Town Meeting and later being elected to the Massachusetts State Senate and as a delegate to the State Constitutional Convention. He was ultimately elected to Congress, but died on July 1, 1925, just before he had taken his seat. A man of wide interests and exceptional ability, he was loyal to his friends and disturbing to his critics. A granite bench on the lawn of the Chi Phi fraternity in Amherst commemorates him suitably, and the inscription does not exaggerate in saying, "His love for Nature, Books, and Life was great." I never go back to Amherst without walking by it and taking off my hat in honor of a very gallant gentleman.

Churchill's literary tastes were comprehensive and his enthusiasm was infectious. He liked Cowper and Byron and Shelley and Keats, but his superlatives were reserved for Wordsworth, and he centered his own theories of Romanticism around that poet's work. When he read from "Tintern Abbey," he was restirring my own love for outdoor life. Without being able to express it, I knew that Nature "never did betray the heart that loved her" and I had already felt that the forests "haunted me like a passion." It is not strange that I was so susceptible to the noble lines when I listened to them from Churchill's lips.

At Christmas, Professor Churchill and I had a conference, in the course of which I rather timidly outlined my hopes. He advised me to enter the Senior Essay Contest on the subject, "Nature in the Poetry of William Wordsworth"— surely a broad topic! I did my best, but I had had no real training in organization, and the prize of $100 was won by my classmate, Ned Gardner. I found my production the other day in our cellar, its pages yellowed with the years. It is crude, carelessly written, and poorly constructed, but the enthusiasm still glows under the bad grammar and the platitudes. On the back, in Churchill's precise handwriting, is his friendly comment, "The intentions are better than the achievement — but don't let that discourage you."

Although Churchill must have been impressed by my boyish hero worship, he was not unreasonably skeptical about my staying powers. "Try a graduate school for a year," he said. "It can't do you any harm, even if you eventually follow the law. And if you do decide to become a teacher, a little more knowledge won't hurt you a bit." It was sound advice, which he implemented by recommending me for a scholarship of $250 at the Columbia University Graduate School, and also urging my father to finance me just a little longer.

It will not be difficult for any one who has read thus far in my confessions to see why my father should hesitate about investing any more of his savings in such a dubious venture. But Professor Churchill was very persuasive. Furthermore at commencement I had enjoyed some minor triumphs, and had won prizes in debating and essay writing. By this date also my younger brother had shown sufficient excitement about the law so that my father could count on him as a future partner and successor. It was, therefore, decided at a family conference that I should pursue my studies further, and under the inspiration which came from Professor Churchill, I was ready to take all knowledge for my province.

Probably I have forgotten, or omitted, many of the incidents which had an influence on my development. Frances Lester Warner, in her book *On a New England Campus* has described how, in a mood of bravado, I joined with a very charming young lady in starting dancing at Mount Holyoke College; and the curious may read the story in that volume. I recall many drives with three of my classmates in a surrey through the Connecticut Valley countryside, and I remember also my first automobile ride in Sid Bixby's dos-à-dos Locomobile — a very unreliable means of transportation. There were no long week ends as there are now, and the students, except for some mild dissipation in "Hamp," remained on the campus. Chapel and church were compulsory, but not disagreeable, and there was no agitation for their abolition. For the majority of us those were carefree days, and at luncheon or dinner, indeed wherever we met in groups, somebody would always start a song.

We were not altogether provincial. One day there arrived in the Alpha Delta Phi House the Reverend Frederick J. Bliss, '80, a specialist in oriental archaeology, who was convalescing from a broken leg and wished to settle down for a few weeks in a quiet spot. My roommate, now the Very Reverend Edwin J. Van Etten, Dean of the Episcopal Cathedral in Boston, invited him to occupy an extra bed with us, and there he stayed for a month. He was a man who had roamed and read widely, and who could talk delightfully about his experiences and ideas. His passion for the moment was George Meredith, and so strong was his influence that I purchased a set of that author in red leather binding on the installment plan and was still paying for it two years after I had left college. I can even now feel the eagerness with which I read for the first time *Richard Feverel* and *The Egoist* and *Diana of the Crossways,* and quoted the brilliant epigrams to "Brother" Bliss as we sat around in the evening before the fire. What Bliss did most for me was to show me the fun which anybody can have from testing his intelligence. The idea is exemplified in the instructional methods of many teachers, from Socrates to Mark Hopkins, and it is fundamental.

During my Amherst days I had four unusual roommates. As a freshman I lived with Harold Coggeshall, my Waterville friend, who made the touchdown which beat Harvard in 1904 and was after that a campus celebrity. Within a few years after his graduation he died of pernicious anemia. The second was Ed Van Etten, whom I have already mentioned. The third was Ernest G. Draper, who after a distinguished career in public service became a member of the Federal Reserve Board in Washington. The fourth was Bruce Barton, the man everybody knows. Some of my education must have come from association with these very different personalities.

We had plenty of guests in the Alpha Delta Phi House. William Butler Yeats came back to us after delivering a lecture in College Hall, and a little group sat up with him literally all night, listening to his comments on literature and life. James K. Hackett, the actor, drove over one Sunday from Northampton and danced for us in his stocking feet. Sir Chentung Liang Cheng, Chinese Ambassador to the United States, appeared one Sunday and amused us by asking politely the cost of everything in our room. All these are memories, vague but very pleasant.

Writing as I do in a time of doubt and despair, when like a doomed race we speak casually of the Decline of the West and the Twilight of the Gods, I find it difficult to recapture the ingenuous optimism of the 1900's. We really believed that the time would shortly come when the war-drum would throb no longer and the battle flags would be permanently furled. We saw nothing startling in the prophecy of John Addington Symonds:

Nation with nation, land with land,
Unarmed shall live as comrades free;
In every pulse and brain shall throb
The pulse of one fraternity.

It is doubtless a mistake to attempt to generalize too far regarding any period. My class at Amherst contained all sorts and conditions of men, some boisterous and some melancholy, some dynamic and some lethargic. But despite their differences, almost none of us was cynical, skeptical, or frightened. In retrospect that generation seems either simple-minded or blind. It has been called by Henry S. Canby, one of my contemporaries, The Age of Confidence — and this unquestionably it was. As a group we had ideals and hopes, and expected somehow to fulfill them. We looked forward after graduation to an agreeable job, a moderate amount of happiness, and not too much suffering.

Our mood of buoyancy was neither thoughtless nor stupid. If we were unaware of the disasters which were to follow in the train of Bismarck and Karl Marx, so were our elders and superiors, Josiah Royce and William James, to say nothing of Professor Garman. If we missed the early rumbles of the storms which were to shake civilization, so did nearly everybody around us. There were not even Cassandras who later could cry, "I told you so!" Where was the evidence to make us pessimistic? We could, if we pleased, travel anywhere without passports, and many of us did so. Although the Japanese had just finished defeating the Russians, that was on the other side of the Pacific, and the atmosphere elsewhere seemed peaceful. The United States, fresh and flushed from the comic opera war with Spain, was espousing the New Imperialism, and historians were not lacking to tell us that we were on the verge of an American Elizabethan Era. College graduates like us did not hunt for jobs — we chose them! If there were economic evils, was not the doughty Teddy Roosevelt out on the rampage against them? If there was crime, was it not being punished? If my education up to 1905 taught me anything, it was that we were marching towards the millennium. As it turned out, we were like people planting their rose gardens over a powder magazine. But we were not conscious of impending perils. It could have been said of us, as of the "little victims" in Gray's "Eton College":

When ignorance is bliss
'Tis folly to be wise.

If we were naïve, so was the Amherst faculty. They taught us very little about the world into which we were going. Their science, it is true, was adequate, but our philosophy had been stereotyped, our economics had been shallow, and our history had no bearing on the present. When I left, I knew nothing about the Balkan States or socialism or Thorstein Veblen. Some of the men in my class, like John Morris Clark and Walter Palmer, became fine scholars in their respective fields. But they had little awareness of things to come. Those of us who were graduated in the Class of 1905 have had to learn much through bitter experience.

At the time of graduation and for fifteen years afterwards I felt no especial gratitude to Amherst, but after the First World War I suddenly and inexplicably found myself remembering it again. I had a modest part in the Centennial Drive for $3,000,000 in 1921; I prepared, at the request of President George D. Olds, the *Amherst Memorial Volume* in 1926; and before long I was returning almost automatically to fraternity initiations and alumni gatherings. I took very keen pride in my first honorary degree, a Doctorate of Letters awarded me by my alma mater in 1929, with the following citation from President Arthur Stanley Pease:

> Claude Moore Fuess, for over twenty years a successful teacher of English, editor and writer in your professional field, yet more widely known by your historical writings in which you have traced the part played in the World War by your town, your college, and your state, as well as of the ancient academy which you serve, and most notably the lives of those distinguished Massachusetts jurists, Rufus Choate and Caleb Cushing; careful in research, discreet in judgment, and felicitous in expression, by virtue of the authority vested in me by the Trustees of Amherst College, I confer upon you the degree of Doctor of Letters.

In 1935, I published my *Amherst, The Story of a New England College,* the research for which taught me much about the evolution of educational thought. More recently I have been Chairman of the Executive Committee of the Alumni Council and President of the Society of the Alumni. For two years I was National President of Alpha Delta Phi, and at this writing I am President of the Amherst Corporate Chapter of that fraternity. I mention these things not in a spirit of boastfulness but to indicate how closely I have been identified with the college and its welfare.

Many autobiographers, including Henry Adams, have asserted that they derived very little out of their college experiences. I have none of this feeling. If I missed something, the fault was largely mine, for being too immature and unresponsive to profit by what was offered. But I have long since concluded that I absorbed unconsciously more than I may have indicated. I held no important offices in my class or in the college. I had no athletic successes. Indeed I was a very inconspicuous member of my class. Yet somehow I emerged after four years less provincial, more tolerant, and more eager for enlightenment. Although I knew very little when I was graduated, I had developed a passion for knowledge. My affection for the college, my devotion to it, is more than mere sentimentality, more than just joining in the familiar songs and cheering the teams. For me Amherst is still an important element in my life, and I am proud to be one of her sons. For me, as for Calvin Coolidge, "Amherst's a good college!"

IV

Getting Ready

COLUMBIA University where I enrolled as a graduate student in the autumn of 1905 was a vast, complex, and rather overwhelming machine, which turned out scholars as a factory turns out shoes, and just about as impersonally. Gone were the leisurely ways of Amherst, with the long "bull-sessions" around the wood fire and the carefree approach to life. Everybody at Columbia seemed to be in a feverish state, plugging for some examination or preparing a report and indifferent to "the sweet serenity of books." These fledgling scholars spent their days and most of their nights trying to eviscerate the volumes in the huge library. Every person had a professional objective, usually symbolized by the mystic letters M.A. or Ph.D. I caught the spirit of the place quickly and began to work as I had never worked before, methodically, persistently, and tirelessly. Perceiving that the competition in graduate school was keen and ruthless, I resolved not to be left behind in what was clearly the survival of the fittest. I was not yet twenty-one, and it seemed to me that life could never wear me out.

But it was not unmitigated labor! Having always been a country boy, I found my first taste of the allurements of the metropolis very exciting. The theater, the opera, and the art galleries were now within easy reach, and contributed new and very pleasant elements to my education. During that winter of 1905–1906 I was a first-nighter at nearly every play presented in the city, including Shaw's *Mrs. Warren's Profession* (suppressed after its first performance on October 31) and *Man and Superman* (which aroused heated discussions on Morningside Heights), Forbes Robertson in *Hamlet* (what a voice he had!), Maude Adams in *Peter Pan,* Sarah Bernhardt in *Camille,* and David Warfield in that tear-jerking romance, *The Music Master.* Most of these shows I saw from the remote "peanut gallery," which was admirably adjusted in cost to my meager exchequer. I heard most of the great operas and studied the paintings in the Metropolitan with all the eagerness of an unsophisticated youth.

I cannot deny also that we had other more mundane diversions — poker games which stretched from Saturday evening until Sunday noon and occasional expeditions to beer halls like Pabst Harlem and Little Hungary. But most of us were too serious to burn the candle overmuch at both ends. The plays and pictures contributed, we thought, to our aesthetic appreciation, and we could justify the time and the money we spent on them. The less refined forms of amusement freshened us up after a wearing week. At any rate, our routine, though exacting, was far from monotonous.

I had selected Columbia rather than Harvard under the advice of Professor Churchill, who felt that the Harvard Department of English was too much dominated by philologists. The faculty at Columbia, however, proved in many respects to be disappointing. The library was there, with its ample facilities, and there was guidance if one deliberately sought it. The instruction, unfortunately, was notably dull; and most of the professors seemed to feel that it was unnecessary to attempt to interest their students.

Among the exceptions was Brander Matthews, who lectured in an offhand manner about literature in general but occasionally broke away from his conventional theme and gossiped about the great and the near great among his acquaintances. A competent playwright and essayist, he never let us forget that he was a man of the world. Legends of his feud with Professor George E. Woodberry were still heard on the Columbia campus. Once Brander took me to the Players' Club to see and hear Mark Twain, to whom he always referred in his lectures as "my dear friend, the greatest living master of the English tongue." At the club Mr. Clemens wore his spectacular white suit, and I, after having shaken his hand, retreated to an obscure corner, befitting my years, and listened with my ears pinned back. The only remark that I remember is the humorist's statement that it was "damned hard being a funny man." It may have been hard for him, but I spent the evening laughing.

Some years later at Andover an argument developed at our table for bachelor teachers on some rare point of grammatical usage. I defended as well as I could the cause of freedom in procedure. The debate culminated in a wager, and it was suggested that I write to Professor Matthews, as an authority, and let him settle the issue. Never was an opponent delivered more completely into my hands, for Brander, after a comprehensively profane denunciation of grammarians as a class, ended by saying, "Tell the fellow to go to Hell — he's a damned quibbling purist!"

I suppose that I was looking at Columbia for teachers like Churchill and Erskine, who regarded teaching as an art worth cultivating: but there were few of them, and when anybody did show any signs of enthusiasm, it was the fashion to disparage him as "superficial." Billy Phelps, my friend of a later period, would have had rough going at Columbia, as he did in his early years at Yale. It almost seemed to some of us as if a pose of indifference was a prerequisite for a junior hoping for promotion on the graduate faculty in English.

It is not irrelevant to suggest that many of these professors had a narrow conception of scholarship. During much of my mature career I have been associated with scholars, and I have myself made some minor contributions to what is vaguely called "learning." The ripe scholar like Professor John Livingston Lowes, who in his critical volume, *The Road to Xanadu,* offered a novel interpretation of a great poem, does something of real importance for culture. But the young scholars in universities who attempt to resurrect a poetaster better decently left buried and the philologists who devote years to a trifling point of grammar are adding little to our knowledge. Groups of such pedants on college faculties cheer one another on and subsist by the device of mutual backscratching. But enough has already been said by William James and others on the evils of doctoral dissertations, which corrupt by deluding the perpetrators into the illusion that they have accomplished something important.

To this indictment of the Columbia faculty I must make one distinguished exception. Professor William P. Trent, then only forty-four years old, was in his prime as scholar and teacher. He wore a beard, not straggly and moth-eaten in appearance, like Brander's, but long, brown, and glossy, like that of Charles I. His eyes had a genial expression, with humor lurking behind them, and he had a resonant and melodious voice with which he loved to read aloud his favorite poems. Trent was eclectic in his tastes, but he was at his best in a course in eighteenth-century literature, beginning with his favorite, Daniel Defoe. There was nothing blasé about Trent. When he recited passages from "Paradise Lost," his eyes glistened, and he rolled polysyllables on his tongue as if he were savoring every modulation. Soon I fell under his special guidance and became his ardent admirer. Later he was a supporter of Germany during the early stages of World War I and, as a consequence, lost many of his former friends. But he did not retire until 1929, and he lived to be seventy-seven. I made a pilgrimage to see him when he was an old man and found him physically shattered but still spicy and caustic.

Professor Trent recommended that I make satire my major field, and under his direction I read in the original Latin the complete works of Juvenal, Horace, and Persius — one of the most difficult assignments I ever undertook. Following up this enterprise, I wrote my master's thesis on "The Satires of Andrew Marvell." It was my first attempt at a scholarly article of any length, and I endeavored to cover all the available source material. Although my thesis was no startling contribution to knowledge, Trent was pleased, and through his sponsorship I was awarded a University Fellowship of $750, which persuaded my father that I might some day be able to support myself by my own efforts.

In June, a friend of mine, Cuthbert Sweeney, who was studying at the Columbia Law School, induced me to join him on a trip to Europe. Not often have two young men had such an inexpensive literary adventure. We sailed on the Anchor Line steamship *Caledonia,* paying exactly $37.50 for the second-class passage of eleven days to Glasgow. In 1950, when my wife and I flew to London, it cost us approximately $300 apiece for the trip overnight from Logan Airport in Boston to Croydon Airport in London. The entire amount which I spent for a summer of travel in 1906 could not have exceeded $350. I suppose that the increase represents progress, but it is difficult to discover exactly how!

Sweeney and I landed at Glasgow in the morning, immediately purchased bicycles, and were off that afternoon for Ayr, thirty-seven miles to the south, to visit the birthplace of Robert Burns. Returning north by an inland route, we pedaled through the Scottish Lake Country to Stirling and Edinburgh, and then down the English east coast, studying every cathedral and ruined castle within our range. After spending ten crowded days in London, we started off for

Cambridge and Oxford and the Cotswolds, stopping each night at little inns where we paid only five shillings for bed and breakfast. Selling our bicycles in London, we proceeded via Newhaven and Dieppe to Paris, where we lived in a huge bare room on the Rue de Bac and walked miles every day conscientiously visiting every museum and even the tombs in Père la Chaise. Not for us Foyot's or Maxim's or the other restaurants for millionaires! We ate along the boulevards, carefully conserving our funds.

After a week in Rotterdam, Amsterdam, and Antwerp, we went by rail to Strassburg and Heidelberg, and walked for three days through the Black Forest. To my delight I found my grandfather's initials chipped in the spire of the Strassburg Cathedral, where he had carved them almost sixty years before. Obeying my father's wishes, I got in touch with my relatives in Annweiler and stepped from the cars in the little Bavarian village to find myself encircled by aunts and uncles and cousins and even the Mayor, all eager to inspect the rich *Amerikaner*. Poor Sweeney and I, who had wondered how we could stretch our Express Checks to get us back to Glasgow, presented a brave outward bearing, although secretly only too conscious of our impecuniosity.

When I returned to my room in Livingston Hall at Columbia in the autumn, I could visualize Rydal Mount and Stoke Poges and King's College Chapel and Kenilworth Castle and countless other places associated with my reading. I have always regarded travel as an important element in education, even if it is only from Boston to Concord and Salem. Whenever I have been asked to give advice to prospective teachers of English literature, I have told them to get to England with all possible speed, even if they have to manicure cows on a cattle boat. Stratford-on-Avon, even when crowded with "trippers," can never seem commonplace to an imaginative mind. *Twelfth Night* is a more enjoyable play seen in the Shakespeare Memorial Theater on the banks of the river which the dramatist knew so well as a boy. Any instructor in English, in school or in college, is more interesting for having walked through the Dorsetshire of Thomas Hardy or eaten lunch at the Cheshire Cheese. Sophisticated tourists may laugh at teachers who wander through cathedrals, guidebook in hand, but there is nothing quite like the thrill which comes from studying for the first time all the architectural details of Westminster Abbey and reading the inscriptions on the tombs.

Filled with an ardor derived from fresh and stimulating experiences, I began my second year at graduate school. My lack of enthusiasm for some of my professors was counteracted by the excitement of reading Chaucer under William Allan Neilson. With his acquiline nose and grizzled Vandyke beard, he resembled a Renaissance courtier, and I liked to watch him as he listened to discussions with subdued and tolerant mirth in his restless, enigmatic eyes. It was said of him rightly that he "made the grim business of learning seem an appealing and blithe adventure." I had the opportunity of meeting him often outside the lecture room, and later I served with him on committees and formed a friendship which lasted until his death in 1946. Although he had a wealth of erudition, he carried it lightly like a flower, and contact with his well-stocked mind was an inspiration to a young man on the verge of disillusionment with some of his professors.

In those days Neilson did not like women in his courses, and deliberately tried to repel them by smoking in his office pipe after pipe of the strongest tobacco, so that he seemed to be haloed by a perpetual nicotinal cloud. Later, when he became president of Smith College, he found himself in a predominantly feminine world, and apparently enjoyed it. It was he who, having occasion to discuss the behavior of the Smith undergraduates, opened a chapel talk by saying, "Young ladies, smoking is a filthy, expensive, and reprehensible habit

— to which I am inordinately addicted!" Neilson confirmed the impression left upon me by Churchill and Trent — that a scholar need not necessarily be a dull fellow. Thus he came to my rescue, without realizing it, at a time when I was growing a little discouraged.

It turned out to be a year of intense and unremitting toil. In preparation for my oral examination for the doctorate I sat up night after night, memorized thousands of dates, and when I faced my inquisitors I was weary and burdened with much useless knowledge. The interrogation covered five hours, with specialists taking turns asking questions. Having been warned in advance that I would probably be quizzed on Thomas Love Peacock and Thomas Lovell Beddoes, I had their works almost by heart. At one point the kindly Professor Trent offered me a cigarette to relieve my tension, and I must add that the attitude of my examiners was uniformly gracious. I had thought that I had reason to be worried, for some candidates had recently been rejected. But when it was all over, I was informed that I had done well — in fact, "Very Well" — and that my residence requirements had been satisfactorily completed.

Presumably I was now equipped with sufficient information and nothing remained for me to do but write my dissertation. I was not attracted by the conventional type of subject, involving the elucidation of some philological puzzle or the revival of some obscure versifier. I recalled that Dr. Johnson, when asked which was the greater poet, Derrick or Smart, replied dogmatically, "Who am I that I should differentiate between a louse and a flea?" I wished to find a more rewarding theme, such as that selected by Ferris Greenslet, in his "Joseph Glanvil" (1900) and by John Erskine, in his "The Elizabethan Lyric" (1903) — the only two earlier Columbia dissertations for which I had any real respect. In prowling about the dark and dusty corners of the university library, I had discovered by sheer luck a forgotten Italian poem called "Il Poema Tartaro," by one Giambattista Casti, and was immediately impressed by its similarity to Byron's "Don Juan," not only in stanzaic form but also in mood and style. In continuing my study of satire I had naturally reached Byron and had become interested in his sources; and when I had probed deeper into the question of material, I was astonished to find how little was known. At any rate I should be dealing with a major literary figure, not a third-rater, and this was a consideration.

It took some argument to convince Professor Trent that I was competent to treat a subject obviously more far-reaching than that of the orthodox dissertation. But when I showed him Casti's poem and pointed out some of the close resemblances between it and Byron's masterpiece, he withdrew his objections. "Fuess, you've got something here," he admitted, and the topic was at once marked down as my property. Unfortunately with my "orals" imminent, I had little time for thorough research, and it was obvious that I would need another full year for the writing of such a comprehensive dissertation.

I was then only in my twenty-third year and in spite of deliberate effort to appear dignified, I was far from sure of myself. As spring came on and I was beginning to look longingly across the Hudson River to the Palisades and the open country beyond, Trent summoned me to his office and said, "Fuess, you really aren't, chronologically speaking, much more than a child, and you haven't had any teaching experience at all. Why wouldn't it be a good idea for you to try yourself out for a year and see whether you can control a classroom? There's a good place open down in Pennsylvania, and I believe you would be wise to consider it. You can come back later and finish your dissertation."

The suggestion appealed to me for two reasons: first, because the burden upon my father had been heavy and I was anxious to become self-supporting; second, because I was skeptical about my possibilities as a teacher. The offer came from George School, a coeducational institution sponsored by the Hicksite, or more liberal branch of the Friends. The headmaster's son, George A. Walton, Jr., who taught English on the faculty, wished to spend a year in travel and study, and his father was eager to engage a substitute who under no circumstances would care to become permanent. I was just that man, for it was now possible for me to accept Professor Carpenter's invitation to return to Columbia in 1908 as an assistant in the Department of English.

And so, in the autumn of 1907, a new and very practical phase of my education started. I found myself, without having taught an hour in my life, the head of a department of three members, with a handsome salary of $1800, with room and board. My two colleagues were women in their forties, college graduates and fine teachers. That they tolerated me is a tribute to their essential kindness; but they did even more by tactfully telling me how to go about my new job. Knowing that it would be fatal to acquire a reputation for being "easy," I assigned to my first section of seniors fourteen English poems to be learned by heart in the first two weeks of the term. Among them were several sonnets, but included also were Gray's "Elegy" and Keat's "Grecian Urn." It never occurred to me until after the class had uttered audible groans and been dismissed that I was morally bound to know the poems myself if I were to retain their respect.

No teacher on the staff smoked, and anyhow I had been assigned a suite in the girls' dormitory and had to be on my best behavior. My only refuge was a beautiful oak grove on the banks of the Neshaminy River, where I soon learned to betake myself after dark and smoke my only pipe of the day. Now I found myself pacing restlessly among the ancient trees, reciting the famous lines. It was a taxing ordeal, but I survived, with the consequence that even now on the slightest provocation I can start off:

It little profits that an idle king,
By this still hearth, among these barren crags,
Match'd with an aged wife, I mete and dole
Unequal laws unto a savage race,
That hoard, and sleep, and feed, and know not me.

Sometimes, as in this case, the discrepancy between my actual situation and the one described in the verses was comical, and any night prowler who heard me would have been frightened out of his wits. But so far as I know my secret has never been revealed until now; and when the pupils began to recite, "Much have I travell'd in the realms of gold," there was I, word and even letter perfect, to prompt the victim and impress him or her with my superior knowledge. The experiment horrified my two department associates, who explained timidly that I had committed one of the unpardonable sins. I have always felt, however, that the members of that class profited by my unintentional cruelty. Best of all my reputation from that moment as a "tough egg" was secure.

This and other less dramatic experiments contributed to my training, and I then and there made the momentous discovery, not yet forgotten, that the quickest way of mastering a subject is to teach it. The efforts which I made to inform myself so that I might keep at least a lap ahead of my pupils did me an immeasurable amount of good; and the process did not cease even when I had years of experience behind me. It may have been hard on the boys and girls, but I had to learn to teach by teaching. Old Dr. Walton was a benevolent and affable soul who was sure that I was doing well so long as I did not trouble him. Thus I was able, with the unconscious co-operation of my students, to work out my own salvation.

Of any science of pedagogy I was blandly ignorant. Never have I taken a course in a school of education, and I have met few first-rate teachers who have done so. Acquaintance with educational psychology may make competent schoolmasters, but cannot turn them into brilliant ones. I had, of course, been exposed to some able teaching in school and college, and in times of stress recalled some of the techniques. But teaching is an art, not a science; and every superior teacher, like every superior artist, though he may begin by imitation, eventually develops his own individual style. The best teaching is not mechanical but personal. Every teacher worth his salt masters the secrets of emphasis and repetition, knows how to introduce anecdotes and reminiscences, and can use humor and criticism at the right moment. He enters the classroom in a mood of alertness, like a man starting on a new adventure. As he proceeds he is quick to shift both tempo and manner if things are not going well. He is ready to galvanize the drowsy with a joke and to stir the indolent by Socratic interrogation. He makes explanations in language which can be understood, answering questions patiently when he believes them to be well meant. By some sixth sense he recognizes the query aimed solely at consuming time, and he eludes the trickery to which healthy American youth resort if they find that a master can be victimized. Like the actor, the teacher must, for an hour in the classroom, throw himself into his part — but he has to walk his stage alone! Rules and systems will avail him little. Only his personality can make him successful. All this I learned gradually, but I was still learning when I taught my last class.

At George School, though I often blundered and blushed at my errors, I decided that I really enjoyed teaching and wished to pursue it as a career. For the previous two years I had been mostly absorbing facts, pursuing a well-defined scholarly path, taking in and seldom giving out. Now I found that explaining a difficult passage to a group of miscellaneous boys and girls was a test of skill and that they were, like an audience, a challenge to the speaker. In my ignorance of procedures I experimented with various devices for holding their attention and even for keeping them awake. I tried subtly to recommend books which would entice them into reading and drive them to the school library. Quaker children are for the most part brought up in simple but cultured homes, indoctrinated early with high ideals of taste and conduct, and are fine material to work with. They know their Bible and are not bewildered when older persons talk to them about the parables and the Beatitudes. I doubt whether in all my career I ever met pupils more responsive than those girls and boys at George School.

I discovered early a fundamental difference in the attitude of the two sexes. Never having had a sister, I was brought up with a romantic conception of girls and even believed, until I saw the George School young ladies at their meals, that they lived on honeydew and probably drank the milk of paradise. When I gave out my first set of marks, I was greeted in my classroom the next morning by a charming girl, who immediately started to weep, eventually almost on my shoulder. "What's the matter with you, Ruth?" I asked, after the deluge of tears. "It's my mark!" she sobbed. I looked at my book and answered, "Why, I gave you a 93 — the second highest grade in the class." "Yes, that's the trouble," was the lachrymose response, "I think I ought to have a 96." I was in a benevolent mood that morning and agreed that I would change the record. She departed very happy. But the good news spread and soon other girls came in, each with her own plausible story. By noon I had altered most of the marks in favor of the fair recipients. The boys, if only they had passed, seemed to feel grateful, and certainly were too proud to make a complaint.

By Thanksgiving I was understandably popular with the female contingent of the undergraduate body — to the consternation of my lady colleagues, who declared that I was a gullible simpleton. They were familiar with the wiles of their own sex, and in their opinion I was destroying all their discipline. Furthermore there was a stampede on the part of the senior girls to be transferred to my divisions. At the opening of the winter term I made a little speech, announcing that the lush days were over and that from then on I should be obdurate, even when deluged with tears.

I learned much in other ways at George School. One member of the staff was a type which I had hitherto regarded as "sissy," for he regularly brought his knitting to faculty meetings and even sometimes darned his own socks. But he was a musical genius who played the piano three or four hours a day — Bach and Chopin and Liszt. He taught me the intricate organization of the sonata and the fugue, and under his gentle tutelage I even ventured into easy compositions for four hands. Soon I was a regular subscriber to the concerts of the Philadelphia Symphony Orchestra, which I understood better because of his professional explanations. For one whose early musical training had been confined largely to playing in the Amherst Mandolin Club and clanging the cymbals in the college band, this was a promotion to the inner circle. My friend brought into my life a new and absorbing interest, which has been both a satisfaction and a solace.

At certain seasons George School was a lovely spot. In the spring the migrating birds, especially the warblers, flew north up the Delaware Valley and I had fun identifying them with the aid of field glasses. In the winter I took long walks along the Neshaminy, through a delightful wooded countryside. One of the teachers, George W. Nutt, had a complete set of Thomas Hardy, and I read in January and February every bit of prose or poetry that he had ever written. To me in these later days he is still the most rewarding of English novelists, and I have nothing but contempt for his disparager, George Moore.

Pleasant though the life was at George School, it did lack excitement, and the discerning Dr. Walton, recognizing in me the symptoms of unrest, would say, "Young man, why don't you go off to the city on Friday night and spend the week end? It will keep you from growing stale." And so back I would go to the familiar Columbia dormitory among my scholarly friends, getting just the respite that I needed. I was the only non-Quaker in the school community, but I conformed to all the local customs; and often on Sunday I would walk to the meeting house at Newtown and marvel at the punctuality with which Dr. Walton, or his charming sister, Mrs. Deborah Stubbs, would rise to speak precisely at the hour of twelve, without any watch or clock in sight to remind them.

My brief sojourn at George School at least enabled me to argue with Perry Smith, Headmaster of the North Shore Country Day School in Chicago, and other defenders of coeducation. The boys whom I met later at Andover were free from the countless distractions which beset young men in institutions where the two sexes are being constantly thrown with one another. The Andover students had tea dances scattered through the term and were allowed to call on the young ladies at Abbot Academy once a week. During the intervals between these diversions they devoted themselves to their masculine pursuits, and I could never see that their attitude towards girls was anything but healthy. My observation leads me to believe that it is normal for boys to wish to have their rugged sports and pastimes by themselves and that it is desirable for them during their tumultuous adolescence to live in a society dominated by males. Never have I heard an Andover undergraduate argue in favor of coeducation;

and I am sure that it encourages a preoccupation with sex rather than an indifference to it.

One could not help admiring the men and women of the Quaker faith. They lived, many of them, beyond the ordinary span of years, and I often met in the forest a sturdy octogenarian chopping down trees, like Adam in *As You Like It,* who was "as a lusty winter, frosty but kindly." They were so simple and sincere, so unostentatiously high-minded, that in their presence I often felt ashamed of my worldliness. They knew the value of leisure, the comfort which follows quiet meditation, the insignificance of material things. As people they had quality. In after years I came to admire Rufus Jones as a perfect representative of the Friends' philosophy — and I know of no finer guide to happy living.

At the close of the school year I departed, feeling that I had been sojourning among the saints. Dr. Walton thanked me cordially for having kept the seat warm for his son, who resumed his position on the faculty and later was elected headmaster in his father's place. From time to time I returned for a day or two to renew my friendships, but one by one the teachers whom I had known disappeared. In the course of time "Young George" himself became "Old George" and finally, after a distinguished career as headmaster, retired. Then I realized that I was no longer in the first flush of youth.

I went to New York to make arrangements for my return to Columbia in the following autumn, and then stopped at Waterville to get ready for a canoe trip which Warner Taylor and I were to take into the Canadian wilderness. We outfitted with Michie & Company in Toronto, had a canoe shipped with us to Temagami Station, and then paddled down the northeast arm of that star-shaped lake to Bear Island, where the famous Dan O'Connor was then the factor. All that summer we paddled and fished, living in the open without guides and sometimes far from any white settlement. I count this, too, as a phase of my education, for although I had been often in the woods as a boy, I had never been quite so far from civilization. The sing of the reel had always sent a tingle up and down my spine, and at Temagami the line was constantly whirling out. We caught mostly small-mouthed black bass — one of the gamiest of fish, especially when you strike a four-pounder on a three-ounce rod.

I came back in early September with a glorious Vandyke beard — which my mother forced me at once to shave off — and reported by telegram to Professor Carpenter. My highest ambition then was, I suppose, to finish my dissertation, get my Ph.D., join the Columbia faculty, and some day take the place of Professor Trent. I little realized how mistaken I was about my future!

V

Finding My Niche

LIKE many people who come from the fresh, uncontaminated ozone of the deep woods into germ-laden civilization, I contracted after my Canadian trip a mean case of tonsillitis, and was lying in bed at Waterville, partly convalescent but still very weak, when a small boy one morning rode up on his bicycle bringing a telegram addressed to me. In those days telegrams were rare in the Fuess family, and my mother waited expectantly while I read it. It was plain and direct:

> CAN YOU COME TO BOSTON TO MEET ME REGARDING POSITION AS INSTRUCTOR IN ENGLISH AT ANDOVER?
>
> ALFRED E. STEARNS

I did at least know where Andover was. As I reread the telegram, I was reminded that Al Stearns, the great Amherst baseball star of the 1890's, was head of an institution called Phillips Academy. But that had no influence on me. I was to be a scholar, and a "prep" school did not stir my interest. The George School interlude had been long enough.

My mind made itself up so automatically that I did not even consult my parents. Hastily scribbling off a brief reply, "Sorry, but not interested," I returned to *The Count of Monte Cristo*. Late in the afternoon the same boy rode up with another yellow envelope. This time the message read: "Can you come as far as Springfield to meet me. Would appreciate it greatly." My father was now home, and I told him briefly what was going on. He felt, like me, that it would be a mistake to consider a secondary school when Columbia, with all its wonderful opportunities, lay before me. I again declined, as politely as possible, and went to sleep without even a thought of the crisis which was happening in my life. The next morning bright and early in came the same boy, with an expression on his face indicating that he was getting a trifle bored. This third message read: "Will you not at least meet me in Albany, at the Ten Eyck Hotel. Will pay all expenses." My father, when he studied this telegram, said, "Claude, this fellow seems to be in earnest. Don't you feel well enough to get up and take the trip to Albany?" I myself was growing a little curious as to what "this man Stearns" had on his mind. Accordingly I sent off a wire agreeing to meet him in Albany and, debilitated though I was, I kept the appointment.

I hasten to interpolate that Al Stearns's desire to talk to me was not due to any resemblance which he had detected between me and Horace Mann or John Dewey. He was up against it! The fall term had hardly begun before one of his best English instructors had resigned in a huff because he had been passed over for the headship of his department. By that date all the private schools had opened, and every available teacher had been engaged. I was probably the only possible candidate in the Eastern area, and Stearns would have offered me the job if I had been even less experienced than I was. All he wanted was somebody with a college degree and not too unprepossessing. Hence his pursuit of his fellow Amherst alumnus.

Al Stearns turned out to be a very persuasive salesman. He frankly admitted his predicament and promptly offered me a salary of $1200, with living quarters and board — very good pay at Andover for a teacher with only one year's experience. I replied unconcernedly that I was already committed to Columbia, and then Al produced his trump card. Professor Carpenter was an Andover graduate, and Stearns had already talked with him on the telephone and convinced him that I would be better off at Phillips Academy for the next year. Therefore, when I explained my situation, Al drew out a telegram from Carpenter advising me to accept the Andover position. Clearly I had to reach a decision in a hurry, and, almost stunned, I agreed to come to Andover on the following day. Before thirty-six hours had passed I was located in Draper Cottage, one of the smaller dormitories, and in the midst of an environment about which I was pitifully ignorant.

Some years later I learned quite by accident that on that same morning Miss Elizabeth Cushing Goodhue, of Andover, who was later to become my wife, was in the Ten Eyck Hotel with her mother, on their way back from a trip to Montreal. When she met Al Stearns in the lobby, she asked, "What in the world are you doing out here just at the time school is opening?" "Oh, I had to come on to see a teacher about a job." "Well," replied Miss Goodhue, "he must have plenty of nerve to make you take such a long trip just to see him." She little knew that she was making her first comment on her prospective husband!

Draper Cottage was populated by ten so-called Commons boys, who were working their way through school and were much more mature than the average undergraduate. Indeed at least two of them were older than I was, and they were full-grown, independent, and unaccustomed to taking orders. They were, however, most courteous and proceeded to enlighten me on various matters of rules and privileges with which I was unfamiliar. It was plain that in their opinion I was not merely an equal but possibly a subordinate — a necessary evil whom they were ready to tolerate so long as

I behaved myself and did not interfere with them. My welcome was disconcerting, after my despotic role in George School; and when at luncheon I met some of my new faculty colleagues, including "Colonel" Horace M. Poynter, they made it clear that my assignment was, for a "greenhorn," a very tough one.

Through that day I followed the wise practice of saying little and listening much. But when I returned to Draper in the evening, not quite sure what course of action to adopt, I was greeted by one of the occupants — the star second baseman on the baseball nine — who was apparently in a state of garrulous intoxication. He reeled up to me and said in a silly mumble, "I want a thousand excuses to go to Lawrence — I jess gotta have 'em!" Shocked, I collected my wits and said as sternly as I could, "Bennett, you go to your room immediately, and I shall report you at once to the principal." With a shamefaced expression he slunk off; and one of the oldest boys in the house — Jim Reilly — who later became a close friend of mine, rushed up and said, "I wouldn't tell the principal about this if I were you. It'll get poor Bennett in a lot of trouble." "I don't care," I cried angrily, and dashed off up the street to inform Al what had happened. He listened patiently, only commenting, "Bennett? That doesn't make sense to me." He did, however, walk back with me to Draper, where a small crowd had gathered, in the midst of which was Georgie Hinman, Instructor in Latin, who was excitedly haranguing the group, to their intense delight. The minute Hinman saw Stearns he burst out in relief, "Mr. Stearns, it's nothing but a society initiation — Fuess didn't understand." I am sure, as I look back, that the incident was my initiation as well as Bennett's.

I was not unfamiliar with fraternities at Amherst, but it never occurred to me that a preparatory school would have such organizations. Poor Bennett, who had been pledged to what was known as P.B.X., now appeared, unquestionably sober and full of apprehension. The Reilly Brothers and the Burdett Brothers — all outstanding athletes and residents of Draper Cottage — had ordered him to put the exhibition on for my benefit, thinking, of course, that I would sense the situation. A full explanation was made. Al laughingly warned the boys not to carry the matter too far, especially with an "outlander" like me, and everything ended amicably.

In case any possible reader of this book may be as uninformed on the subject as I was in 1908, I will say that the two Phillips Academies — one at Andover and the other at Exeter, in New Hampshire — founded in the Revolutionary period by members of the same family, are the oldest and the most completely indigenous of the great American independent schools. Andover, opened in 1778 in the calamitous winter of Valley Forge, is the older of the two, but they have gone along for nearly a century and three quarters of friendly rivalry. They have remained approximately the same in size, objectives, and endowment, and when at certain periods one has forged slightly ahead of the other, new leaders and benefactors have appeared to rectify the discrepancy.

Both started under the sponsorship of Harvard men, but when Harvard in the early nineteenth century turned towards Unitarianism, Phillips Academy — the official and legal name of the Andover school — was tied up with Andover Theological Seminary and, remaining true to its original Calvinistic Congregationalism, began to send more and more boys to conservative Yale. Unlike Winchester, Eton, and Harrow, Andover and Exeter have always aimed to send all their students to college; and in 1908 an overwhelming majority of the students were intending to go on to Harvard, Yale, Princeton, Dartmouth, Williams, Amherst, and the better known eastern higher institutions. It would be fair to say, however, that at the period when I arrived the predominant influence at Andover was from New Haven. Indeed then, and for many years afterwards, one tenth of the Yale undergraduate body had prepared at Andover, and many of the great Yale athletes, like the Blisses, Hinkey, Bloomer, Kilpatrick, Morse, Murphy, and Daly, were Andover men.

Phillips Academy opened in 1908 with an enrollment of 490 students and a faculty of 30 members. It was beginning to move into a new era under the energizing leadership of Alfred E. Stearns, who had been elected principal in 1903, at the age of thirty-two. During the months following the death of Principal Cecil F. P. Bancroft, on October 4, 1901, the school passed through an interregnum, when no one was sure just what would happen and the discipline was much relaxed. Stearns, after graduating from Phillips Academy and Amherst and teaching for a short time at the Hill School, had returned to Andover, partly to study in the Theological Seminary but also to work under his uncle, Dr. Bancroft. He shortly became baseball coach, registrar, teacher, and eventually personal secretary to the enfeebled principal, and was regarded, in spite of his youth, as the logical heir-apparent. He stepped into a position of authority gradually after Bancroft's death, serving as vice-principal before his election as principal. He was vigorous, courageous, imaginative, and very popular, especially among the students, who admired his athletic ability, and he had a very well-developed sense of humor.

In 1908, although he had been in office only five years, Stearns had already accomplished what seemed like miracles. For a century Phillips Academy and Andover Theological Seminary had existed within a stone's throw of one another under the same Board of Trustees, who spent most of their deliberations on the higher institution. The Seminary, conservative in its policies even when it was founded, had begun to lose ground in the 1880's, when a notorious heresy trial revealed its position as a citadel of obsolete theological orthodoxy. By the close of the century the number on its faculty was almost as large as the student body, and its beautiful buildings were almost deserted. Meanwhile the Academy had grown in enrollment and prestige, and was looking in an acquisitive mood at the plant across the street which was not being put to productive use.

One of Stearns's first jobs had been to create a separate Board of Trustees for Phillips Academy, and then to arrange, after some difficult negotiations, for the transfer of the Seminary property, including two large dormitories, a lecture building, a library, a chapel, and several very beautiful residential houses, to the Academy, together with about two hundred acres of land on Andover Hill. All this required purchase money, and Stearns, with his former roommate and friend, James C. Sawyer, who was treasurer of the school, undertook to raise the funds. Often the two cooled their heels in the outer offices of millionaires, and occasionally they were ejected without a hearing. The two made a wonderful team — Sawyer with his charm and tact and wide acquaintance and Stearns with his moral earnestness. It was a partnership of the Cavalier and the Puritan. "We were both beggars," Al used to say, "and sometimes we pleaded with all our souls and came out with a hundred dollars!"

By 1908, Andover Hill belonged to and was Phillips Academy. The Seminary, all except the library, had been moved to Cambridge, and what had started a century before as a protest against Harvard and its Unitarianism was now located in the camp of the enemy. Stearns tore down or moved the two rows of ugly wooden dormitories called the Latin and English Commons, and the ground where they had stood was graded and sodded. The transformation was complete.

Phillips Academy had flourished for years with inadequate equipment, and some of its dormitories were better suited to a slum district than a school. James G. Blaine, when he was in the cabinet, came to Andover with his sons to look over the institution. Principal Bancroft escorted him about the grounds, and when the tour was over the statesman said, "Well, Doctor, I've made up my mind to enroll my boys here — if you will permit me." "Good," responded Bancroft. "And now would you object to telling me how you happened to make your decision?" "Certainly not," answered Blaine. "Any school which can build up such a fine reputation in spite of such wretched buildings and equipment must have something — and I want my family to find out what it is."

Now, by a lucky turn of fate, Phillips Academy had secured most of what it needed. It took some time to effect the transition. The removal of the dust-covered Seminary books from Brechin Hall was slow, but the school by 1910 had its own librarian, and the ground floor of the building provided much-needed office space for the school administrators. At last the boys could all be housed in dormitories controlled by the trustees, and the landlady system, with all its disadvantages, could be eliminated. The policy of housing all the students under direct faculty supervision was of incalculable service in eliminating disciplinary problems and bringing about order on the campus.

Again and again I have heard Al Stearns tell, with grim humor, of the situation which he had to face during his first five years. The undergraduates were on the average much older than they are today, more independent, and very jealous of what they regarded as their prerogatives. They played in sports against Yale and Princeton and Amherst — often defeating them, especially in baseball — and consequently felt that they were entitled to the freedom and privileges of college men. The boys who were working their way through school had plenty of independence. Often they were good athletes, and they certainly monopolized the school offices. I have never seen in operation a democracy more complete than that which had been built up at Andover. If there was any aristocracy, it was not the result of wealth or social position, but was created by the so-called Commons boys, living in Brick House, Clement House, and Draper Cottage.

With characteristic wisdom Mr. Stearns soon abolished the separate Commons houses and assigned the scholarship students to various dormitories scattered over the Hill. After that, rich and poor boys were located on the same corridor and mingled with one another as they had never done under the earlier policy of segregation.

Al had undergone two or three rather ghastly experiences shortly after becoming principal. An unfortunate case of mass cribbing on the entrance examinations for Princeton had brought the school some undesirable publicity. In 1905 a large group of undergraduates, incensed at the manager of the Phillips Inn because it was reported that he had divulged the name of an undergraduate "wolf" who had kissed a waitress, formed a parade one warm spring evening, marched to the Inn, seized the manager, and ducked him in the nearby shallow Rabbit Pond. Stearns, who was in Pittsburgh at the time, was recalled by telegram and came back to find a faculty investigation under way and the student body sullen and uncommunicative. Finally the decision was reached to expel some thirty boys whose complicity could be proved — many of them prominent in campus affairs. The news leaked out, and the next morning before chapel service, which was held in those days at 7:45, nearly the entire school assembled across the street, where they were harangued by their leaders and urged to remain away in protest.

Al often told me how he walked over to the Main Building where chapel was held, found it deserted by students, and waited with some of the faculty, wondering what he would do if a strike actually occurred. The bell began to toll, and still no move was made from the throng. But when only a minute was left, a break came in the ranks. A few boys started off, clearly terrified of consequences. Soon the whole crowd was in movement, and when the bell had ceased ringing, every boy was in his seat. "That," said Stearns, "was the decisive point in my career as principal. If I had lost that battle, I should have had to resign." He had some fear that the "ducking episode" — as it has always been called — might have a detrimental effect on the next year's registration, but as so often happens, doubtful fathers and mothers concluded that a school must be all right which could take such prompt and drastic action to meet an emergency. After that incident, the undergraduates decided that the principal was a strong man, and behaved accordingly.

The principal was indeed a strong man. It took plenty of courage for a young man still under forty to face 450 rather irresponsible undergraduates, some of them as old as the average college sophomore, and win their confidence even when he had to inflict punishment. For some time he felt as if he were sitting on a slumbering but still active volcano. When I first knew him, he walked around the grounds each night to make sure that all the boys were in their rooms and not out on a rampage. Shortly after I arrived, I was taken by a faculty colleague to a rather famous night club called Ferncroft, on the North Shore. As I was casually glancing over the register, I noticed to my astonishment the names of eminent professors in the Theological Seminary and of an elderly and very pious gentleman on the Academy faculty, with opprobrious nicknames attached — all signed, as I quickly discovered, by wandering Andover students. Much of this deviltry was eliminated after I came to the school, by the very simple process of direct faculty supervision.

In some of my first classes were pupils who were older than I was, and I was afraid that I might not be able to get them under control. I remember vividly one magnificent athlete, well over six feet tall with arms stretching down almost to his knees, and hands like hams. He played tackle on the football eleven, and he could have plucked me easily by main strength from my place behind the desk. But he was always docile, except on the football gridiron, and struggled painfully with his books. Finally, after spending two years vainly trying to pass the work of the lowest class, he was asked by the principal, in the words of the euphemism so familiar to all Andover men, to "sever his connection with the Academy." What amounted then to a "double standard" for athletes disappeared early in Stearn's administration.

My admiration and affection for Al Stearns make it difficult for me to characterize him objectively. What he was will appear more and more as this narrative proceeds, for he was literally my "guide, counselor, and friend," and I viewed him only a little this side of idolatry. He was definitely a man's man, apparently rather embarrassed with women and never quite at home at formal social functions. He was tall and angular, with a shock of reddish hair which gradually during his administration turned to a glorious pure white, a long nose (or "beak," as he called it), and a resolute jaw. In spite of accidents which prevented him from playing much football at Amherst, he was one of the great athletes of his generation, and had many offers to play professional baseball with the major leagues. Until middle life, he invariably pitched for the alumni against the school nine at commencement and was tremendously applauded when he struck out one of his students, as he did quite frequently. On his fiftieth birthday, June 6, 1921, he pitched six innings against the school team and won for the alumni.

As time went on, I came to know Al better and better, for we had many tastes in common. I went often to his camp on Second Connecticut Lake in northern New Hampshire. On my first visit, evidently to try me out, he and Larry Shields, after talking at supper about the ferocity of the local wildcats, called me at dusk to the window and pointed out one of the savage creatures — a stuffed animal which they had prepared to frighten greenhorns. When I rushed for a rifle to slay the beast, his delight was unbounded. I recall his amusement when I once, while fishing, missed my footing and went bobbing and floating like a cork down Perry Stream. He was a fine sportsman, never complaining about poor weather or bad luck and always doing more than his share of the chores. Nor was he a prig or an ascetic in his personal habits but very human and ready to join in the fun.

After I became alumni secretary, we went on speaking trips together, twice across the continent, and he was a perfect traveling companion, always trying to preempt the upper berth and leaving the more comfortable lower one to me. It was difficult to get ahead of him in courtesy or sacrifice, and he was constantly on the watch for the pleasure of those around him.

One outstanding trait was his moral fervor. His prayers in morning chapel, always extemporaneous, were very moving, and I can still remember his fervent and frequent exhortation, "Keep us, O Lord, from those things which are base and sordid and mean and vile." He was in some respects an evangelist and spoke like a modern Savonarola, denouncing the sins of our society. Caring more for the spiritual than the intellectual aspects of education, he was frankly not much interested in psychological theories or experimental changes. In the Headmasters Association, as we shall see, he was a stalwart member of the Old Guard, along with Endicott Peabody and Horace Taft, and had a good deal of fun at the expense of what he called the "Teachers' College Crowd."

Al was clearly governed more by his emotions than by his reason. He was impulsive and quick-tempered, apt to make snap judgments which he later regretted. He seemed to me very much like Andrew Jackson, sympathetic with the underdog, loyal to his friends, even when they betrayed his trust, and more strongly affected by personalities than by ideas. Like Jackson also he was at heart a simple person, disliking pomp and circumstance and allowing himself to be publicized only with the utmost reluctance. His was the power which comes from strong character and right instincts, backed by a consistent and uncompromising Christian faith.

The quality of the man is illustrated by the long list of his friends from many walks of life, including bishops, bankers, college presidents, industrialists, guides, and janitors. The austerity which he showed in the pulpit was no index of his appealing humanity. Those early years at Andover were hard ones, but he won the victory. By 1908 the boys knew that he was the master, and the faculty and alumni were sure that the school was in the right hands.

VI

Personalities and Policies

ALTHOUGH I had no realization of it in 1908, I was to remain at Phillips Academy for forty years — twenty-five as instructor in English, with many subsidiary jobs, and fifteen as headmaster. I soon came to love both the school and the town, their traditions and their people, and I rejoiced in the surrounding countryside. The opportunities offered by the school were so great that, in spite of invitations to join college faculties, and calls to headmasterships, I decided that I would be happier where I was. Andover became my geographical and spiritual home. I enjoyed the friendships which I made and the continuing education which they brought; and I have never for one moment regretted the stroke of chance which placed me in that pleasant and stimulating environment.

Perhaps my impressions of the Academy during my early years there may throw some light on American secondary education in the twentieth century. No one could doubt that the teaching staff was exceptionally strong. They kept the standards high. Incompetence was simply not tolerated. Yet the members differed markedly in training, character, and attitude. Among the many older instructors of outstanding ability with whom I became intimate I would name three — Charles H. Forbes, Allan R. Benner, and Archibald Freeman — who had come to Phillips Academy in the early nineties, fresh from college, and remained there for the rest of their professional careers. They were, of course, somewhat senior to Stearns and treated him, when he came back to the Hill in 1897, like a younger brother. His promotion to the principalship naturally altered their relations for his new position required some official deference; but I think that he never quite got over looking up to them as superior to him in practical knowledge. I soon noticed that he often yielded to them on matters of curricular policy.

Charlie Forbes in Latin and "Zeus" Benner in Greek, continued ably the classical tradition which had made Andover famous. Whenever Stearns showed any signs of capitulating to insistent "modernism" they kept him orthodox. Forbes was a ruddy-faced, thick-set man, of highly social propensities, whose home was an entertainment center for his countless friends. As a host in his own drawing room he was affable and generous, and his frequent parties were distinguished by a lavishness which I had seldom seen. In his thinking he was broad rather than deep, clever rather than profound, but he possessed a wide culture outside of his own special field, and he was a brisk and convincing talker whose philosophy of life was clear and well-ordered. He had traveled and read with discrimination, and was a most diverting raconteur. After his death I tried to express my affection for him and his gracious wife, Nellie, in an article entitled "Going Out to the Forbeses." Charlie made the *Aeneid* an instrument for a liberal education on many topics, and like every first-rate teacher, he taught more than his subject. In those days when recitation sections were large, he met nearly every member of the senior class, and the influence of his urbane and civilized mind was felt over the campus. It meant everything to me to be brought into contact with the Forbeses, who had so much to give and were apparently not bored by a junior who admired them unstintedly and openly.

Zeus Benner was a shy and sensitive scholar who, to use his

own phrase, had never been trapped into matrimony. Once when he was a guest at a hospitable home in the village, his hostess requested him to escort an attractive young teacher at Abbot Academy back to her apartment. He flushed, and blowing out his cheeks like Dr. Johnson, replied, "Yes, I am willing to do so — if you will tell her that I mean nothing by it!" Benner was a Harvard graduate, and one of the finest gentlemen I have ever known. He was co-operative in his political views, belonging to the right wing of the Republican party. During the New Deal period, when he was particularly unhappy, he went down, as he always did, to get his mail at the local post office. It was closed for Washington's Birthday, and Benner was locked out. As he came down the steps, some one heard him mumbling, "Damn this Roosevelt administration!"

By 1908, Greek was no longer a required subject in the Andover curriculum, and Zeus frequently told me that he regarded this as the beginning of the downfall of American education. Nevertheless he continued to have pupils and to exert a salutary influence on the boys who elected his courses. He made many of them happy by taking them on canoe trips up the Shawsheen River and inviting them to dinner and the theater in Boston. In his later years he led, I think, a rather lonely life, for he had grown too old for easy companionship with youth, and he felt that the world had passed him by. But to the end he had a nobility of mind and presence which were most impressive.

Archie Freeman, Head of the Department of History, was, like Forbes, a Brown graduate, but the two men had little else in common except that they were both superb teachers. Forbes was rotund, tolerant, and conservative; Freeman was thin, highly specialized in his interests, and liberal in his philosophy. Freeman was a "strict constructionist," who believed in enforcing all school regulations to the letter, but he also had a rare sense of humor and a lambent wit which enlivened many a faculty meeting, and his conversation was delightful. Before I arrived a disagreement had arisen between Forbes and Freeman which defied all the efforts of their friends to bring them together. Tactful hostesses saw to it that they were never invited together to the same dinner party. Forbes would, I am sure, have been willing to see the breach healed, but Freeman was implacable. Freeman it was who encouraged my ventures into political biography, and I owe him a very great debt.

Freeman and his closest friend, James G. Graham (Jimmy), who taught chemistry were both bachelors and lived on opposite sides of the same dormitory. They were inveterate practical jokers, and nobody knew who would be the next victim. Once while their fellow teacher, George W. Benedict, afterwards a professor at Brown, went out for a few hours, the two men entered his study, removed the large coal stove which heated it, and substituted a very small stove, which they carefully attached to the stovepipe. Benedict's astonishment when he beheld the transformation was described as having been both fluent and fiery. If the undergraduates at Andover had only known of the antics of their dignified instructors, they would have perceived that teachers, even when outwardly formidable, are but children of a larger growth. When one of the students asked Freeman why there was a spring on the entrance door to the dormitory, that instructor replied that it was an instrument which registered whenever a boy left the building after eight o'clock. Years later, when the youth returned as a prosperous alumnus, he told Freeman, "You know, I actually believed what you said about that door spring, and whenever I went out after hours I always opened a window and crawled out rather than use the door!"

Forbes, Benner, and Freeman were not only first-rate teachers but also scholars, great readers of books and ponderers on events, the most stimulating company possible for a novice ambitious to succeed. I cannot exaggerate the influence which they had on my susceptible mind. With them I must mention two others whose friendship was both a spur and a solace. Markham W. Stackpole had come to Phillips Academy, at Stearns's urgent invitation, in 1907, to accept the position of school minister and help to build up the religious life of the undergraduates. He and his wife, Agnes, rented what was then the Phelps House, the beautiful Bulfinch residence directly across from the main campus. I have never met a nobler character than Mark Stackpole. He never indulged in malicious gossip or had a mean or vulgar thought. To some he seemed austere and reserved, especially in his later life, but his heart was warm and his spirit full of animation. Within a few months he had, through his own contagious enthusiasm, aroused my interest in the as yet unwritten history of Phillips Academy; and it was at his instigation that I prepared and published in 1917 my book, *An Old New England School.*

Mark was versatile and very much alive. He and his family enjoyed informal charades, and at Thanksgiving the whole house was given over to the guests, who were free to roam everywhere in quest of stage properties — fur coats, silk hats, sheets, and even potted plants. Before the evening was over the Phelps House was a shambles, but even the long-suffering inmates had had a happy evening. Mark liked to walk, and often we would start out cross country, without deviation for swamps or streams, for some designated point, such as Prospect Hill or Rattlesnake Hill. With him I covered every path or wood road in the countryside, finding such out-of-the-way spots as the soapstone quarry, the black tarn, and the sandy dunes known mysteriously as the Land of Nod. As we strode along, we would recite passages from famous orations which we had memorized at school: Wendell Phillips on "Daniel O'Connell," Henry W. Grady on "The New South," and Robert G. Ingersoll on "James A. Garfield"; and once, as I burst forth in a magnificent paragraph ending: "Never till Duty, Stern Daughter of the Voice of God, shall cease to speak can the work of the Ironsides be ended!" a farm laborer rose up from behind a stone wall, shouted, "Good God Almighty!" and ran as briskly as he could across the meadow. Later Mark, although forty-six and beyond the age limit for service, secured in 1917 a special dispensation and enlisted as Chaplain of the 102nd Field Artillery of the Yankee Division and was overseas for twenty-six months. He was in most of the major American engagements, served gallantly under fire, and returned with shattered nerves from which he never fully recovered. For me Mark Stackpole was the embodiment of conscience, and I would have trusted his judgment on any moral issue.

At my first meal in the dining hall after my arrival, the man sitting at the head of the table reserved for bachelor members of the faculty was Horace Martin Poynter, already known as Colonel because of his Kentucky origin. Six years older than I, he had been an instructor in Latin at the Academy since 1902, and in that brief period had built up a reputation for severity in the classroom which had made the undergraduate loafers regard him as a holy terror. His insistence on accuracy and thoroughness and his impatience with mediocrity had created a tradition. But his adherence to exacting standards won him the admiration of the younger group of teachers who sat together in the dining hall. We liked him all the better because he would not compromise or conciliate, but stood by his pedagogical guns. As a matter of fact, he was by nature a very kindly, indeed a rather sentimental type of man, and, like Dr. Johnson, had nothing of the bear about him but the skin. I have known him to spend precious hours outside of the classroom with a slow, faithful boy, refusing to accept any compensation.

Even in those far-off days the Colonel was an unabashed pessimist, with the conviction, expressed in picturesque language, that the school and the world, including himself, were on their way to hell. Once when we were watching a steam shovel at its deadly work in excavating for a new building, he remarked, "Well, Jack, it won't be long before they'll be shoveling the dirt in on you and me!" To observations of this nature, as he and I grew older and older, I made reply in the words of the poet:

The good die young,
And they whose hearts are dry as summer dust
Burn to the socket.

But Poynter's melancholy was only superficial: although he was *tristis in modo,* he was *laetus in re.* He had an amazing fund of anecdotes, a new one for each occasion, and he was the most delightful company even when he growled *de profundis.* He loved games, especially bridge and billiards and golf, invariably announcing before each contest that he was certain to lose. It was he who, during a golf match at the Abenaqui Club, at Rye Beach, New Hampshire, when his caddy stepped in front of him as he was about to drive, shouted, "Get out of my way, son. I don't mind killing you, but I don't want to get my ball covered with blood."

The faculty atmosphere was one of frank cordiality. Having come direct from George School, where smoking was not permitted on the campus, I moved warily at first, not knowing what to expect. But at my first meeting with Archie Freeman, he drew out a cigar and handed it to me. "Is it all right for me to smoke this?" I asked, still a little uncertain. "That's what it's for," he answered, and I was put at ease immediately. There was no hypocrisy among the faculty members.

They behaved like normal members of society, not like beings set apart. It was a community, furthermore, where one quickly acquired the "first name" habit — except towards the elder statesmen, Graves, McCurdy, and Eaton, who seemed too remote for me to give them anything but their proper titles. So far as I could see, everybody wanted to help me. It was easily discernible that I was inexperienced and naïve, but nobody seemed to mind. Nobody offered me any direct advice as to how to teach, but I kept my eyes and ears open and tried to keep from making too many blunders.

I observed within a week that the standards of teaching, the classroom morale, were very high. Misbehavior was not tolerated, and "freshness" was punished with incredible rapidity. The inexcusable sin, from the viewpoint of both boys and faculty, was for an instructor to be an "easy mark." I was astonished at my first faculty meeting to find how ruthless the teachers were. We sat, perhaps thirty of us, in none too comfortable chairs around the four walls of the principal's office in Brechin Hall, while name after name was brought up for discussion. Such comments as "lazy loafer," "not college material," "never should have been admitted," were tossed about easily and without any animosity. The feeling was general that any boy who couldn't or wouldn't make the grade should be asked to withdraw, and very little attempt was made in those days to ascertain why he was failing. The mere fact that he was flunking was sufficient.

Now and then Mr. Stearns would twist in his chair as some particularly scathing indictment was made by a caustic master. Later I was to discover, sitting myself behind the headmaster's desk, how often well-intentioned teachers could condemn a boy without realization of the various factors which affect an adolescent's moods and progress. The "sink or swim" idea was, however, in those days regarded as Andover's proud possession, and I can remember myself boasting that our faculty made no allowances, not even for the son of the president of the Board of Trustees. I recall that at the end of a rather brief post-Christmas faculty meeting one of the older members remarked casually, "This is an unusual meeting — we haven't fired anybody!" Whereupon Jimmy Graham looked up and said, "I've got a candidate. I move that Randolph be fired. He hasn't done a stitch of work since vacation." Believe it or not, after some perfunctory discussion the boy was dropped, and nobody seemed to be particularly disturbed. As it turned out, the young man doubtless deserved his fate, but the manner of his expulsion rankled in my heart for many years.

As I learned later, it is very easy for a teacher, momentarily exasperated, to wish to get rid of an unpromising or mischievous pupil. He forgets, however, that the burden of carrying out the sentence rests not on him but on the headmaster, who probably knows more than anybody else about the factors involved and who is aware of the army of sisters and cousins and aunts who will be affected. As headmaster I often, after asking a father to withdraw his son, could not sleep that night, so conscious was I of the fallibility of human judgments.

Fortunately the system at Andover has since become far more intelligent. Boys are now studied carefully from every angle, psychological and physiological, and there are no offhand dismissals. Cases do exist, of course, where the offense is so flagrant that it cannot be disregarded. But the wise teacher learns to make allowances for the idiosyncrasies of adolescence and understands that development in boys moves in phases. An indiscretion is not a sin. A master in a school must acquire patience, remembering that plenty of annoying boys have turned into most respectable adults. This basic fact was not emphasized when I first attended Andover faculty meetings.

Teachers, like other men, may be divided into two different groups. One is made up of "strict constructionists," who trust in clearly expressed rules, firmly enforced, without any allowance for circumstances. Regarding these, Albert Einstein has said, "To me the worst thing seems to be for a school principally to work with methods of fear, force, and artificial authority." The other group believes in a certain degree of flexibility, based on a careful consideration of motives and conditions. The famous Exeter dictum, "This school has no rules until they are broken," has much to recommend it. In my early days at Andover, "bounds" were very carefully marked on a map which was distributed to the students, and "out of bounds without permission" was regarded as a very serious infraction of the regulations. Two teachers taking a walk observed an undergraduate crossing a bridge into forbidden territory and reported him to the office. When he was interviewed by the principal, the lad explained that his hat had blown across the little stream and that he had chased it "out of bounds." This excuse was sustained by the two classmates who were with him, but when the case was brought before the full faculty, a majority voted for his expulsion. In this instance the principal for some reason confided to me his doubts of the wisdom or justice of our action; but he added that the two teachers who reported the offense were of such strong influence with their colleagues that he felt it to be injudicious to overrule the decision. I must add that such drastic action would not be taken today.

The younger men on the faculty were naturally too timid to say very much in the presence of their elders. Furthermore, to tell the truth, we were ourselves rather proud of being connected with a school which would tolerate no monkey business. And it is true that the system, although it would now be regarded as barbaric, did produce a group of very independent, very mature, graduates. It was survival not necessarily of the "fittest" but certainly of the "best-adjusted," and we had no reason to be ashamed of the results. Many men for whom I have the highest respect look back nostalgically on their Andover experience with the feeling, "Well, some injustice may have been done, but it was good for most of us." On the other hand, some of the victims were permanently embittered. It was easy to believe that being "fired" saved many a boy who through punishment was awakened to a sense of the meaning of life. But I am sure that very few teachers would wish to return to a system which brought unhappiness to so many.

A very large proportion of the curriculum was devoted to the study of language, especially Latin, and even in the modern languages the emphasis was on visual, not auditory, instruction. As I have previously stated, Andover had a strong classical tradition; and Latin, from Caesar through Cicero to Virgil, was not only a basic but a compulsory subject. When President Eliot, Abram Flexner, and other educational iconoclasts expressed doubt as to the value of Latin for everybody, Forbes led the other members of the Latin Department in defense of their cause. They could not well stress their most effective argument — that the best teaching in those days was being done in the classics. Rather they maintained that Latin, and to some extent Greek, were indispensable adjuncts of the highest culture. Professor Forbes, who ranged in his senior classroom over all history and philosophy, did not realize that Latin as taught in the first year was often no more valuable than the repetition of numbers and addresses in the telephone book. Many a small boy with a naturally inquisitive mind, when subjected to incessant drill in conjugations and declensions, was driven to hate foreign languages. I personally knew dozens of boys who suffered — and rebelled. But the doctrine that it was good for a boy to study subjects which he didn't like — that it brought iron into his soul — was still prevalent. The hour came when more and more voices were raised against drillmaster methods and when doubt was expressed whether the recitation of case endings and of prepositions taking the dative really improved the mind. Albert Einstein, whom I have quoted before, once wrote, "The most important motive for work in the school and in life is the pleasure in work, pleasure in its results and the knowledge of the value of the result to the community." Although I lacked the self-assurance to come out publicly in favor of interest as an incentive, I had many an argument with my friends, the supporters of the established order; and I had a secret feeling, even in the 1920's, that both Benner and Forbes knew only too well that they were fighting for a cause which was already lost.

I should be guilty of concealment if I did not present this phase of my reactions. I must now add that what I admired most about my colleagues as I came to know them was the way in which they used their subjects as a key to life. The teacher of algebra covered much more than his limited mathematical field, by relating figures and formulas to the world around him and what was happening in it. The teacher of French did far more than have his pupils memorize the irregular verbs. He tried to show them something of France and of the French mind in operation. The faculty may have been, as some of them suggested, too highly departmentalized, but this was only on paper in the catalogue. Most of them ranged far and wide in their digressions. Poynter would apply a passage in Caesar to a situation in the war with Germany. Forbes often took his *Aeneid* as a text for something resembling a sermon. Yet his pupils passed their College Board examinations without sitting up all night with wet towels around their foreheads. They had developed a general ability for independent thinking which was far more important than the acquisition of special knowledge.

As my year at Andover drew to a close, I was again forced to make a decision, for I was once more invited by Professor Carpenter to take a position at Columbia and President Harris asked me to return to Amherst as an instructor. By this time, however, I had discovered how fortunate I was to have landed at Phillips Academy. With my fellow English teacher, Henry N. Sanborn, I was editing my first book, *English Narrative Poems,* which had been accepted by the Macmillan Company and was to appear that autumn as one of the Pocket American and English Classics. Furthermore my salary had been increased, and Mr. Stearns had let me know that I was not doing badly. Consequently I declined the offers from Columbia and Amherst, and set off in late June on the steamship *Berlin* for Naples, with three friends of my New York days — Bill Otis, Al Stout, and Art Bauer. We spent the summer traveling inexpensively through Italy, Switzerland, Germany, France, Holland, and England, being joined along the route by my close friend, Warner Taylor. In the fall I found that my quarters in Draper Cottage had been improved by the addition of a modern bathroom, so that I no longer had to resort to the huge tin tub in the basement when I wished to get clean. Soon *English Narrative Poems* came out, and I was the proudest budding author in the United States. My share of the so-called honorarium was only $100, but the important matter was that for the first time my name appeared on the title page of a book.

In my second year at Andover I became engaged to Miss Goodhue, who lived in the town, but we agreed that we would not marry until I had completed my dissertation and received my doctorate. Accordingly in the summer of 1910 I accepted a very lucrative offer to go to Europe as a tutor for John Harbison McLennan, of Louisville, one of my Andover students who needed some help with Virgil before he could make Yale. With Mrs. McLennan, her two small daughters, and John, I sailed on the *Berengaria,* in such luxury as I had never before enjoyed, and eventually settled down with my pupil at the Hotel Randolph, in Oxford. It was a delightful summer, for we did not study more than three hours in the morning and spent the remainder of the day punting on the Isis, swimming, and bicycling over the Oxfordshire countryside, sometimes far into the Cotswolds.

Wishing to carry on some research in the Bodleian Library, I presented myself one morning to Dr. Nicholson, the librarian, with my credentials. I told him I was investigating English satire and had my degree of A.M. from Columbia. "You mean your M.A.," he snorted. "No," I replied, "that isn't what they call it in America!" "Well," he growled, "if you are such a fool as not to know that your degree is an M.A., you don't deserve the privileges of this library." Back I went to the Randolph Hotel — a saddened and discouraged young scholar.

The next afternoon I went with Mrs. McLennan to call on Sir William Osler, then Regius Professor at Oxford, at his residence at 13 Norham Gardens. I was only twenty-four years old, shy by nature and certainly very much flustered at the prospect of meeting the great man. He was then sixty, at the height of his international reputation — an erect figure, with most impressive drooping mustachios, a stiff wing collar, a receding forehead, and very brilliant dark eyes. He received Mrs. McLennan cordially as an old friend, and soon I was listening spellbound as he displayed his wonderful collection of Whitmania, smoothing the volumes affectionately as he told me how he attended Whitman in 1886. He asked me why I was in Oxford, and I found myself plaintively describing my grim encounter with the guardian of the Bodleian Library. "Why," he burst out indignantly, "I'm one of Nicholson's bosses. He ought not to have treated you like that." I learned then that Osler was not only *ex officio* a curator of the library, but also a member of the standing committee, which met there every Friday afternoon. "You come with me tomorrow morning," he said, "and we'll fix that old fossil!"

The next morning promptly at ten I called again at the Osler home, and he walked with me to the library. Striding straight into the lair of the library watchdog, he said, "Dr. Nicholson, I want to introduce a young American friend of mine who wishes to study here." The inhospitable crab of the day before smiled blandly, shook my hand as if I were President of the Royal Society, and responded, "Certainly, Sir William, we'll do everything in our power to facilitate the gentleman's researches." From that moment, whenever I crossed the sacred threshold, the librarian literally dogged my steps — whether I was A.M. or M.A. — asking anxiously whether I was getting the service I required. Never did contempt change more quickly to obsequiousness, and all through the kindly intervention of a man whom I then barely knew.

When we returned in September, John, to my delight, passed his entrance examination in Latin; and after a brief visit to Andover, I returned to the familiar atmosphere of Livingston Hall to finish my dissertation. I had saved some money, which I supplemented by tutoring and by teaching German for a few weeks in the Collegiate School. But my time was spent mostly on my dissertation, and I allowed nothing to interfere with that important project. Fortunately my topic — "*Lord Byron as a Satirist in Verse*" — was an interesting one, offering plenty of material, and I felt that in a slight way I was making a contribution to knowledge and not merely marking time. In June the dissertation was approved and sent to the publisher, and I was finally awarded my degree of Doctor of Philosophy in June 1912. In those days the doctoral dissertations in English had to be published at the expense of the candidate, and when I had paid the printer's bill I had hardly a dollar in the bank.

In June, 1911, Miss Goodhue and I were married at Andover and spent our honeymoon at the Birches, a hotel colony on an island in Lake Mooselookmeguntic in Maine. On the day after our arrival we were canoeing, and my bride, to keep herself occupied, dropped overboard a line with a plebeian worm-baited hook, hoping to attract a stray perch. Suddenly a terrific tug nearly drew her overboard, and she hastily handed the tackle to me. We had no landing net or gaff, and finally I asked her to paddle slowly along the shore until we had exhausted or drowned our catch. After what must have been over half an hour, we approached the dock and I slowly drew in a weary salmon which weighed on authentic scales almost eight pounds — the largest caught that season in those waters. The huge fish was planked that evening for our dinner, and Mrs. Fuess, who so far as I know had never before held a line or rod in her hand, was the heroine of the summer!

When we returned in September, we settled down in a house of our own just off the campus, and I resumed the work as a teacher which I was to carry on, with some intermissions, until 1933. On April 13, 1912, the night when the *Titanic* struck an iceberg and went down with the loss of hundreds of lives, my son and only child, John Cushing Fuess, was born. He was later educated at Andover and Harvard, spent two years teaching at the Brooks School, and then entered the foreign service. He has since held posts in Mexico City, Belfast, Auckland, Cape Town, Milan, and Washington, having traveled more extensively than any other member of the family.

I was now twenty-seven, with a doctorate and a family and a job which demanded all my attention and satisfied all my needs. In 1913, we moved to a new school dormitory, John

Phelps Taylor Hall; and in 1915 we were transferred to Tucker House, a huge ugly Victorian residence, where, with six or seven undergraduates annually under my charge, we remained for seventeen years.

I was to see very little of Columbia again until, in 1934, the university awarded me the honorary degree of Doctor of Literature. I had been asked also to deliver the Phi Beta Kappa oration, in the course of which I had occasion to mention Carl Schurz, whose biography I had just completed. In one passage in particular I referred to Schurz's statue on Morningside Heights, picturing him rather dramatically as gazing out over the metropolis which had been the scene of so many of his activities. By great good luck I walked over in the morning before the hour of my address in order to have one last look at the statue, and discovered — what I had completely forgotten — that the great reformer had his back turned on the city and was gazing toward the university. I hastily altered the paragraph to fit the actual situation and thus avoided an egregious and inexcusable blunder.

I remember the conferring of degrees as an impressive ceremony held outdoors in the open space in front of the old library before thousands of spectators. I felt proud indeed to be thus again associated with the great university where I had spent plenty of toiling hours and midnight electricity in earning my Doctorate of Philosophy. It was much easier to become a Doctor of Literature.

VII

Teaching English

ALTHOUGH it now seems incredible, the Phillips Academy catalogue for 1908–1909 proves beyond a doubt that only four English instructors were provided for 489 undergraduates. The classes were, of course, very large — indeed I remember having one section of fifty-three, a number which in these days would be regarded as impossible for one teacher to handle. Frankly I found it rather stimulating to have an audience tucked away on window ledges, and I felt like an actor facing a packed house. It was only when the themes piled up that I wished for fewer pupils.

My room was a huge affair, remodeled from the former chapel of Andover Theological Seminary, with ceilings eighteen feet high, embrasures for the windows, and wooden desks, each seating two, of an ancient variety. On the tops were carved the words of generations of Andover students — some of them minatory, like the constantly recurring "To Hell with Exeter!" others of an amatory nature, like "Pete Loves Ruth," together with a heart pierced by an arrow or a crude attempt to reproduce a female profile. The white painted walls had in the beginning no decorations whatever, but I managed before long to cover them in part with maps and pictures. Behind my desk — which stood on a slightly elevated platform — was a window niche in which some earlier occupant had placed a bearded plaster bust, presumably of Plato. This I was able to use as a symbolic portraiture of whatever author we were studying; it served at various periods for Shakespeare, for Alfred, Lord Tennyson, and even for Robert Frost. All that was required was a little imagination on the part of my listeners. One of them, with an irony which must have been more than unconscious, perpetrated a couplet which I have not forgotten:

I see the bust of Plato on the shelf —
Methinks that Claudie should be there himself.

I derived much from observing my elders and superiors, as a tyro profits by watching master craftsmen. My immediate chief, Arthur Willis Leonard, was one of the finest gentlemen I ever knew. He was a quiet, unassuming Princeton graduate, neat in his dress and in his mental habits, a scholar by temperament and an artist in his profession. He could read beautifully, and I often paused outside his recitation room to hear his melodious voice declaiming the soliloquies of Hamlet. He and I worked side by side for many years, during which my respect for him constantly increased.

I learned much also pragmatically, through a process of trial and error, and endeavored to profit by my mistakes. I discovered early that the secret of all good teaching is the revival of motivation. The good teacher makes his pupils wish to learn. We should aim to preserve that instinctive curiosity which impels the child of seven or eight to keep asking "What?" or "Why?" or "How?" Instead we have allowed him to feel that the acquisition of knowledge — at least in school — is distasteful and unimportant. It is the teacher's business to uncover a buried natural trait. In our civilization the normal youth of sixteen has been hardened to resist instruction and submits to it unwillingly. That this is so may be due to wrong methods or to wrong material — or both.

I often tried to seduce into reading a boy who had come

to believe that it was an unmanly occupation. He would shy off like a colt when approached directly; but if I could only get him to listen to a paragraph from *Virginibus Puerisque* or even *John McNab* and stir him a little, I might find later that he had taken the volume out of the library and enjoyed it. It is my experience that any healthy lad will work his head off on a job which attracts him. The problem for the teacher, then, would seem to be simple. Find some ingenious device for arousing the pupil's interest and making him realize that books can be as fascinating as their modern competitors, the radio, television, and the movies. The kindling can be done only if the teacher is himself aflame. With an elusive student I have often felt like a fisherman on Squam Lake, experimenting with different kinds of bait. The hellgrammite fails, and also the crawfish — but put a frog on the hook and "Zip!" the bass is yours!

I labored for weeks with one of the toughest pupils I ever confronted — a giant tackle on the eleven and a complete extrovert in his mentality. He was by turns scornful, obstinate, and resigned, until one afternoon by chance I recited to the class Joyce Kilmer's "Trees." I heard him several days later discussing with two of the undergraduate "grinds" the line, "Who intimately live with rain" — which he said was a perfect description of what had happened to him on a camping trip the summer before. At last I had him, and a few doses of Kipling and later of Robert Frost almost converted him into a rather shamefaced reader of poetry.

Andover students wished to be treated with respect. There is a story, probably apocryphal, of the lad on a train who when asked, "Are you a Groton boy?" replied, "No, I'm an Andover man!" My students wanted me to understand that they had put away childish things. Once I learned a lesson which kept me from superciliousness. I had spent several minutes explaining to a boy the stanzaic construction of Shelley's

"Ode to the West Wind," and when he failed to apprehend my remarks, I spoke to him too caustically about his deficiencies. He looked a trifle disconcerted, but made no reply. A few days later, I was attempting desperately on a very cold morning to start my Dodge when the same lad, passing the garage door and observing my futile maneuvers, came in and asked, "Can I help you, sir?" Embarrassed at being caught thus helpless, I grunted a noncommittal response; whereupon he lifted the radiator hood, peered into the bowels of the engine, took from his pocket a tiny screw driver, made one or two turns, and said, "I think it'll start now, sir." Sure enough, it did! Then he expounded to me some mystery of the carburetor which I could not comprehend. Observing my perplexity, he directed my attention to the mechanism itself, and, without the slightest trace of annoyance, showed me what had been wrong. He was a better teacher than I had been. After that, when a boy wrinkled his forehead over the difference between a metaphor and a synecdoche, I remembered the carburetor, moderated my wrath, and started again.

It is very important for the teacher to put himself in the place of his pupils and imagine how they feel. The boy is a sentient human being, sensitive and emotional and with a keen sense of justice. The teacher, bulwarked by his position behind the desk and by all the power of entrenched tradition, has a marked advantage over his pupils. This he should not abuse. Sneers and sarcasm have no place in the enlightened classroom, and only engender resentment. The teacher who brings a laugh at the expense of one of his pupils has probably lost him forever. And why not? How would the instructor feel if he were the victim?

By an inexplicable paradox, casual and trivial remarks are often remembered when important points, reiterated and emphasized, are forgotten. On a train going to New York I was greeted by one of my former students who, after some preliminary conversation, said, "Mr. Fuess, you were the finest teacher I ever had, and you made a lasting impression on me." Naturally my chest swelled with pride, and I asked, "What are some of the things that you recall best?" "Well," he answered, "I have never forgotten that Keats was born in a livery stable." Nothing about the "Grecian Urn" or "A thing of beauty is a joy forever!" I refrained from inquiring how frequently that startling bit of information had helped him in his career as a manufacturer of clothespins.

When I began teaching at Phillips Academy, certain books were still "required reading" for admission to college — among them *Macbeth,* Milton's "Minor Poems," Macaulay's "Essay on Johnson," and Burke's speech "On Conciliation with the Colonies." I regret to confess that for some years I became little better than the drillmaster whom I have so vigorously condemned. Every boy in my classes had to make a careful outline of Burke's famous speech, paragraph by paragraph, until he virtually knew it by heart. It took me some time to realize that however significant it may be as an historical and oratorical masterpiece, this oration is not the proper diet for adolescent minds. Milton's "Lycidas" is a noble elegy, but not the best approach to English poetry for those who are only recently literate. The hour arrived when I longed to break loose as a teacher and introduce my boys to more lively literature, even if it were only *Huckleberry Finn,* but it just couldn't be done under the existing system. When the College Entrance Examination Board altered the requirements, the situation changed very much for the better.

I had been brought up, furthermore, under an unnutritious diet of formal grammar, including the diagramming of sentences on the blackboard; and I still carried with me, rather against my better judgment, a conviction that it was necessary for a complete education. I did, however, have my saner moments, especially when one of my colleagues voiced some obiter dictum on the obnoxious sentence, "I knew it to be he." Wendell Willkie lost the vote of many an English teacher when, in his acceptance speech, he was heard over the radio to say, "This reception has meant much to Mrs. Willkie and I." But my confidence in formal grammar as a means of making boys or men speak correctly has diminished with the years. For this heresy I make no apologies.

By the time I had been in Andover five years a liberalizing movement had been started, chiefly through the agency of the College Entrance Examination Board, whose tests had by 1915 replaced almost entirely the separate college entrance examinations which prevailed in the first decade of the century. Leonard and I had before this tried the experiment of giving the seniors a textbook in the history of English literature, using an excellent volume by Moody and Lovett. We stressed particularly the personal traits of the authors and attempted to make a broad survey of English writers, from Chaucer down to Kipling, with readings from typical works. This method was criticized by some of the faculty because it anticipated courses which were to be later taken in college, but I am certain that our students went to Harvard and Yale exceptionally well prepared in that field. With my increasing interest in biography — which was soon to become an absorbing passion — I was delighted that we were sending out graduates with a sense of the personalities in English literature as well as a knowledge of its continuity.

Part of our job was to get our boys to write. One very young teacher, who did not linger very long with us, remarked to me as we were walking back from dinner, "It's hard teaching these roughnecks style!" Leonard and I made little effort to turn out Walter Paters or Robert Louis Stevensons. Any boy who is destined to write needs only a few suggestions and an occasional warning. He will find himself somehow, like an apprentice artist, in God's good time! But we did believe that we could help the average school citizen to express his ideas simply and clearly. Mere drill on grammar never made a writer. A student may understand all about gerunds and indirect objects without being able to produce a respectable sentence. Gradually we dared to neglect the traditional categories of Unity, Coherence, and Emphasis, and fell back on simpler concepts, such as Clearness, Variety, and Force.

When I became more ambitious, I ventured to ask them to compose in verse, occasionally with fascinating results; and I have in my files a collection of several more than creditable sonnets and quatrains. It was one of my boys who rejoiced my heart by producing this authentic heroic couplet:

Her eyes are jade, her neck is like the swan —
And that's the neck I do my necking on.

Another matter which interested us greatly was that of oral English. My experience at George School had convinced me that mere pleasure in sound was a first step towards the appreciation of poetry. Accordingly we asked each boy to memorize and recite before the class a passage from some great writer — very often a sonnet by Wordsworth or Keats or a short poem like "She Was a Phantom of Delight." It consumed precious minutes in the recitation hour, but I am certain that it was worth while. My students told me that these selections came in very conveniently on the College Board Examinations, for their quotations seemed to indicate a profound and extensive knowledge of the anthologies. But this was purely incidental. I know that the lines linger still with many of my old boys who have little time nowadays for anything but business.

I met one of them two or three years ago while walking across Boston Common. Since I had last seen him his waistline had obviously grown larger, and he was visibly puffing as he stopped to shake my hand. Then he smiled and began to recite:

O! that this too too solid flesh would melt,
Thaw and resolve itself into a dew. . . .

The quotation carried me back twenty years, to a time when he as a slender youth had risen to recite Hamlet's famous soliloquy, and I said to him, "Well, Bill, it was worth while learning it, wasn't it?"

It is a pity in my opinion that more time is not spent in school on public speaking and the proper management of the voice. On the walls of the lecture room at Amherst where I sat under Professor Genung, author of the famous "Rhetoric," were Latin words which may be freely translated, "He who knows but cannot express what he knows is as if he knew nothing." These might well be inscribed in letters of gold in every English classroom. We teachers should do all in our power to make our students articulate, able not only to prepare committee reports but also to stand on their feet and convince an audience. Silence may be golden, but strong silent men are easily misinterpreted.

How much actual writing should a student be asked to do? The daily theme as usually administered soon becomes a bore and ceases to have any value. I quickly discovered also that work prepared outside the classroom, often done with the aid of the dormitory Bright Boy, sheds little light on a student's ability. Two or three paragraphs written by a pupil completely "on his own," even though classroom time is utilized for the project, will tell a teacher more about his student's stylistic weaknesses than a whole folio of "formal themes." Some simple hints about the use of dependent clauses and participial phrases, in small doses and on the spot, are better than huge smears of red or blue pencil. The object should be to make the student write less — and better!

The time arrived about 1920, when alert teachers began talking about Précis Writing — which was merely a new term for an old method. As a means of jarring students into thought, it had, and has, an important place in an English teacher's program. It compels them to weigh the value of different words and phrases, and thus really to exercise their own judgment. The fact that the College Entrance Examination Board began experimenting with questions of the précis type inevitably gave the technique prestige, and soon it was being tested all over the country, but especially in the private schools. Many conventional teachers didn't like the précis, largely because questions of this type were unpredictable and left the examinee dependent on his own individual ability. "Cramming" for précis questions was almost impossible, except for instructors with the gift of second sight.

The same general comment could be made upon the "comprehensive" or "new plan" type of examination, which brought dismay to teachers whose reputations had been built up by their careful preparation of candidates for the "restricted" tests. It was a joy at last to be able to read *Othello* and *Romeo and Juliet,* and even *Antony and Cleopatra* and *The Tempest,* knowing that pupils who had comprehended these plays were equipped to face questions on the drama. The comprehensive examination, which included the précis, was actually a symbol of a shift in educational thought from rigidity to flexibility, from narrowness to breadth, from emphasis on content to emphasis on choice, and was therefore welcome to those of us who desired greater freedom. Under the new system as it eventually developed, most intelligent teachers felt a sense of liberation, as if a new and marvelous vista were being opened up. Unfortunately a combination of inertia and ignorance prevented the widespread adoption of the comprehensive examination. The English departments of some New England colleges still preferred an examination on specified books, and they were aided and abetted by secondary school teachers who had thrived under the old system. Thus the movement never moved beyond allowing schools and candidates to choose between the comprehensive and restricted plans.

Just as some of us were beginning to see light ahead, along came a deep fog, in the shape of objective tests. These aptitude and achievement tests have, I must admit, been very useful, especially to college admission officers, who now have a measuring rod of relatively high predictive accuracy. But the advocates of objective tests did a great disservice to English teachers by minimizing the importance of the familiar essay type of question. Having concluded that this had no significance for admission officers, they proceeded to declare that it had no value for teachers. What they really said amounted to the assumption that nobody can be taught to write — or rather can *learn* to write. Much more proof must be presented before I can be persuaded that assigned themes in the classroom, accompanied or followed by constructive comments, will not enable boys and girls to express themselves more clearly on paper.

When in the 1920's Edward S. Harkness provided the funds for smaller classrooms and a larger number of instructors at Exeter, he started a trend which had a powerful impact on English teaching throughout American secondary education. In 1932, at Andover, I tried the experiment of offering a small seminar for able seniors. The table was not oblong or oval, but in the shape of a small cross, around which sat a select group of fourteen boys. The atmosphere was completely informal, and we tried to make the room in Samuel Phillips Hall cheerful by flowers and pictures contributed by the members. For half a year we read one novel every two weeks, with an opportunity for full discussion; and we covered in all, ten books, including Hardy's *The Mayor of Casterbridge,*

Galsworthy's *The Man of Property,* and Walpole's *The Wooden Horse.* It was the general feeling among the members that in content it was the best course they had ever taken, and I still hear from Andover graduates who recollect it with satisfaction.

Largely because of the success of this experiment, we were able to secure, through the generosity of Mr. Harkness, a separate building devoted to English, with eighteen small classrooms, numerous conference rooms, and a larger debating hall seating about one hundred and fifty. Classroom sections are seldom more than fifteen, and in many cases the pupils sit around a table like the directors of a bank. There are several obvious advantages. Disciplinary problems — which had never been troublesome in Andover classrooms — were reduced to nil in a group where the teacher was on the same level with his students. The free interchange of ideas was fostered, and each member received much more personal attention from the master. Under this system, so to speak, each participant gets more for his money.

The devil's advocate, however, may argue that a first-rate teacher has an opportunity of meeting only about fifty boys and therefore loses some of the influence which he exerted when he taught an entire senior class. It was unfortunate, for example, that Leonard's inspiring teaching could not be diffused over a larger group. Furthermore the plan is so expensive that only the wealthiest schools can install it, and it cannot, unless taxes are greatly increased, be established in the public schools.

I had a share also in the movement for dividing pupils, on the basis of their aptitude and demonstrated accomplishment, into "Fast," "Medium," and "Slow" divisions. Before long I had convinced myself that the plan of segregating students who were both exceptionally able and willing was for them very profitable. It is important, of course, that nobody should be forced into such a division against his desires and that the grading should not reduce the chances of a boy's receiving honor marks. But with these minor reservations, I am in favor of allowing students to proceed as rapidly as they can and wish to go. This is Nature's way, and it should be adopted by the schools.

The so-called "Slow Divisions" have never been popular with brilliant teachers. Moreover some conscientious pupils always resent being assigned to them and complain to their parents of unfair treatment. On the other hand, many boys who are not rapid readers and find it difficult to complete normal lessons manage to get along creditably when strenuous competition is removed. If the element of ignominy can be eliminated, the plan is basically sound.

The whole problem of the so-called "slow boy" has been simplified considerably by the studies of wise physicians and psychiatrists. The high standards of admission to Phillips Academy almost automatically kept dunces out. But there were always boys who were labeled by the faculty as "stupid" or "lazy," and the question was what to do with them.

In the 1930's some of the teachers supported me in adopting a new attitude towards these delinquents. Before asking them to withdraw and thus transferring the responsibility to other more tolerant schools, we deliberately tried to find out the reason for the low marks. Emotional disturbances, lack of motivation, poor health, family dissension — all these, we discovered, often kept a boy from doing good work. But we also noticed, after doing some testing, that we had in the student body certain boys who just didn't know how to read. The American Optical Company generously equipped our infirmary with a metronoscope and an opthalmograph, and we undertook through Dr. Gallagher, our school physician, some pioneer research into the cause of slow reading. The next step was to organize remedial classes for those who were in difficulties. We were not always successful, of course, but the improvement more than justified the experiment.

The chief and lasting consequence, in my judgment, was to start the faculty speculating on the reasons for failure. It was no longer enough to blame low grades on just plain cussedness or human depravity, or to vote disciplinary measures. We tried to get at the root of things, and thereby sometimes achieved an almost miraculous reform. It was one of the great moments in educational evolution when teachers commenced to ask, "What is the real reason why Ned's marks are so low?"

Before I left Phillips Academy in 1948, we had reached the point where we had one English teacher to every forty boys, and the four of us who were in the department in 1908 had grown to sixteen. But the same old discussions as to aims and methods were being carried on, and the same wide variations in energy, in techniques, and in fundamental philosophy still existed. The former domination of the curriculum by English had been succeeded in the 1920's by an increasing emphasis on the social sciences, particularly history. That was followed at the outbreak of the Second World War by a very practical stressing of mathematics and science. Meanwhile, although English is hardly relegated to the second rank, there is a feeling that perhaps the large proportion of time spent on it does not bring commensurate results. To some extent I share this feeling, for too much of the present compulsory English course of four years is spent on needless repetition. A better spirit of co-operation between English teachers and instructors in other fields could save a considerable amount of time for the student preparing for college.

It was impossible for me as I began to feel more at home to keep from producing textbooks; and by so doing I learned what was popular and what was not in my professional field. Leonard and I began with *A High School Spelling Book* (1913), in which we undertook to air some of our theories on that very delicate and much overrated subject. *Good Writ-*

ing (1922) was our attempt to tell the world about some of the methods which we had developed at Phillips Academy. Finally *Practical Précis Writing* (1926), also published by Harcourt, Brace & Company, was very up-to-date in its approach and to some degree popularized a new technique in the field of English. Leonard and I did plenty of talking about methods and materials, and were always ready to experiment with novel ideas.

The editing of various texts brought me in a little much needed money and added to my store of knowledge. I find that I "did" in 1914 a volume of *Selected Letters* for Houghton Mifflin Company and a collection of *Selected Short Stories* for the Charles E. Merrill Company, as well as *Selections for Oral Reading* for the Macmillan Pocket Classics. When the College Entrance Examination Board included among its options "a collection of essays," I was Johnny-on-the-spot with *Selected Essays,* another item in the Riverside Literature Series, commonly known as the R.L.S. In 1922, Harold Crawford Stearns, my younger associate in the English department and a poet of some distinction, collaborated with me in editing *The Little Book of Society Verse,* published by Houghton Mifflin Company, in which, without thinking of classroom use, we included the finest specimens of a genre which we both liked. This later appeared in a de luxe edition and had a considerable sale. Stearns and I a year later were responsible for still another anthology, *Selections from the Victorian Poets,* he covering Browning and Swinburne while I took Tennyson and Arnold. In this case we tried out each poem in our classes and were able to predict the impression which it would make on pupils of seventeen or eighteen. In 1926, at the insistence of Professor Thorndike, I edited Dana's *Two Years Before the Mast,* for the Macmillan Company, acquiring thereby an enormous amount of miscellaneous and useless information regarding sailing vessels. Finally, in 1932, with still another colleague, Alan R. Blackmer, I tried my luck with *Hamlet,* for Houghton Mifflin Company. I am inclined to believe that Blackmer and I added little to the significant literature on the subject, but we did to our own satisfaction indicate how the tragedy should be interpreted to schoolboys.

As I gaze at the row of thin textbooks in which I have had a share, they seem to represent an immense amount of hard labor, especially when it is remembered that I produced during that period several good-sized biographies. My primary interest was always teaching, and day in and day out I had to be in Pearson A, preparing Andover seniors for college. But I had some capacity for toiling long hours at high speed, and usually I would be up at five o'clock in the morning, thus getting two hours or more of work on my typewriter before setting out for my classroom. I also had my summers free and tried to utilize every moment of that valuable time.

I am sure that teachers themselves and the quality of their work have greatly improved since I faced my first class at Phillips Academy. The instructors whom I meet at professional gatherings are more rugged, less pedantic, and worthier of the respect of their pupils. Teaching today is attracting some of the ablest graduates from our colleges and universities. Teaching methods, thanks to some of the revelations of modern psychology, are less crude than they were in 1908. I was once guilty of stating publicly that anybody could learn to spell if he wished to do so badly enough — and this with the examples of Macaulay and Stevenson before me! Now I realize that this was a dogmatic statement based on complete ignorance, of which I should have been ashamed. If I have learned nothing else from my experience it is that in education there are vast areas which we have not yet even penetrated. The teacher who thinks he knows it all is only on the outer border of the holy shrine.

My classroom teaching necessarily ceased abruptly in March

1933, when I became headmaster, and has never been resumed. The demands of the administrative post made it impossible for me to meet classes regularly, and the best I could do was to deliver an occasional informal lecture. Yet in many respects I was happier as a teacher than I have been since. I took a passionate delight in finding ways to stimulate boys to think and write clearly and to appreciate the best in literature. I enjoyed the personal contacts with my pupils. A headmaster, however benevolent, is always regarded as a possible instrument of discipline, and boys except as a last resort do not confide in him. With a teacher it is different. True, he also is in a position of power, but the undergraduates see him at close quarters every day and soon lose their sense of fear. While I was teaching at Andover my house would be filled with boys every evening. When I became headmaster, they would accept invitations and apparently enjoy themselves; but they seldom came of their own accord, they were obviously on guard, and they were visibly cautious about responding to my honest gestures of friendship.

My experience, possibly my prejudice, makes me regard teaching as one of the noblest of professions. Several great teachers have influenced me, and always for the better; and I know of many other cases where a timely word of warning or encouragement has altered the course of a young man's career. It is indeed a strange anomaly that parents will pay out large sums to physicians who heal their children's bodies and yet begrudge adequate salaries to the men and women who have control over their minds and spirits. In these days when antagonistic ideologies are struggling for domination, it is of tremendous importance to the coming generation that it should be brought up under the guidance of men whose thinking is on a high plane and whose words and conduct set an example for those who sit under them. Such an environment I can testify was to be found at Phillips Academy.

VIII

War as a Phase of Education

BECAUSE no one in my college generation ever dreamed that his country would be in a European war in his time, the gradual entrance of the United States into the struggle against Germany was a disconcerting and disrupting experience. At Phillips Academy we were closer to it than most schools, for Henry L. Stimson, Secretary of War under Taft, was a member of the Board of Trustees and brought up General Leonard Wood to speak on "Preparedness" as early as the autumn of 1914. Principal Stearns, with his crusading spirit, saw clearly the moral issues involved; and in the early winter of 1917 an Andover Ambulance Unit went overseas, with two members of the teaching staff in charge. This was, of course, before our formal declaration of a state of war with Germany.

After we had entered the war, every citizen had his duty to consider. When the school opened in the fall of 1917, an academy battalion was formed, and nearly all the physically able undergraduates, together with many of the faculty, went into khaki and drilled on the campus. In the good old Horatio Alger tradition I enlisted in the ranks and worked my way up — through sheer merit! — to a captaincy. While I was a buck private, a fat rather slow-witted lad who, however, had once attended a military school, "rode" me properly, taking a sweet revenge for every F I had given him in the classroom. It was all in good fun, and I enjoyed it as much as he. But the drilling was child's play, and as the situation became more critical I had to consider what I should do. I had a wife and small son, but I was only thirty-three and it did seem as if I might be useful somewhere. My well-intentioned efforts met at first with ludicrous results.

General Adolphus W. Greely, of arctic exploration fame, was a friend of my wife's family, and I made a date to see him in Washington at the Cosmos Club. He was a stately figure of a man, tall, with a magnificent white beard, looking like an elderly Jupiter or Neptune. After we had chatted for a while in general terms, he said, "I know just what you ought to be — a captain in the air corps. Come along up the street." I was certainly startled, realizing that I knew nothing whatever about aviation, but I could hardly desert the old gentleman; so off we went about three blocks away to the headquarters of the air corps, while I tried vainly to protest as I followed in his wake through the door straight to the office of the commanding colonel. General Greely walked up to his desk and said with dignity, "Colonel, here is a young friend of mine whom I should like to have commissioned in the air service." The colonel stared at me politely, taking in my bald head and heavy spectacles, and then drooped his left eye at me with what looked suspiciously like a wink. Seeing that the general was not observing me, I tried to wink back, and a faint smile played across the colonel's face. Then he replied, "That's fine, General Greely. Can you leave me with this young fellow while I examine him briefly, and he'll report to you later." The general retreated saying, "Thank you, I'll just stroll back to the club and wait."

When he had departed, I hastened to explain my predicament, but the colonel understood perfectly. Going over to the opposite wall, he said, "Now, Mr. Fuess, take off your glasses." Then he held up an army manual, printed in small type, and asked, "Can you read this without difficulty?" "Honestly, Colonel," I replied, "I can hardly see the book." He came back, sat down at his desk, and gazing at me with the utmost apparent seriousness, announced, "My dear sir, I regret deeply that because of defective eyesight, you cannot qualify for a commission in the air corps." I replied, "Colonel, I knew perfectly well that I couldn't get a commission. I came here only because General Greely insisted on bringing me." "I know, I know," he responded. "And now we'll try to pacify that grand old man." He scribbled off a few lines on a card and added, "You give this to him, and perhaps he'll forgive me." When I reported the results to General Greely, he burst out, "This damned army has all gone to hell! I never heard of such picayune treatment; you'd make a wonderful officer!" He was finally quieted, and I returned to Andover, with a feeling that my quest was hopeless.

Once more I tried, this time for a commission in the Trench Mortar Service, but was rejected because of an alleged heart murmur. Then in late March, acting on a hint from a friend, I went to Washington to consult Frederick P. Keppel, Assistant Secretary of War, whom I had known at Columbia. I had hardly started to explain my situation when he broke in, "Fuess, you're in luck. You hurry over to the Cosmos Club, and ask for Walter Dill Scott. You'll see some other men there. Don't say too much, but do exactly what you are told." I hurried to the club, and was shown into a big room where a group of perhaps forty men had evidently just finished lunch. I sat down in a vacant chair at the far end of the table just as a tall distinguished-looking gentleman was explaining that a test was about to be given. There were pads and pencils before each place. He called attention to the directions, and the next minute I found myself for the first time in several years taking an examination instead of giving one. I followed orders and did my best, not realizing I was participating in one of the first demonstrations of a test prepared by the famous Committee on Classification of Personnel in the Army and that the presiding officer was an eminent practical psychologist. When he had finished, President Scott said, "These papers will be checked, and the results announced in about two weeks. The top man will have to give a dinner for the crowd."

I returned, somewhat puzzled, to the State, War, and Navy Building, where Secretary Keppel informed me that I was to go to Newport News with a certain Captain Royal Mattice and await further instructions. "Learn all you can," he advised, "it may help you later." At Newport News I spent a dreary rainy ten days, assisting with the embarkation troops. Then one morning came a telegram notifying me to go back to Washington at once and report to Secretary Keppel. He greeted me with a vigorous handshake and the remark, "Congratulations, Fuess — you made the highest mark on the new tests and that entitles you to the toughest assignment. You must be ready to take the next train for Jacksonville, Florida, for Camp Joseph E. Johnston." He then explained that I had been appointed by the War Department as Civilian Chief of Personnel, with instructions to straighten out a situation which was rapidly becoming intolerable. The commanding officer was incompetent, the camp was without discipline, and I was supposed tactfully but firmly to clean things up. Never was a young English teacher, with no practical experience, more completely "on the spot." Knowing nothing of the army or of military procedure, I must confess that I was terrified. But the incident was typical of what I was to meet during the next ten months — perhaps the most decisive and assuredly the most dramatic in my strange education.

On a warm morning in late March 1918, I stepped from my Pullman in Jacksonville into an atmosphere of tulips and magnolias, Spanish moss, live oaks, and all the exotic accessories of the semitropics. An orderly was waiting to drive me out to the newly constructed camp on the banks of the St.

John's River, and I proceeded without delay to the office of the Camp Commander, Colonel Charles W. Willard. He was sitting with his boots up on the desk, his army hat on his head, chewing tobacco vigorously and spitting with incredible accuracy into a cuspidor. As I was introduced, he glared ferociously and demanded, "What in hell do you want?" Unused to such a greeting, I replied, "Colonel, I bring a communication from the Secretary of War," and handed him my orders. Its contents obviously astonished him, for I was not an impressive figure and I could see that he was considering whether I could be an imposter. He looked up, surveyed me carefully, and remarked, "What God-damned fool thing will they do next?"

This was hardly a query which I was able to answer. I did, however, want to propitiate the Old Man, so I said, "I know, Colonel, that it must seem peculiar to you, and I'll admit that it's funny to me. But we both have to carry through instructions, and I'll bother you as little as I can." That was that! But I learned shortly that Colonel Willard for the moment had only one genuine interest. He thought of himself as doing the assignment of a brigadier general, and he wanted the pay and prerequisites of that rank. Indeed as I observed him, he spent an inordinate amount of time writing to the War Department in the hope of having his status rectified. It now suddenly occurred to him that, as an emissary from Washington, I might have some influence, and appeasement became his policy. He could not assume an amiability which was foreign to his temperament, but he did become moderately cooperative.

My first task was to set up a personnel office on a scale large enough to serve a body of men which at the maximum numbered more than 50,000. Since I was unfamiliar even with routine administrative procedure, I resorted to every legitimate subterfuge to conceal my colossal ignorance. I did, however, find rather quickly three or four young college graduates of high intelligence who helped me build an organization. Soon the blueprint of the personnel office aroused the grudging admiration of even Colonel Willard, and a similar chart appeared on the wall of his headquarters.

In many respects Camp Joseph E. Johnston was unique. In its early stages it was a quartermaster camp, organized to train, equip, and send out what were known as supply companies. There was hardly a professional fighting man in the camp. Schools had been set up to instruct recruits in what might be called the business aspect of war, carried on by carpenters, electricians, telegraphers, butchers, storekeepers, plumbers, and representatives of other trades. We even formed a number of Graves Registration Units, each consisting of one sergeant, one corporal, and two privates, under command of a second lieutenant. In the summer it became also a center for the Motor Transport Corps and at once assumed a more rugged character with the advent of countless truck and taxi drivers.

Under the existing conditions military drill beyond a few necessary formations was not required, and the discipline of the camp, as I had been warned, was unspeakably bad. Nor did Colonel Willard, except by growling and cursing, do anything to improve it. He had issued an order that his own chauffeur-driven automobile, bearing his insignia as commanding officer, should be saluted whether he was in it or not; and on several occasions I was amused by seeing a group of buck privates, after investigating to find whether the Old Man was inside, thumb their noses at the car as it went by.

The next step after setting up the office organization was to devise some workable method of assigning men where they belonged. The maladjustments were pathetically numerous. When the glad news spread that my department was trying to put square pegs into square holes, long lines of disgruntled soldiers formed outside — with the permission of their company officers — to beg to have their cases investigated. One of the most brilliant classical scholars I ever knew was cutting up meat with a cleaver in the butcher shop. A top-ranking mechanical engineer was doing a cook's job in a small officers' mess. Here and there I came across people with whom I was acquainted — nearly all of them in jobs for which they were not fitted. How they had been so terribly mishandled I could never find out, except that when an officer wanted a cook he just went out and picked the first man he saw. The most experienced cook in camp, who had been a chef at the Waldorf, had been drafted by the band, because he had put down as one of his minor qualifications, "playing cornet."

It was an incredible muddle, and nothing remained but to set doggedly to work and patiently try to straighten things out, as an angler unravels a tangled fish line. For weeks I was in my office fourteen hours or more a day, and it seemed to me that I had hardly gone to sleep before I was at it again. We brought into use the new Trade Tests recently devised by the CCP; and when a man claimed to be a riveter, we could in a few minutes determine roughly the degree of his proficiency. When the Motor Transport Corps arrived we built the highest hill for miles around by the simple process of excavating with bulldozers and piling up the earth. On this we set up a maze of stakes through which drivers could guide their trucks and thus demonstrate their skill in emergencies. While the tests were far from exact and required constant checking, they did accomplish much in helping us to reach a decision. At least we no longer put former truck drivers into the school for bookkeepers.

Among our more difficult jobs was the commissioning of officers, and week by week we studied the qualification cards, hunting out men with the experience and education which presumably made them officer material. On one occasion in the late summer of 1918, when we had in our judgment exhausted the available candidates, I received a telegram signed simply "Pershing," reading, "Request you commission immediately two hundred Second Lieutenants for duty overseas." Eager in my humble way to maintain standards, I wired, "Impossible to find two hundred qualified men for commissions as requested." Promptly came back what might be regarded as a categorical imperative. "You will commission immediately two hundred men as Second Lieutenants." Not wishing to be court-martialed, I set up a Board of Three and under the moss-dripping live oaks we interviewed one after one the sad possibilities. The criterion of even a high school education had to be disregarded. We virtually accepted anybody who appeared not too stupid and could understand English. Naturally many of them were astounded, never having dreamed that they might become officers. As I saw them later dressed in their brand new uniforms, they looked somewhat better, but I was always glad that the war ended before they were called upon to "do their stuff."

I was impressed in Florida, as I have been since more than once, by the inability of many apparently well set-up young men to meet emergencies or face responsibility. The hospital at Camp Johnston was full of officers with shattered nerves. One morning as I stepped out of my barracks I found the body of a second lieutenant lying under a live oak, his revolver on the ground beside him. He left a note to his wife saying that he just couldn't bear up under the burden which had descended upon him — the command of a Graves Registration Unit of four men. All over camp were fellows who had managed somehow to get along in civilian life with somebody to tell them what to do but who broke down when that support was lacking. Many of them had been clerks in stores or helpers in gasoline stations, where they had never been obliged to make decisions. This experience taught me to realize that the percentage of potential neurotics in any American community must be very high — and the troops whom I saw were not destined for front line combat.

Colonel Willard was superseded by Major General Duval, commonly known in the army as the "Bear Cat" — a retired officer who had patriotically offered his services and had been a fine leader, but who in 1918 was old and tired and died at the camp before many weeks had passed. His first order was for a reorganization of the Receiving Camp, in which at that moment were located more than 20,000 inductees, most of them Negroes, who were kept occupied by grubbing palmettos with mattocks. The general order providing that the camp should be reorganized in new units necessitated a vast amount of paper work, with the shuffling and transfer of thousands of cards. I had no sleep for two nights supervising the arrangements. On the morning when the Great Shift was to be executed, I stationed myself with General Duval on a little mound six or eight feet high to watch the proceedings. At eight o'clock a cannon was shot off, and everybody started to move, with his personal belongings, to his new outfit. The result was absolute bedlam, like that described in Milton's "Paradise Lost":

> *Infernal noise! war seemed a civil game*
> *To this uproar; horrid confusion heaped*
> *Upon confusion rose!*

For most of the morning puzzled soldiers wandered here and there, hunting their new positions. That afternoon the unit commanders sent in their reports; and when they had all been checked, more than three hundred men could not be accounted for. It took two weeks to straighten out the mess so that we knew where we were; and even then some of the colored troops were never found, having vanished apparently into the Floridian obscurity. At that period, according to camp gossip, Florida sheriffs were given a reward of fifty dollars for each alleged deserter returned to the service; and it was commonly asserted that many a local official, when hard up for cash, merely went out and picked up a few colored boys and brought them in to the camp.

Some of the incidents at Camp Johnston, like the one just related, hovered between comedy and tragedy. Shortly after the Motor Transport Corps began to use the camp, a certain colonel appeared announcing that he had been given authority to form a *corps d'élite,* composed of prominent clubmen in New York and Philadelphia, between thirty-five and forty-five, with incomes of $25,000 or more. To each of these whom he interviewed he promised a commission as major in the Motor Transport Corps. Soon by twos and threes the prospective officers reported to the camp — usually stout and bald and obviously quite out of condition. At first nobody knew what to do with them, for we had received no instructions from Washington. When the number of recruits had increased to about forty, I called on Colonel Willard and asked him what should be done. The storm of profanity which burst from his lips was even more scorching than usual. "Take the bastards out and drill 'em," he shouted. "Give 'em the works!" I protested that this was cruelty, but succeeded only in rousing him to more violent imprecations. So, under a tough old army sergeant, the group were assembled on the parade ground and put through, on some scorching July days, a full quota of setting-up exercises. The poor fellows dropped to the ground one after another, exhausted and unable to carry on. Some of them objected that they had not been told what was ahead of them, but most did their best, thinking that this was an essential part of army discipline. Nevertheless the havoc was great, and the resentment of the victims mounted from day to day. Very few of the contingent finished the ordeal without disaster, and the fabulous *corps d'élite* never became a reality.

In the following January, when I was in Washington, I read in the paper that an unknown ruffian had assaulted the imaginative colonel as he was stepping from a cab and knocked him down. The news item declared that the outrage had been perpetrated by a discharged soldier with a "fancied grudge." I am sure, although I cannot prove it, that this was the revenge of one of the survivors of that unfortunate group.

Camp Johnston was in several respects unique. It was filled with good businessmen who were trying their best to avoid combat duty by joining up with the Service of Supply. Numerous malingerers fell ill when they ascertained through the grapevine that they were about to be assigned to companies destined for France. Sickness at home, family obligations, all the customary excuses were advanced, until we in my office became at times disgusted with the whole human race. On my staff was a first lieutenant whose father-in-law was a local merchant of considerable wealth. When the news reached him that his son-in-law had been selected for overseas duty, the old gentleman came out to call on me and, in the course of our conversation, said, "Mr. Fuess, I just can't have that boy leave this country — my wife would die!" I explained patiently that no discrimination had been made against the young man, that the order was routine, and that war was war. After much expostulation, he drew from his pocket a little slip, unfolded it, and slid it along to me on the desk, saying, "Would this make any difference?" I looked at it. It was a check for $1000, made out to me. I stood up and without saying a word, pressed a button; but before anybody could answer the ring, the old fellow was out of the room. It is only fair to add that the son-in-law made no protest of his own and was entirely unaware of what his wife's father had done. This was the most flagrant of several instances of attempted bribery in my experience.

In late July I was unexpectedly summoned to Washington and there instructed to settle down in a building on Virginia Avenue and prepare the figures for what was called the "Fourth Phase" operation of the war. I have never known to this day why I was selected, except that I was supposed to be informed on the relative proportion of men required in each branch of the Service of Supply for the effective working of a division in the field. With my associates I functioned in front of a huge blackboard, where we made calculations, aware that we were doing a job of improvization. I have always been thankful that the "Fourth Phase" did not reach Europe, for I was afraid that some blunder on my part might leave a regiment stranded without a cook or a stove. At any rate I did the best I could through the blistering August days, and then returned to my Jacksonville post, much astonished and certainly wiser.

In September, at the insistence of the War Department, I was commissioned as a major in the Quartermaster Corps, still with the understanding that I was to be an unattached rover, under special instructions from the Secretary of War. Meanwhile, through the enervating Florida summer, I had been losing pound after pound and had little appetite for anything but milk and eggs. I was thus an easy victim to the dreaded influenza when it struck the camp in early autumn, 1918. One day I was carried off to the hospital where that night the officer on one side of me died at eleven o'clock and the one on the other side at two. My convalescence was aided by a remarkable Jesuit priest, Father Talmadge, who spent two hours or more each day by my bedside, arguing that Coventry Patmore and Aubrey de Vere, Roman Catholic poets of the nineteenth century, were at least on the same level as the Protestants, Tennyson and Browning. The good Father would quote *in extenso* from his two favorites and I from mine, until the patients in the adjoining beds would rise up in profane protest. The issue was never satisfactorily settled, but the controversy gave me an interest in continuing to live.

Somehow I recovered from the attack, was discharged from the hospital, and returned to my duties; but in three or four days I felt some disquieting sensations and consulted the camp surgeon. After a cursory examination, he said gravely, "Major Fuess, something is wrong with your ticker, and I am ordering you to take the first train back to Andover. Have your orderly accompany you as far as Washington, and make no more exertion than you can possibly help. I warn you that it's about fifty-fifty whether you reach home alive." This was disturbing news, and it looked as if my education, as yet hardly begun, would shortly terminate with a "Requiescat in Pace" under the elms in the Phillips Academy cemetery.

As things turned out, the journey back was uneventful. In the Washington Union Station I was put into a wheel chair and taken to a compartment in the Boston train; and at the Back Bay station I was met with an ambulance and driven out to the Tucker House, where I was deposited and soon warned by a heart specialist not to move hand or foot any more than I could help. On Armistice Day, while the bells rang out and the Andover students paraded in the early morning through the streets, I still lay inert, incapable of action. Fortunately I had plenty of recuperative power, and rest in bed followed by a gradual increase in exercise accomplished marvelous results. Fifteen or more years later my physician, after giving me my first electric cardiogram, reported that I had what he described as a "heart block," the result of some earlier infection; and after probing into my history, he concluded that it was either congenital or the aftermath of my bout with influenza — probably the latter. Fortunately I have never since had any similar symptoms.

In early December I was back in Washington, under orders, to write a history of the Quartermaster Corps during the war. Captain Hardin Craig, later Professor of English at Leland Stanford University, and I were assigned to quarters in the State, War, and Navy Building — Room 510 I think it was — and there paced up and down, smoking ounces of tobacco and dictating to stenographers chapters of our masterpiece. So far as I know the mimeographed sheets are still gathering dust on some shelf in the archives. After Craig and I deposited our manuscript with the quartermaster general we never heard again from our production. We felt at times like the unfortunate victim in Conan Doyle's *The Red-Headed League,* whose daily copying was so futile.

In January 1919, with no further duties to perform, I was honorably discharged and returned to Andover, where for many months my wife had been acting as proctor for the boys in our house. My place as an English instructor had been filled for the year, but within a week I was committed to new enterprises which were almost as strange to me as war and were to teach me almost as much.

Many of the incidents at Camp Johnston are still vivid in my memory after all these years. Every evening after supper a group of us would sit on the bank of the St. John's River, watching the sun go down over the live oaks and the rather sickly looking palm trees and the muddy water, so full of alligators that nobody in the camp was allowed to bathe in it. Just as the sun was sinking, Dr. Robert L. Cooley, of Milwaukee, who had general charge of the Quartermaster Schools, would say in a doleful voice, "Well, boys, one acre of old Wisconsin is worth the whole God-damned state of Florida!" It was a ceremony which we all enjoyed.

Major General Duval was an inveterate kidder who made all his subordinates his victims. He pretended that I was very susceptible to female charms and made up stories to suit his fun. Once as we were driving in his car to Atlantic Beach for a brief respite from our busy life, he said, "Fuess, you ought not to spend so much of your time in those Jacksonville dance halls. Somebody will get wise." This time I was a little nettled and responded, "Well, General, that blonde I saw you with at Keith's last evening was no lily." He was so much astonished that he was almost speechless, but he turned and glared at me and finally ejaculated, "Fuess, sometimes I think you don't realize who I am!" It was a squelch which I did not forget in a hurry. Thereafter I understood that in the army the authority of a superior is unlimited, even in jokes.

Up to the time that I went to Camp Johnston, my life had been parochial in scope, largely academic, and much of it spent among boys. Then fate tossed me into the midst of a confused world of fifty thousand men, a large proportion of them not even high school graduates, but all of them American citizens, with the rights and privileges which belong to that status. Unconsciously I learned a new language, so rough and profane that for months after my return my wife would rebuke me, "Oh, Jack, can't you get rid of that awful army talk?" I had to learn to hold my own with some of the "toughest babies" I have ever seen. I had to play stud poker with a face completely masking my inner emotions. I discovered that in that camp community nothing counted but results. The hard-boiled quartermaster sergeants, now to their astonishment suddenly promoted to be captains, had always been intolerant of weakness.

Some of the lowest aspects of human nature were, as I have indicated, revealed at Camp Johnston. Fat-bellied officers "in the know" carried off government building materials and even constructed houses from them for themselves. Graft was prevalent among the retailers that supplied the camp with provisions. Thefts and assaults were common, and the guardhouse was filled nightly with offenders. But there was also an extraordinary amount of unselfishness and genuine patriotism, even in unexpected quarters; and I can never forget some of the kindnesses extended to us by some of the citizens of Jacksonville.

The administrative heads of the various schools established in the camp were men with academic or collegiate backgrounds, but capable of adjustment without too much difficulty to a new environment. Watching them I reached the conclusion that in wartime, resourcefulness and aggressiveness are supreme virtues. It was necessary for those making decisions to forget tradition and precedent and resort to common sense. What the camp needed was a nucleus of Robinson Crusoes — and it had a good many.

Watching some of my associates at Camp Johnston, I found many reasons for agreeing with Frederick P. Keppel, when he declared at the fiftieth anniversary of the Columbia Chapter of Phi Beta Kappa that war is "a practical test of scholarship." He added that the scholar must "if he is to serve effectively learn to think and to deal with all sorts of conditions of men; he must bear with their amazing ignorances and profit by their equally amazing knowledge of things of which he is ignorant." All this I can corroborate after working intimately with teachers suddenly projected into an army camp.

The work done at Camp Johnston in trying out the theoretical tests devised by the CCP was to have far-reaching consequences. Laboratory experts in the field of psychology discovered the defects of the earlier tests and gradually improved them. Leaders like Walter Dill Scott, Walter V. Bingham, John J. Coss, Beardsley Ruml, and others made a contribution which was both corrective and constructive. The A–12 and V–12 examinations used so effectively in World War II were based on the cruder tests which we employed at Camp Johnston.

Furthermore the whole broad theory of fitting the man to the job was, with some fumbling and plenty of mistakes, shown to be practicable in Jacksonville. Even "old-timers" could perceive that it was wasteful to turn an expert plumber into a storekeeper and an electrical engineer into a drummer. Before the spring of 1918 attempts were being made to set newly inducted privates at tasks for which they were equipped. Once the principle was established, the development of details was only a question of time.

We had the satisfaction of experimenting on a large scale with what might be called "universal training." Thousands of young men received instruction in matters of personal hygiene and even learned a trade. I then and there reached the conviction — which I have never abandoned — that the educational value of twelve months spent by a young man in making a useful contribution to the state is high. In large areas of the country the public school systems accomplish less than is supposed. Even when military drill is not paramount, there is plenty of work to be done in building bridges, draining swamps, and constructing roads; and I have no doubt that important projects, unhappily too long postponed, could be accomplished by this superabundant manpower. I know that many of the young men at Camp Johnston felt that they were being given a chance for training such as would ordinarily have been denied them. And for me those months were probably the most profitable of my life.

IX

Widening Interests

PROFESSOR John J. Coss, of Columbia, an influential member of the Committee on Classification of Personnel in the Army, once said to me after resuming his university duties when the war was over, "Jack, it's hard to return to a milk diet after living on raw meat." I knew exactly what he meant, and I must admit that I had much of the same feeling at first as I took off my uniform and settled down in Andover at the opening of 1919, hoping that there might be enough for me to do and that it would absorb all my energies. There soon was plenty.

To make it clear how my life at Andover widened at this juncture, I must necessarily build a little background. When I accepted the position on the faculty in 1908, I began almost at once to take an interest in the long history and splendid traditions of Phillips Academy. The school had published for some years a little quarterly magazine called the *Phillips Bulletin,* and in 1913 I was asked by Mr. Stearns to assume its editorship. No invitation could have been more opportune, for I was trying to learn how to write. It was at this time that I formed a close friendship with James C. Sawyer, Treasurer of the Academy. Jim was a born antiquarian, an insatiable lover of the past. He had a passion for old things, especially when they were beautiful, and an amazing memory for facts and dates and incidents. As he caressed with his sensitive fingers the mahogany balustrade of a Bulfinch house, he infected me with his own delight, and I tried to understand what he saw and felt. By mere contact with a gentleman of his aesthetic tastes, I learned much that was to be for me a stimulus and solace through the years.

I have used the term "gentleman" because Jim was about the most perfect specimen of that genus I have ever encountered. He conformed to Newman's famous definition by never willingly inflicting pain, but it was instinctive with him to be gracious, sympathetic, and tactful, and to draw out the best in others. Much of his irresistible personal charm lay in his deep-seated cheerfulness and easygoing temperament. His mere presence was an antidote to pessimism, for he had a profound conviction that everything would turn out all right. Fortunately most of his career as treasurer was spent in days when a steadily flowing river of money came in from the school's generous benefactors. When a pressing need arose, he would say, "I'll get the cash somehow" — and he usually did. During the lean 1930's Jim was unhappy, for he did not relish cheeseparing and counting pennies.

Jim once went with Al Stearns on a begging errand to Mr. Piel, of brewery fame, who had had sons in the school. After he had explained for some minutes the need for an endowment, Mr. Piel responded in his strong German accent, "And vot iss diss endowment — a dormitory?" Undismayed, Jim went on to discuss some of his budgetary difficulties. When he had finished, the old gentleman inquired, "Do I understand that you have been running along for some years mit a deficit?" "Yes, we have," admitted Jim. "Vell," retorted Mr. Piel, "Vy don't you chenge de menagement?" Needless to add, that mission was not successful.

Backed by Mark Stackpole and Jim Sawyer, I commenced gathering notes on the history of the school and writing in the *Bulletin* short sketches of the former principals. My material accumulated rapidly, and the manuscript of my book was completed late in 1916. *An Old New England School* was published by Houghton Mifflin early in the following spring. Naturally I was excited, for it was my first major publication, and I had put into it a vast amount of research and labor. Some of it was pioneer work, requiring the poring over almost indecipherable records; and I was rather proud of the fact that I had accomplished the writing while carrying on a full schedule of teaching.

Meanwhile I also became Secretary of the Alumni Fund, a job which fitted well into the editorship of the *Bulletin* and which also gave me a wide acquaintanceship with the graduates. The war came along as a kind of strange interlude, and when I returned the trustees asked me to prepare a volume which was eventually entitled *Phillips Academy in the Great War.* It was published by Yale University Press in the summer of 1919 — one of the quickest pieces of writing I ever did.

It has seemed my destiny to be the local chronicler of persons and events. In 1921 I published a volume called *Andover in the World War,* dealing with the contribution made by the town. I have already mentioned the *Amherst Memorial Volume,* which appeared in 1926. Meanwhile I helped to form Andover Post, Number 8, of the American Legion, and in 1923 was elected State Historian of the Legion. In that capacity I wrote and published *A History of the American Legion in Massachusetts.*

It was my function as alumni secretary to raise what was called the alumni fund, which had been becoming increasingly important in balancing the treasurer's budget. At the close of the war, prices rose, and it was evident that steps should be taken at once to avert financial catastrophe. Furthermore the main Academy building was in such a state that it had to be torn down, which of course made it necessary to replace it with a more modern structure. In the spring of 1919 the trustees were discussing seriously the advisability of starting a campaign to raise money for the new building and for teachers' salaries. Plans were drawn up, methods were discussed, and by the time school opened in the autumn it was settled that I was to be the executive secretary of the project and must for several months abandon my classroom work.

It would be absurd for me to devote space to a purely local money raising campaign if it had not had a wider significance. No independent school had as yet undertaken such a venture. In what was written and spoken we tried to speak for all secondary education. The arguments which we used for raising salaries were applicable anywhere in the United States. The stress which we laid on the dignity of the profession was needed in Texas as well as in Massachusetts. The future not only of Phillips Academy but also of all private secondary schools was at stake. What was done by Andover in 1919–1920, and for some years afterward, gave courage and hope to many headmasters.

The next few months were very exciting. We didn't know much about organizing a campaign, but as amateurs we learned rapidly by trial and error. Luckily we had among our alumni some leaders who were unaccustomed to failure and who behaved from the beginning as if success were inevitable. We called our project the "Building and Endowment Fund." On September 23 we held a preliminary dinner at the University Club in New York, at which we were able to report an advance gift of $100,000, two others of $50,000 each, and a few of smaller size, making a comfortable reserve of $250,000. I learned as the result of experience that every drive should have a nest egg before it gets underway. Soon we opened an office in Room 1817 of the Forty-second Street Building in New York City, and Dr. Stearns, Mr. Sawyer, and I commuted back and forth between

Andover and the metropolis, feeling very busy indeed. The New York spark plug for Andover was George B. Case, a lawyer who dropped in at headquarters every morning on his way to Wall Street. We divided the country into twelve divisions, each with its own chairman. In New York, Frederic C. Walcott, later United States Senator from Connecticut, who had just returned from prolonged war service, took three months off to work for American education and acted as chairman of the important Middle Atlantic division. In the background but always quietly dominant was Thomas Cochran, of J. P. Morgan and Company, who was shortly to make Andover the major interest of his life.

During this, my first experience with top businessmen, I was tremendously impressed with their alertness, audacity, and resourcefulness. Nothing was regarded by them as impossible. They began by giving very generously themselves. Then they went vigorously at the task of soliciting others. Typical of their methods was a small luncheon to which Mr. Cochran invited a wealthy Connecticut alumnus. Except for Dr. Stearns and me, the guests were all millionaires, and the victim, as he cast his eyes around, soon saw what was expected of him. As light dawned, he turned to Mr. Case and said, "I get the point, George. How much is this going to cost me?" "We'll let you off for $20,000," replied Case; and before the prospect was allowed to depart, he had pledged himself for that amount.

Everybody knew that the fund's ace was Dr. Stearns, and even at the risk of wearing him out, a schedule of speaking engagements was arranged which would carry him to every Andover center in the nation. I was deputed to accompany him and talk about the practical details of the drive, while Al furnished the inspiration. Before we set out, George Case cornered me and said, "Now, Jack, it's your main business to take care of Al. You see to it that he always travels in a drawing room, that no expense is spared to make him comfortable, and that he doesn't get too tired. If anything happens to him, we'll blame it on you!" I had reason to feel my responsibility, for the principal never watched out for his own health and was indifferent to deprivations. Left to himself he would have sat in a day coach and eaten nothing but hamburgers.

In his talks, Dr. Stearns took the broad position that in pleading for higher teachers' salaries at Andover, he was enhancing the prestige of all American secondary schools, both public and private. He stressed the point made so frequently today that the spread of Bolshevistic and Communistic doctrines in schools could be blocked mainly by keeping teachers satisfied with their lot under the free enterprise system. Some passages in his formal speech described the difficulties faced by teachers in trying to make both ends meet; and he was so eloquent that I, as a member of the profession, often found the tears coming to my eyes. Occasionally, when Al could not attend a meeting, I used his very words and gestures, although much less effectively. Dallas Lore Sharpe had recently made a stinging and quite illogical attack on American private schools, which Al refuted with the vigor of a revivalist. As a spokesman for American secondary education, Dr. Stearns was in his element. He reminded me in his fervor of President Woodrow Wilson, whose tragic breakdown had occurred just before our campaign opened.

Talking so much on the same subject, Al and I had naturally our favorite stories, which we told and heard again and again. One which seemed very much to the point was the tale of the Dumb Dora, who after being shown around a silver fox farm, said to the proprietor, "All this is perfectly fascinating; and now will you answer me one question — how many times a year do you skin these foxes?" "Not more than three or four times," replied the manager. "It makes them nervous!" Alumni quickly saw the relevancy of this anecdote and always applauded, with sincere appreciation of its grim humor.

After a few days of expansive hospitality, Stearns and I grew hardened to the ordeal. Fortunately our digestive apparatus survived the endless succession of hurried breakfasts, elaborate luncheons, crowded cocktail parties, and prolonged dinners. I soon learned the trick of holding a highball glass in my hand throughout an afternoon, letting the ice melt and allowing the glass occasionally to be refilled with water. One feature of nearly every dinner was the singing of "Lord Jeffery Amherst" by Al and me, as a conclusion to the festivities — a remarkable blend of sentiment and cacophony as the Andover alumni joined in the stirring college song.

Our first short trip covered Buffalo, Cleveland, Detroit, Chicago, St. Paul, Minneapolis, and Milwaukee, and then back to New York in early November. It was the period right after the winning of the great war, when the mood of the American people was optimistic and men and women were expansive in their hospitality. Dr. Stearns, furthermore, was at the height of his popularity, and the alumni viewed his career with a natural pride. The sponsorship of the campaign was so distinguished that our leading graduates in every city felt impelled to participate. It was the best psychological moment possible for our enterprise.

On November 2, 1920 an Andover Smoker was held at the Yale Club in New York, with movies of school life shown for the first time. The progress of the drive, indicated on a huge thermometer, showed that more than half a million dollars had already been raised, and it was clear that things were going well. After returning that night to Andover to vote, Stearns and I set out on a longer journey which was to take us to several cities where meetings of Andover alumni had never before been held. We went first to Pittsburgh, then to St. Louis, Kansas City, Omaha, Denver, and Colorado Springs, being entertained lavishly and delightfully wherever we stopped.

For both of us this trip beyond the Mississippi, across the plains, and into the mountains was a fascinating adventure, every minute of which we enjoyed. We reached Denver on November 6, in the midst of a driving snowstorm which covered the ground eight inches deep and made the ranges stern and sombre. Even more unforgettable than Pike's Peak to me was an evening spent with Tyson Dines, a Denver attorney who resembled Daniel Webster. In a darkened room, lighted only by a fire blazing on the hearth, he recited Longfellow's sonnet, "The Cross of Snow," beginning with the lines, "In the long, sleepless watches of the night" and ending:

There is a mountain in the distant West
That, sun-defying, in its deep ravines
Displays a cross of snow upon its side.
Such is the cross I wear upon my breast
These eighteen years, through all the changing scenes
And seasons, changeless since the day she died.

His restrained but vibrant emotion, his deep-lined features in the shadow, made us feel as if we were in the presence of some major prophet.

We crossed the Rockies by way of the Denver and Rio Grande Railroad, through the Royal Gorge to Salt Lake City and then down the Feather River Canyon to Oakland and San Francisco, where we were the guests of William H. Crocker and Sam Morse. At that point we had previously agreed to separate, one going south and the other north. But I now had instructions not to allow the principal out of my care, and accordingly we tossed a coin to decide in which direction we should proceed. Fate made the dime come down "heads," and we bought tickets for Portland and Seattle. The warmth with which we were greeted there convinced us that we had made no mistake.

Much good was accomplished by this trip, the first ever undertaken on such a scale by representatives of an independent school. The alumni, many of whom had not been back to the Hill since graduation, were obviously interested in the news about the teachers — Mac and Pap and Charlie. The amount contributed by the various groups was not great, but their loyalty was stimulated and several of them who had been out of touch with the school began considering Andover for their sons. For Al and me, as we moved from one metropolis to another, the Academy assumed the aspect of a national institution. We never had any doubt that the trip was worth the money and energy that it cost.

We returned east by way of Vancouver, Victoria, the Canadian Rockies, Moose Jaw, and St. Paul, reaching Andover on Thanksgiving morning. During our absence four men — Oliver G. Jennings, Alfred I. Dupont, Fred T. Murphy, and Thomas Cochran — had agreed to give $100,000 apiece. The original plan had been to close the New York office on November 22, but it became clear that the time set was too short. By January 9, 1920, the amount reported from headquarters was $1,065,021.17, and it was agreed that the date for the Victory Dinner should be set for January 28. The usual telegrams were sent out in every direction urging each leader to clean up his section. On the morning of January 28 only about $1,265,000 could be added up on the New York records, but in the course of the day many alumni increased their pledges, and the committee had a pleasant surprise up their sleeves in the shape of one new gift of $100,000 and the removal of certain conditions originally attached to three donations of $50,000 each. With such providence, the dinner could not have been a failure, and the announcement was joyfully made that the total sum of

$1,531,632.17 had been raised. The drive had succeeded.

It is pleasant to record that the benefits from the new fund were immediately felt by the faculty. A flat increase of 10 per cent in salaries, as of January 1, 1920, was made as soon as the success of the campaign was assured, and another raise of the same proportions was voted on April 1. The pledge made to the teachers was thus fulfilled. Furthermore the example set by Phillips Academy had a salutary effect on the policies of many other independent schools. Dr. Stearns spoke at commencement of "the depth and sincerity and length and breadth of the loyalty of old Andover men" and gave thanks that the faculty, with this definite and tangible encouragement, could "continue their work undismayed."

Knowing that one third of the fund had been raised specifically for construction, everybody on the Hill was looking forward to the day when the badly needed school building would be ready. Where should it be located? The conventional choice would have been a site on the west side of Main Street, traditionally occupied by Phillips Academy. At this point, however, George B. Case, with his restless and far-sighted mind, studied possibilities and offered a daring suggestion. He could visualize an extensive and attractive development on the other side of Main Street, on land controlled for a century by Andover Theological Seminary but recently purchased by Phillips Academy. Why not move Pearson Hall (formerly the Seminary's Bartlet Chapel), open up a broad vista, and construct the new main building on the ridge to the east, the highest point on the Hill? It was an audacious conception to shift a brick structure two stories high, tear down its ugly bell tower, and restore its original external design created by the great architect, Charles Bulfinch, in 1818. One morning Case led his fellow trustees to a position on the slope where he could explain his project and show where a new quadrangle could be laid out. Then and there he converted them, and the future expansion of Phillips Academy was assured.

In February 1921, exactly a year after the Victory Celebration, a crucial meeting was held at Andover. Many ideas were proposed and considered, but the opinion had spread that Case was right. Clearly if his plan were followed, other modern buildings must eventually be erected in that area, but that did not disturb him or his friend, Thomas Cochran. The trustees, as if hypnotized by Case and Cochran, found themselves talking in terms which would have frightened them ten years before. It took some time and much debate to reach an agreement on details, but the basic concept was never altered.

From that moment in 1921 events moved rapidly. Confident of the future, the trustees voted to erect a new dormitory, to be called Osgood Johnson Hall, rounding out the quadrangle on the west side of Main Street. Samuel L. Fuller announced his wish to build a Memorial Tower, commemorating the ninety boys and men, alumni of Phillips Academy, who had given their lives in the recent war. He had been stationed for a period in Fiesole, where he could hear the bells of Florence ringing out from the valley below; and in an idealistic mood he decided to give Andover a bell tower — "something absolutely useless!" The cornerstone was laid in the spring of 1922, on the old training ground — a spot which fitted perfectly into Case's plan. On the day before the dedication of the Tower I was walking by and lifted the cloth hiding the inscription to find out whether all was well. To my horror I noticed the word DESCENDANT was spelled DESCENDENT. Although the hour was late I called the architect, who immediately ordered a new block of stone to replace the one on which the mistake had been made. The cutter worked all night, and the next morning the new stone was set in place of the old. Not until years later did I tell Mr. Fuller how narrowly we escaped the ridicule of all good spellers!

Mr. Case himself gave to the school, in memory of his son, George Bowen Case, Jr., what was officially known as the Case Memorial Building but is locally called the "Cage," — a huge, glass-covered structure for indoor athletics but which has also been used for large dinners and for commencement activities. This was dedicated in June 1923. In June 1924, came the formal dedication of the new recitation building called Samuel Phillips Hall, in honor of the founder. With its tall white pillars and imposing façade it dominated the campus scene. The Andover renaissance was well on its way.

Before the movement thus begun was finished, buildings had sprung up on the Andover campus as if under a magician's wand. A chapel and a library, an administration building and an art gallery, a science laboratory and a dining hall — these, and many more, gave new vitality to an old institution. What brought this about? It could not have been done without money, and the 1920's were a period of exceptional prosperity for many people. Ordinary men were becoming well to do. The wealthy were growing wealthier. But the money was made productive by men of vision, who themselves created the spirit of the age, and who had the will and capacity to form plans and carry them out.

It is the fashion nowadays to condemn the Coolidge Era as a time of materialism and social injustice. I can only say that the educational benefactors whom I knew did not waste their substance in riotous living or grind down the working man. Harkness, Morrow, James, Folger, Lamont, Cochran, and many others were thinking constantly of how their money could be put to wise purposes. They felt their responsibility. Many rich men lost everything in the panic of 1929. The philanthropists whom I have mentioned were not wiser than they knew. Rather they were well aware of the consequences of what they were doing. Long after the Great Depression had swept away vast fortunes, the buildings on the campuses of American schools and colleges showed that some men had left good behind them. As these philanthropists looked around they could feel that they still had what they had given.

X

Tom Cochran and the Golden Age

THOMAS COCHRAN was in many respects the most picturesque figure I ever met. Although he wore the conventional banker's garb, stiff collar and all, his language, his manner, and his thoughts followed no normal pattern. His career in finance had been meteoric, for he had been a poor boy who worked his way through Phillips Academy and Yale; yet by 1917 he had become a partner in J. P. Morgan and Company and during the ensuing period of rapid money making he profited by that inexplicable sixth sense which enables speculative men under favorable conditions to amass fortunes. But he was never interested merely in piling up stocks and bonds. His wife died in 1914, four years after his marriage, leaving him no children to inherit his wealth. His constructive brain sought a sound and lasting use for his money, and he finally decided to invest in young manhood. Even as an Andover undergraduate he had written letters expressing his hope that he might some day do something for his old school. Accordingly, with all the intensity of his dynamic nature, he made himself in the 1920's Phillips Academy's guardian and golden angel. Eventually he widened his philanthropies to include other independent secondary schools of the same general type as Andover. The story is one of almost incredible drama and romance.

During our Building and Endowment Fund campaign of 1919–1920, in which he took an active part, he one day picked up my book, *An Old New England School* and seemed to be turning its pages rather lazily. A week later he drew me aside and said in his forceful way, "Jack, why haven't we capitalized on our history? I never knew that George Washington and those old fellows like Paul Revere and Oliver Wendell Holmes had anything to do with this place. A school with a background like ours should tell the world about it!" An idea had germinated which was to fructify the remainder of his life. With the elation of an explorer he discovered that Andover had unique traditions, that it was linked in many ways with American history, and he resolved that he would tell others what he had learned. Nearly all of his magnificent generosity stemmed from his desire to make the most of the school's intangible assets. He would do the tangible part himself.

It is not easy to elucidate the exact process through which Tom's conception of education broadened and deepened. He certainly did not rationalize his program until many features of it had been for some time in operation. His early donations to Phillips Academy were casual and unsystematic. He was always governed by his emotions rather than his reason, but intuition had with him all the authority of logic. Ultimately, however, his philosophy took coherent form and fitted a visible design, although even then there were aberrations which puzzled those around him.

To conceive an idea was, with Cochran, to take prompt steps to carry it out. He had the most restless as well as the most persistent mind I have ever watched in action. One project after another raced through his imagination; but when he had once reached a decision or embarked on a program, he could not be diverted from it; and he was intolerant of any delay, no matter how legitimate the explanation. I think of him in the words of James P. Webber's sonnet on Harlan P. Amen, as one who

Wrought with tireless hand through crowded days
Like one who hastened lest the eternal sleep
Should steal upon him ere his work was done.

While he was waiting for one of his dreams to take shape, he kept pressing builders and secretaries to hasten. Meanwhile he infected others with his own mood of hurry, until those in his vicinity were running around like ants in all directions. His favorite sentence was, "We've got to get things done!" After he was elected a trustee of the Academy in 1923, he had a good excuse for coming to Andover and could, of course, speak with more authority.

For some years Guy Lowell, of Boston — the school's very competent architect — had been erecting on the campus buildings which were faithful to the Georgian-Colonial tradition. But Tom did not like Samuel Phillips Hall, and when a new science building was contemplated, he was dissatisfied with Lowell's drawings. One evening at the principal's house, Miss Grace Clemons spoke of Charles Platt as a brilliant architect recognized as a specialist on the American Colonial Period. With his usual speed Tom called Mr. Platt by telephone the next morning and soon brought him to Andover as a consultant. Fortunately Mr. Platt was not only an architect but an artist and a landscape gardener, peculiarly suited to Tom's expansive temperament. Platt's imagination knew no bounds, and his adventurous spirit surmounted every obstacle. Cochran persuaded his colleagues on the Board that Platt had just the genius they needed. Platt cared nothing about costs, and neither did Cochran.

Walking with Cochran under the stately elms and studying the inimitable rust color of the brick in the Bulfinch buildings, Platt convinced him that beauty should be more stressed in the education of boys. "Why not surround them with the very best in architecture and nature and the fine arts?" asked Mr. Platt. "Why not a bird sanctuary, a really fine library, a topnotch art gallery, a good Colonial church with an organ? Why not a few broad vistas, some lawns and terraces, even some notable lectures and concerts — all the instruments of culture? I'd just like to try my hand at it." All this sounds a little bombastic as I report it, but Platt made it seem inevitable. Phase by phase under Platt's constant tutelage the conception seemed more and more practicable. Tom was converted and with his own enthusiasm enkindled the hearts of even the more conservative trustees until they were ready to support him in his noble madness. At his own expense and with Platt's co-operation Cochran had a model made of the campus, showing every major tree and every existing building, together with tiny reproductions of each proposed change and addition, so that the trustees and alumni could visualize his concept. The miracle was that before he died nearly all his projects had been carried out. The Andover campus will always be Platt's enduring monument.

A stroke of good fortune brought four members of the class of 1890 at Phillips Academy — Case, Cochran, Sawyer, and Stearns — working together for the lasting good of their school. Case, although more practical and realistic than the others, had plenty of vision; Cochran, in addition to his money, thought in large terms; Sawyer was a man of excellent, indeed almost infallible taste, with a feeling for what was appropriate; and Stearns, although himself not artistic, often served as a corrective when Platt wanted to uproot everything. Cochran was unquestionably obstinate and at times irritating to a traditionalist like Stearns. One leading member of the Board, a professor at Harvard, consistently opposed Platt's plans for a new brick chapel. Tom said nothing at the moment; but shortly he invited the professor to New York for a week, entertained him lavishly, and introduced him to a flock of distinguished people. "I'll have that fellow eating out of my hand," he said once to Stearns and me. And he did! When the matter was brought up before the Board, the professor upheld the Platt design, and Al, who had simpler tastes and did not altogether like the drawings, was obliged to give way.

The impulsiveness with which Tom reached and announced his decisions was startling to more pedestrian souls. I was living at that period in the Tucker House — a glaring specimen of what used to be called "New Jersey Renaissance" — located on the corner of Main and Phillips Streets. Platt and Cochran were standing one morning on the steps of Samuel Phillips Hall looking towards the west where my house was blocking the view. "That monstrosity is in the way," remarked Platt. "Very well," responded Cochran, with an imperial wave of the hand, "we'll have it moved at once!" The next morning I was notified that my house was to be transferred to a less conspicuous position. Sure enough, within a few days the three-story residence was on rollers and was shifted, crockery, furniture, books, and all, to a new site back in the fields — all at a cost of more than $20,000.

Nothing daunted Mr. Platt. A large brick dormitory, three stories in height, was moved from its site on Phillips Street, turned around, and faced in the opposite direction on a spot at least three hundred yards away. Elms two centuries old were uprooted and carted to new locations, where in a few years they looked as if they had stood forever. The Phillips Inn, constructed of heavy stone, was actually transferred to a spot down the street, and a new Inn, of brick, rose on the old site. The principal's house, a fine wooden mansion built in 1829, occupied the ground which Cochran wanted for his chapel. In this case Stearns was really annoyed at what he considered a kind of desecration, but his protests had little effect. Cochran was so persistent that Al, unwilling to start a violent controversy, yielded and allowed his house to be moved. Even the most loyal reverer of the past, looking at the Cochran Chapel today, is forced to admit that Platt was right.

Of Cochran's major building projects on Andover Hill — all of them designed by Mr. Platt — the most important were George Washington Hall (1926), the administrative center, in the lobby of which hangs the Gilbert Stuart portrait of Washington purchased by Cochran for $40,000; Paul Revere Hall (1929), a magnificent new dormitory for seniors; the Oliver Wendell Holmes Library (1929), given in the name of his sister and brothers; the Addison Gallery of American Art (1931), dedicated to a friend, Mrs. Keturah Addison Cobb; and the Cochran Chapel (1932). Cochran also contributed sums of considerable size towards the erection of Samuel F. B. Morse Hall (1928), the science building; the dining hall (1930); the Andover Inn (1930); and the heating plant, an unromantic but very essential feature of the school equipment. In naming these structures Tom deliberately aimed to bring out the relationship between the school and the nation. Washington sent to Phillips Academy his nephew and eight grand-nephews; Paul Revere designed the school seal; Morse and Holmes were graduates. Cochran wished to name one building for John Hancock, who signed the Academy's Act of Incorporation, but in this instance was blocked by Professor Ropes, of Harvard, who pointed out that Hancock had embezzled the funds of that institution and was therefore not worthy of commemoration. After Professor Ropes's denunciation, a copy of a portrait of Hancock which Cochran had procured for the new building was quietly relegated to my office, where it hung for years behind the door in a place where Ropes would presumably not see it. The incident explains why Phillips Academy has no Hancock Hall.

Bliss Perry, in his autobiography, *And Gladly Teach,* refers to the "grandiose new buildings" of Phillips Academy which have "destroyed the charm of the once quiet hilltop." With this adjective I cannot agree. Here Charles Platt did the most comprehensive and brilliant work of his career, and the buildings, displaying variety and unity, have a noble relevance and an intimate relationship to one another which every visitor is bound to notice. Platt did not make the hilltop less quiet. That was done before him by the trolley car and later by the automobile. The charm is different from what it was in the 1880's, but it still exists, enhanced by the architect's genius.

Cochran did his best to restore the peace of former days by getting the Commonwealth to construct a bypass which would reduce the extensive traffic on Main Street through the heart of the modern school. Mr. Henry S. Hopper, then comptroller and an indispensable authority on local detail, informed Cochran that Governor Frank G. Allen was a personal friend of Mr. Philip L. Reed, a member of the Andover Board of Trustees. Hopper suggested, however, that before further steps were taken some preliminary plans be prepared, and Cochran sent him $2500 for that purpose. Engineers proceeded then to make drawings showing a possible route for the new road. When these were ready, Reed arranged for a conference between the Governor and the State Commissioner of Public Works on the one hand and Phillips Academy representatives on the other. The group met at the State House, lunched at the Parker House, and then motored out in a caravan to inspect the proposed route for the new highway. It was a very cold day in January, and everybody was glad to get back to George Washington Hall, where the discussion was resumed under less frigid conditions.

Commissioner Lyman finally agreed to build the road if the Andover Trustees conveyed to the Commonwealth a 100-foot right of way, approximately five miles in length, and would also pay the cost of construction of one mile of road.

It was a fine bargain for the Commonwealth but very expensive for Tom Cochran. Hopper was the skillful intermediary in the acquisition of the land, which involved 56 separate deeds and a total of 400 acres. Tom was constantly pressing for more speedy action, but Hopper measured up to all the demands, and the legal transfers were accomplished in a surprisingly short time. When the job was over, Cochran invited Hopper and several other coadjutors to be his guests on a trip to Europe in April, 1930, to celebrate a feat which was, I think, unprecedented in the annals of the Commonwealth. Today, as I drive along the broad bypass, I never fail to think of the perseverance with which Cochran achieved his purposes.

Equally illustrative of his impetuosity and pertinacity is the story of the Cochran Wild Life Sanctuary. Jack Miner and Fred Walcott had talked with Tom more than once about waterfowl; and one evening when Cochran and his satellites were sitting on the terrace at the Andover Inn, Walcott suggested that Rabbit Pond might well be developed into a stopping place for migrating birds. John Stewart, the witty proprietor of the Inn and a favorite of Tom's, acted on the hint and induced a local sportsman named Dick Hoyer to draft a possible program. As a consequence Stewart was promptly instructed to build a duck house on the shore of the pond and buy a number of species. There was so much good-natured "jollying" that Stewart, who enjoyed practical jokes as much as Tom did, started off for Stamford, Connecticut, where he purchased a considerable number of ducks and geese at Cochran's expense. On the road back some of the cages fell apart, with the result that when Stewart drove up to the Inn, his car was incredibly filthy. Tom happened to be on hand to watch the subsequent proceedings and found plenty of amusement in them.

When the ducks and geese became too numerous to be

cared for at Rabbit Pond, Tom asked Olmsted Brothers to plan two small artificial ponds in the area to the east. At the same time he requested Hopper to obtain options on land in the immediate vicinity. Fourteen property owners were concerned, and when the news was whispered around that Mr. Cochran was buying more land, the price quickly mounted. Fortunately Hopper had already acquired most of what was necessary for the project. A wire fence ten feet above ground and six feet below — to keep out dogs and rodents — was set up around the area, and it was then planted extensively with pines, laurel, and rhododendron. Some years later it was further improved by the addition of the "Bobby Thompson Swimming Pool," donated by Mr. and Mrs. Charles D. Thompson in memory of their son, the first Andover graduate to lose his life in the Second World War. The pines are now tall; the laurel and rhododendron offer a colorful display when they are in flower; and several charming stone memorials have been set up here and there through the woods. Although the breeding of birds has been abandoned, many varieties, especially of gay-plumaged pheasants, may be detected in the underbrush. It is a place of peace, of recreation for large numbers of boys and of delight for visitors. It may even be more enduring than towers and porticoes.

One morning Tom called me to the treasurer's office, which he made his Andover headquarters, and said, "Jack, we don't make enough of our distinguished alumni. I want you to scout around and find as many portraits as possible of graduates and then have Alec James copy them. I'll pay him $1000 apiece, and then maybe he can take that trip abroad that he's wanted to have so long." "How many shall I try to get?" I asked. "Oh, hell, make it a couple of dozen, if you can find good ones," he answered. In that offhand but characteristic fashion I was despatched on missions which carried me all over the East. Alec, who was a portrait painter of distinction, rather enjoyed the prospect of such an informal, although wholesale, adventure. We heard that in a Boston suburb was a fine portrait of an eminent abolitionist who had been a student at Phillips Academy in the 1820's. Alec and I, with two companions, started out one afternoon in my open Dodge car, having taken the precaution of insuring the valuable work of art for $10,000. It turned out that the picture was actually a very poor chromo of a handsome but much bewhiskered gentleman. As we drove back, Alec remarked: "This is really a great chance for me. I'll make him a combination of William Cullen Bryant and Walt Whitman." At one point in the proceedings we wired the subject's niece about his eyes, and were told that they were "steel-gray." I must admit that Alec took some liberties with the rather crude original, but the completed copy revealed a countenance almost obscured by hair. When the niece later visited Andover, she stood in front of Alec's copy for a long time and then said, with appreciation, "That's uncle to the life!"

The portraits ordered in this impetuous fashion were one by one completed and hung on the walls and along the corridors of the buildings, to their manifest improvement. John Phillips and Josiah Quincy, Nathaniel P. Willis and John Thornton Kirkland, Robert Rantoul and William H. Moody, Ray Palmer and William A. Stearns — these and many other leading Americans looked down on the boys of a later generation. In the same spirit Tom employed Stuart Travis to draft a pictorial map of the school grounds, with little inserts showing picturesque incidents in its history. Among these were depicted the visits of Washington and Lafayette and Webster to Andover. When Thomas W. Lamont examined the map and found there a picture of the "Godlike Dan'l" in his tall beaver hat, he said to his partner, "Tom,

I knew that you were unscrupulous in what you did for Andover, but honestly I never dreamed that you would steal one of our Exeter graduates and put him in an Andover group."

The hour arrived when Cochran's interest spread beyond brick and granite and canvas to the very fundamentals of education, as presented in the teacher. Here Al Stearns's influence was paramount, for he knew through experience that the faculty is the energizing factor in any school. Suddenly it occurred to Cochran, after listening to a speech by the principal, that although a fine equipment and first-class tools are important, they are so only when utilized by well-informed, wise, and inspiring instructors. Again with him to think was to act. "We must," he declared oracularly, "be able to attract to Phillips Academy any teacher in the United States — if we want him badly enough." To this end he made several of his gifts contingent upon the establishment of ten teaching foundations of $160,000 each, providing annual salaries of $8000; and he harassed some of his opulent friends, particularly Edward S. Harkness, until in sheer self-defense they contributed to his scheme. He had begun by wishing to have the finest buildings possible. Now with these he must have the best available teachers.

In the prosperous summer of 1929, just preceding the catastrophic slump in the stock market, Tom's energies reached their peak. He had publicly declared to reporters that prices were not too high and evidently saw no reason why the golden flow should not continue indefinitely. In a letter dated June 20 and addressed to his "Dear Fellow Laborers" — who included not only Stearns, Sawyer, and Hopper, but also Augustus P. Thompson, an Andover and Yale friend whom Tom in his whimsical way had created "Warden of the Sanctuary" — he listed twenty-nine different projects, some significant and some trivial, which were on his docket. They ranged from the demolition of Brechin Hall (an architectural atrocity which had been the library of Andover Theological Seminary) to the procurement of a huge armillary sphere, or glorified sundial designed by Paul Manship and the purchase of a stuffed Great Auk (which had cost him $3000 at a London auction).

During this gorgeous period, Cochran taught those around him — of whom I, in a very subordinate way, was one — to think in terms of millions. Nothing seemed impossible! If he had decided to build a replica of King's College Chapel on the campus, nobody would have been much astonished. His every visit to Andover was followed by some change in the location of buildings, the digging of cellar holes for new structures, and the appearance of more steam shovels and bulldozers. From the moment that he appeared things moved faster. He played a practical joke on Gus Thompson; he humorously berated Mr. Hopper for some entirely imaginary delinquency; he approved of a proposal for a series of motion pictures of undergraduate life; he criticized the make-up of the catalogue and made suggestions to the headmaster for its revision; he strode about the grounds with Charles Platt and listened to the latter's recommendations; he even insisted, against Dr. Stearns's protest, on changing his title from "principal" to headmaster; and during the intervals between these bits of business he was sitting in the treasurer's office joking with anybody who came along, including clerks and janitors.

Tom Cochran had a highly individual personality. His language at times was, as I have intimated, shockingly picturesque. He would refer to some of his more conservative colleagues on the Board of Trustees as "old dodoes" and describe his closest friends in epithets which would have been insulting if not accompanied by his expansive smile. His favorite verb when he was aroused was to "bastardize." When thwarted in any way he would storm about in an apparent burst of uncontrollable rage, saying, "I'll bastardize the son-of-a-bitch!" and then the sunshine would follow the storm and he would beam genially at those around him. He was also one of the most thoughtful of men, continually making presents and doing kind deeds. Jim Sawyer found outside his house one Christmas morning a brand-new automobile registered in his name — a gift from Tom. To another friend he sent a set of rare books on his birthday. At heart he was a sentimentalist, but how he did hate to have his secret weaknesses revealed!

The one hundred fiftieth anniversary of the founding of Phillips Academy, occurring opportunely in 1928, gave Mr. Cochran precisely the excuse he wanted for focusing public attention on American independent schools. If it hadn't been for Tom the occasion would doubtless have been just another local celebration. He gave it almost national significance. Two years before the event he began talking and planning. "Of course we must have the President of the United States," he announced, "and I'll see to it that he comes." It is indicative of our respect for Tom that no one who heard that quiet assertion doubted that the promise would be fulfilled.

I was drafted to be the active manager of the affair, and for many months my teaching suffered, in quantity if not in quality, for I was never sure when I would be summoned to New York to discuss some detail or assigned a mission which would absorb my time for a week. I had to take charge of the publicity, arrange the details of the program, attend to countless routine items, always trying to anticipate what I felt would be Tom's wishes. I even published another book, *Men of Andover,* containing short biographies of certain Andover celebrities. It is a wonder that I survived, for following in Tom's wake was at best an exhausting experience.

After consulting meteorological records over a long period, we finally selected May 18 and 19 as the dates most likely to guarantee good weather, and then prayed hopefully that all might be well. As the great day drew near, even President Coolidge's private secretaries denied reports that he was to take a trip to New England. Tom, however, smiled blandly and authorized me to have the invitations and programs printed, and I went ahead, convinced that nothing could go wrong. Sure enough, the word arrived through Ted Clark, the President's secretary, that Mr. Coolidge was working on his speech. Then the news came that he would be arriving by special train, with Mrs. Coolidge; and shortly Colonel Starling, of the Secret Service, descended upon us to check on the route for the parade and the other arrangements. He stayed at my house for two days and regaled my family with some of the thrilling tales later published in his book, *Starling of the White House.*

On Friday afternoon, May 18, in the Great Quadrangle recently completed, the exercises were opened with addresses by college presidents. But alas, President Angell, of Yale, had finished and President Hibben, of Princeton, had hardly begun before the threatening rain really descended, and the audience had to move indoors to the auditorium of George Washington Hall. The weather prophets had all gone wrong.

On the next morning, however, the skies were brighter, and everybody was on edge with excitement. Dr. Stearns, Mr. Cochran, and others of the committee were at the station, together with a detachment of very amateurish cavalry officers, two of whom fell off their mounts as the locomotive steamed in. The Governor of the Commonwealth, Alvan T. Fuller, with his wife, was at the headmaster's house to greet the President and Mrs. Coolidge, to whom Dr. Stearns presented two gold medals designed especially for the occasion. At eleven o'clock, following the academic procession, the

President, from a platform in front of Samuel Phillips Hall, addressed a throng of twenty thousand people in one of his best oratorical efforts.

Among the passages which attracted attention in Mr. Coolidge's speech was the following:

> The world will have little use for those who are right only part of the time. Whatever may be the standards of the classroom, practical life will require more than 60 per cent or 70 per cent for a passing mark. The standards of the world are not like those set by the faculty, but more closely resemble those set by the student body themselves. They are not at all concerned with a member of the musical organizations who can strike only 90 per cent of the notes. They do not tolerate the man on the diamond who catches only 80 per cent of the balls. The standards which the student body set are high. They want accuracy that is well-nigh complete.

On the Monday morning following this address the boys in my senior English class were discussing recent events, and one of the brighter pupils, referring to this paragraph, said, "The President didn't say anything about batting averages, did he? And I wonder what proportion of his decisions since he entered public office have been right?" I could only say, "Bill, all I know is that any executive who is right in his decisions three fourths of the time is a first-rate administrator." This judgment has been confirmed by many businessmen whom I have consulted on the subject.

Being in some degree responsible for the success of an occasion which meant so much to the school and to Tom Cochran, I was in a mood of constant excitement until the last guest had departed; but some humorous incidents relieved the tension. When the procession reached the platform, a little confusion arose, as a consequence of which the Honorable James J. Davis, Secretary of Labor, and another gentleman occupied the seats intended for Governor and Mrs. Fuller. While I was walking about to see that everything was in order, I noticed the President's index finger crooking at me as though summoning me to his presence. Hastening to him, I leaned down, and he whispered in my ear, "Governor of Commonwealth belongs in front row." Mr. Coolidge was a stickler for protocol. He had himself been governor, and he was absolutely right. Fortunately the situation was easy to explain to Mr. Davis, and the Governor and his wife were soon in their proper places. I may add that Mr. Fuller, with characteristic tact, did all in his power to soften my embarrassment.

My friend, Dr. Alfred V. Kidder, the eminent archaeologist, was standing on the outskirts of the crowd and reached into his hip pocket for his pipe, only to have his hand enclosed by another as large as a ham. Then came the ominous words, "Don't make a move!" It was the redoubtable Colonel Starling himself, who led Kidder aside, quietly "frisked" him for concealed weapons, and warned him to be careful not to commit any overt act. The colonel obviously stood for no nonsense, even from the best-dressed spectators.

In the headmaster's office, where he retired for a few moments before joining the procession, Mr. Coolidge smoked one of his favorite "little cigars." When he left, a hero-worshipping secretary placed the butt in a glass test tube and put it in the office safe, with an appropriate inscription. And there it was, when last I knew anything about it, preserved for an admiring posterity!

The President's speech was excellent, but the two best addresses of that loquacious celebration were made by schoolmen — Lewis Perry, of Exeter, who was never happier in his remarks, and Frederic B. Malim, the Master of Wellington College, in England. Mr. Malim closed his talk with some verses from the Psalms, adapted to the occasion, beginning, "I was glad when they said unto me, Let us go into the house of the Lord," and ending, "Yea, for the sake of the house of the Lord our God, we will seek to do thee good." His speech was simple, sincere, and very moving — an appropriate conclusion for the greetings of the guests of the day.

At the luncheon in the Case Memorial Building on Saturday Dr. Stearns, as was fitting, was to say the last word. As he sat there at the head table, Tom Cochran, obviously under a strain, kept tossing little scribbled slips of paper with suggestions for Al to use in his concluding remarks. As a pile of these notes accumulated in front of the principal, I could see him gazing at them in perplexity. He had prepared his speech carefully in advance. It had been distributed to the press. Now Cochran was disrupting all his plans. When Al rose, he did his best to incorporate the new material, but no one could possibly have digested the miscellaneous ideas which Tom had placed before him.

The Phillips Academy Sesquicentennial was unquestionably the most important event up to that date in American private secondary education. No school had ever attempted a celebration on such a large scale. A distinguished group of college presidents representing Harvard, Yale, Dartmouth, Princeton, Cornell, and Amherst put themselves on record in praise of the independent school and its place in our society. The presence of the President of the United States gave the affair prestige. I regretted myself that we did not invite some of the leaders in public secondary education, but the committee decided that the list should be restricted. At any rate the publicity for the independent schools was beneficial to all of them. They gained in confidence, in self-respect, and in dignity. Many people, often for the first time, understood how much these institutions had contributed to American life and character.

For Phillips Academy the sesquicentennial was a climax, but for Cochran it was only a dramatic beginning. Soon he gave anonymously a capital fund of one million dollars, the income of which was to be used in perpetuity to beautify the grounds. At commencement in 1929, it was announced that the gifts to the Academy for the year amounted to nearly five million dollars, most of it from Mr. Cochran. During the same period, in a mood of frank optimism, he made several new commitments. Then in October began the succession of crashes in the stock market. Some of Andover's wealthiest alumni found themselves in positions of financial embarrassment. But although Tom must have lost plenty, he never faltered in carrying through his projects. "I still have a little currency left," was all he said, and he met every obligation. The Addison Gallery was opened with a simple ceremony on May 16, 1931. The Cochran Chapel, the last and perhaps the noblest of his benefactions, was dedicated on Sunday, May 8, 1932.

The total amount of Tom's gifts to Phillips Academy has been estimated as rather more than eleven million dollars. Although the Depression had to some extent altered his plans, he had actually achieved his primary purpose of transforming Andover into a place of beauty. He had provided the school with everything but a new gymnasium and a new infirmary — and the latter had been promised by one of the trustees. Very few philanthropists have been able to watch and direct their projects over so many years. Having furnished Andover with what it needed, he now intended to broaden his generosity to include other independent schools, particularly Deerfield Academy. But this the state of his health would not allow.

Henry Adams said of Theodore Roosevelt, "His restless and combative energy was more than abnormal," and added, "He was pure act." The same could have been said of Thomas Cochran. For some years Tom had suffered from intermittent attacks of mental disturbance, and his excitability was well known to his friends at Andover. Even while afflicted with his moods of extreme melancholia, however, he continued to think in terms of the future. In 1932 came a more serious breakdown, and he was condemned to be an invalid, isolated by a physician's decree from his associates and tragically aware that his active days were over. A little while before his death in the autumn of 1936 he sent in his check for five dollars to the Alumni Fund, writing me in longhand that it was all he could afford. He died believing that he was impoverished. He did, however, leave approximately three million dollars, of which one quarter was allotted to fulfill a pledge to the Addison Gallery. Almost his last words were, "All I want is rest and peace."

Tom Cochran was the ideal benefactor. As a money raiser he could cajole and bully a victim with compelling persistence. As a donor he was farsighted, discriminating, and tactful, with occasional whimsical lapses. In a playful mood he established a capital fund of $10,000 to provide for an annual concert named for his friend, Jim Sawyer, who disliked music. When a trustee inadvertently remarked that Al Stearns hadn't been commemorated in any such fashion, Cochran replied, "Well, Al doesn't like lectures — I'll give another $10,000 for a Stearns Lecture." The school has been having Sawyer Concerts and Stearns Lectures ever since.

Tom was extraordinarily sensitive to criticism. When a self-important member of the faculty was heard declaring that he didn't like the location of the Armillary Sphere, Cochran gave orders the next morning to have it shifted to another spot on the campus. When Mr. Platt casually remarked that the two dormitories, Bartlet and Foxcroft, would be better proportioned if they were only three stories high instead of four, Tom broke out, "Look here — you take off the top story, and do it damned quick!" Except for his teaching foundations, he left no dead hand to trouble posterity. He had his prejudices, but they did not control his decisions.

He placed very few restrictions on his gifts, and these have seldom been annoying.

Without our being aware of it, the dedication of the Cochran Chapel in 1932 marked the end of an era. Mr. Cochran never came back to the Hill again. In December 1931, Dr. Stearns suddenly collapsed in a faculty meeting, was carried to the hospital, and underwent a serious kidney operation. During his enforced absence Professor Forbes, the very efficient head of the Latin Department, was appointed acting headmaster. On January 1, 1933, Dr. Stearns, then in Italy, sent home a letter of resignation. A few weeks later Professor James Hardy Ropes, President of the Board of Trustees, died; and on March 12, Professor Forbes had a fatal heart attack. It did indeed look as if everything and everybody were collapsing at once. Under such inauspicious conditions I became Headmaster of Phillips Academy.

XI

Destiny Turns the Wheel

WHENEVER a young teacher asks me, "How can I become a headmaster?" my first reaction is to inquire, "Why such a foolish ambition? The burdens are heavy, the grief is constant, and the rewards are nebulous!" But if he persists, I can only answer, "Nobody knows. Headmasters are recruited from all walks of life — not only from teaching but from business, from school and college deans, from the ministry, and even from the army. No specific form of training leads to school administration. Furthermore luck, good or bad, has a lot to do with it."

In the late autumn of 1932, Stanley King, who had just been inaugurated as President of Amherst College, asked me to come to see him and then offered me a Professorship of Biography at Amherst, at a generous salary, with complete freedom to write and teach as much as I pleased. I was to be resident on the campus, with a position in the field of biography similar to that occupied by Robert Frost in poetry. After my wife and I had talked it over, we made up our minds that perhaps we were ready to make a change. I had done about all I could do as a teacher of English and was moving rapidly towards history as my major interest. Here was my chance!

While the Amherst matter was still in abeyance, I made a trip to New York by train and found myself talking in the parlor car with General Edward L. Logan, the eminent commander of the 26th (Yankee) Division in the First World War. At Providence the porter came through announcing, "Calvin Coolidge is dead!" That was on January 6, 1933. As we rode on, General Logan and I exchanged stories about Mr. Coolidge, and when I reached the University Club in New York I drafted an outline for an article on the ex-President which I submitted on my return to Edward A. Weeks, editor of the *Atlantic*. He looked it over and asked quickly, "Why don't you do a biography of Coolidge?" I was already committed to a biography of Henry Cabot Lodge, but that task had for several reasons become distasteful, and the idea of writing about a fellow Amherst man was most appealing. Furthermore it occurred to me that Amherst would be the perfect place in which to carry on research about Coolidge and steep myself in the proper atmosphere.

As the weeks went on, the project seemed more and more attractive. In early March I made an engagement with Mrs. Coolidge at Northampton and persuaded my friend, Horace M. Poynter, to accompany me. We spent two days in the Connecticut Valley, seeing Mrs. Coolidge three times, and on Sunday afternoon, March 12, we drove back to Andover with my plans all settled for an indefinite future. As we stepped out of the automobile in front of the Phelps House, Elsie Poynter appeared in tears and said, "Jack, Charlie Forbes is dead, and the trustees are waiting to see you in Jim Sawyer's library."

Although Forbes, the acting headmaster, had not been well, this news was staggering, and I could hardly believe that another major disaster had happened to the Academy. At the treasurer's house I found Judge Elias B. Bishop (who had only recently been elected President of the Board of Trustees), Alfred L. Ripley (former President of the Board), Mr. Sawyer, and one or two others, sitting around in very solemn conclave. After telling me the details, Judge Bishop —

whom I then didn't know very well — glared at me and said, "Fuess, we've decided that you are to take over the school tomorrow morning!" "But I can't," I protested. "I've made different plans. I'm going to Amherst as a professor." "Nonsense!" replied the judge. "You've just got to help us out here." "Do you mean to say," I asked, "that I've got to be headmaster whether I want to be or not?" "Not necessarily headmaster," came the answer. "This doesn't mean that you're not going to be headmaster; on the other hand it doesn't mean that you're going to be." I was tired and hungry and emotionally shattered, and perhaps may be forgiven for coming back vigorously "You're damned right it doesn't!" Then Judge Bishop, with a quizzical expression on his face, inquired, "Fuess, do you often say *damn?*" "Not too often," I rejoined "but when I do say it, I mean it!" The judge leaned over, patted my knee, and said "Young fellow, you're a man after my own heart!" That was the beginning of my close friendship with one of the most generous, humorous, and fairminded of men. The next morning I walked over to the headmaster's office, took my seat with my knees shaking on the platform at morning chapel, and explained to the boys the situation. I continued to sit on that platform, with varying degrees of timidity, until June 1948.

There is no moral to this story. I became a headmaster in spite of my designs or desires. That is what happens to most headmasters. Very few start out their careers with the announced intention of becoming the administrative heads of schools. By far the largest proportion come direct from the teaching profession, as I did. Perry and Saltonstall at Exeter, Heely at Lawrenceville, Kittredge at St. Paul's, Arthur B. Perry at Milton, and many others were teachers before being elected to headmasterships. From the Deerfield Academy faculty have been drafted several headmasters, including Eames of Governor Dummer, Wickenden of Tabor, Allen of Hebron, Poor of Fountain Valley, and Hagaman of Holderness. A man who has gone through the mill as an instructor should, as a headmaster, be able to talk the same professional lingo as his teaching staff. Until I tried to run Phillips Academy, I never realized how much protection a Phi Beta Kappa key and a doctorate could offer.

As I have intimated, I had no inauguration or formal investiture. One week I was quite contentedly preparing seniors for the College Entrance Board examinations; the next I was sitting behind a desk in an office in George Washington Hall, endeavoring to regain my bearings. My friend, G. Grenville Benedict, hastened back from Bermuda to take my place as teacher and ultimately became the very reliable Dean of Students. The situation in some respects was critical, for the school had been shaken by a succession of unparalleled misfortunes, and it was necessary to restore confidence. Fortunately for me, I was well known on the campus, and even those who didn't like me preferred to take a chance with my familiar defects rather than risk somebody entirely new. Thus I had the initial strong support of both faculty and boys.

It seemed to be essential to dramatize the new administration in some appealing way. With unprecedented rapidity we broke with tradition by shifting the hour of morning chapel from 7:45 to 10 and abolishing the second compulsory Sunday service. These reforms were both long overdue and very popular. Because I was not, like most of my predecessors, a clergyman, I recognized the desirability of placing somebody at once in direct charge of the Academy's religious activities. Accordingly I asked my younger friend, the Reverend A. Graham Baldwin, then on the staff in the Department of Religion, to fill the position of school minister. His acceptance was a guarantee that I need have no worries about a field in which I was certainly without experience. I believed then — and still believe — that the school physician and the school minister occupy unique positions and must be selected with the greatest care. No man could have been more co-operative than Gray Baldwin — or better suited to his job.

Baldwin was hardly settled in the Cochran Chapel before he called one morning at my office, sat down, and said, "Jack, wouldn't it be a good idea for you to join the church?" "Why, Gray," I responded proudly and reproachfully, "I joined the Presbyterian Church at the age of eight in Waterville, New York, and can even repeat part of the catechism." A smile of relief passed across his face, and then he said, "That's fine — now why not get yourself transferred to the Church of Christ in Phillips Academy?" This seemed to me sensible, and he went away happy. I then wrote a letter to the minister of the Waterville church requesting a transfer, but no reply came. Baldwin would stop in my office three or four times a week and invariably ask whether the necessary document had arrived; and I had to confess that it had not. Finally I communicated directly with my brother, who explained that the present local minister was new and unacquainted with his responsibilities; and the next time Baldwin propounded the familiar query I was able to take from my desk a Manila envelope and hand it to him. He opened it, read a few lines, and then began to laugh. "What is there funny," I asked, "about a church transfer?" "Well, read it yourself," he retaliated. I took it from him. It was an impressive-looking sheet of parchment, adorned with gilt letters certifying that Claude Moore Fuess was herewith transferred from the First Presbyterian Church of Waterville, New York, to the Church of Christ in Phillips Academy. But down at the bottom the cautious clergyman had typed the sentence, "We know nothing of the conduct of this man for the past thirty years." I had the document framed and it hung for years on the wall of my office, as a reminder that pride goeth before a fall.

To my delight the Faculty Curriculum Committee passed

with amazing unanimity a revised curriculum, placing Latin upon an elective instead of a required basis and providing for a compulsory History Sequence, with ancient history in the junior year, European history in the lower middle year, English history in the upper middle year, and American history in the senior year. Under the old program, few boys had taken more than one course in history and many had taken none at all.

As a member of the Curriculum Committee I had been trying for three or four years to have these changes made, but they had been blocked in the end by two members of the Board of Trustees. One of them had said at a meeting of the Board in 1931, "American history will become a compulsory subject at Andover only over my dead body!" Within a year he was in his grave, and American history was a required subject — and has been ever since.

It is wise for any school, no matter how well established, to re-examine its curriculum at least every ten years and make what changes seem to be desirable. The course of study should not be allowed to become static, and at different periods different subjects require different emphases. The hour had unquestionably arrived at Andover for the abandonment of compulsory Latin. It was distasteful to many students, and in the existing state of the world other subjects assumed greater importance. I do not intend here to add my contribution to the already too long dispute over the value of Latin for adolescent boys. The faculty felt that there were boys in Phillips Academy to whom a modern foreign language offered a greater reward than Greek or Latin, and this the revised curriculum permitted them to take.

With the recent opening of the Addison Gallery and the installation of the magnificent Cassavant Frères Organ in the Cochran Chapel, Andover was at last equipped to institute required courses in the appreciation of art and music. I must confess that I felt like shouting when the faculty finally agreed to allow this experiment to be tried.

While these changes were taking place, I was still acting headmaster, with the possibility increasing that I might have to face the prospect of being elected permanently to that position. During the spring vacation my wife and I went to the Partridge Inn, at Augusta, Georgia, where I tried each of the four fine golf courses, including the famous Bobby Jones course, which I was delighted to play one morning in 89. Each evening we would sit before the log fire, usually with my father's boyhood friend, Frank L. Babbott, and try to decide whether, if it were offered to me, I would accept the headmastership. Mr. Babbott, a graduate of Amherst in the Class of 1878, was strong for my going back to the college. My wife, however, who had lived in Andover most of her life, obviously preferred to stay there — although she promised to abide by my decision. I returned to Andover for the spring term with my mind still in a turmoil and with my problem still unsettled. Although I was aware that the trustees were carrying on an investigation of possible candidates, I was much too busy to concern myself about that. So far as I knew the Amherst job was still open, and I was ready for it.

One May morning Judge Bishop came unexpectedly into my office and said, "Fuess, we've been looking over quite a number of other fellows, but all of us know that we really want you, and we're going to elect you permanently at the next meeting. What have you got to say about that?" As he was speaking, I was aware that I would have to accept. I had committed myself to projects which I didn't wish to abandon. I had begun to enjoy getting things done. It seemed to me that if I had any real mission in life, it was probably at Andover. Almost without a pretense of reflection, I replied, "All right, Judge Bishop — if you want me, I'll take the job!"

Some questions of housing had to be discussed, for Judge

Bishop wanted us to move out of the ugly and poorly located Tucker House into the beautiful Phelps House, built by Bulfinch in 1810 for the President of Andover Theological Seminary and the most attractive residence on the campus. My friends, the Poynters, who were then renting it from the trustees, with characteristic abnegation consented to occupy other quarters. At the meeting of the trustees on May 28 I was instructed to be available in my office on the ground floor of George Washington Hall. While I waited, I was formally elected headmaster and was then escorted upstairs to the Trustees' Room by my friends, Philip L. Reed and Lloyd D. Brace. When my acceptance was publicly announced, the boys gathered at Bulfinch Hall and, headed by their band, marched to my house to cheer me. About all I could say was, "This has been a co-operative year, and I hope there will be many more co-operative years to come." At the commencement in June I tried to sum up my own views by saying:

> To me education is the process of so broadening and intensifying a person's latent intellectual, artistic, and moral power as to enable him to develop his capacity for enjoyment, to increase his efficiency and his capacity for service, and to enlarge his aesthetic and spiritual resources.

One of my difficult problems was how to conduct religious services, for until I was elected headmaster I was unaccustomed to liturgies and litanies. I did believe, however, that it was the duty of a headmaster to place himself squarely and unequivocably behind the religious program of the school, and I resolved to do my part in both chapel and church exercises. Accordingly I presided at these whenever I was in Andover. Often, too, I pronounced the prayers but never extemporaneously, for I recognized the literary quality of the Episcopal prayer book and always used it whenever possible. Once in my early experience on the platform I actually forgot the Lord's Prayer, but the boys carried on without my leadership. After that, I had several typed copies made and framed under glass so that one would be available wherever it might be needed. I have heard several clergymen confess that they have forgotten the familiar words; and even Bishop Lawrence told me that he was never free from the fear that the words might fade from his memory.

I still feel that compulsory chapel and church are very desirable in schools. The mere assembling of the entire undergraduate body at least once a day is in itself important and makes for community fellowship. Beyond and above that is the fact that for a few minutes the boys are lifted above their ordinary surroundings into a higher atmosphere. The program can be very simple — a short prayer, a hymn, a brief scripture reading, perhaps a simple talk — but these do at least remind them that life has its spiritual values.

As my older readers will remember, the country in 1933 was in a mood for changes, and it was not difficult at Andover to effect what I regarded as improvements in procedure. When we opened in the autumn, we tried to greet the new students in a friendly manner and make them feel at home. Basically we wanted to pay more attention to each boy as an individual — to test his aptitudes, to advise him wisely, and to help him adjust himself to the society of which he was a unit. We gave the Senior Council more power and attempted to create a closer relationship between pupil and teacher. We made some experiments in small classroom sections, and the trustees, in order to test the idea thoroughly, allowed me to enlarge the teaching staff. Soon we were bringing in a new group of first-rate teachers and increasing the ratio of masters to boys with amazing rapidity. In April 1934, by arrangement with Exeter, the two Phillips Academies announced a flat rate fee, covering every expense, instead of the former separate items for room, board, and tuition. This was a reform which increased the revenue for the school and also made parents much happier.

One of the major changes was brought about in the field of disciplinary cases. We decided to give the accused lad a hearing, and if he were guilty, we discussed punishments with an eye on the school morale and also the consequences for the victim. On the faculty were still survivors of the old regime who wanted a rigid code strictly enforced; but a majority were ready to make the experiment of examining each case on its merits. At any rate, the matter occasioned some fruitful debate, and in the end the liberals had a free hand.

One of my keenest interests then and later was in the health of the undergraduates. Dr. Peirson S. Page, who for years had been not only school physician but also Director of Athletics, was preparing to retire, and came to me himself to recommend that we find a younger man to take his place. We were fortunate to draw from the Hill School Dr. J. Roswell Gallagher — a doctor with a fresh approach, a passion for research, and a knowledge of adolescent psychology which eventually made him the foremost man in that field in the independent schools. At just the right moment, furthermore, we received a bequest from Mrs. Frederick F. Dennis of more than $300,000 — enough in those days to allow us to build a modern addition to the obsolescent infirmary and to construct a new dormitory, Rockwell House, for the smaller boys. The new infirmary was completed in the autumn of 1935, with approximately seventy-five beds, and the school was embarked on a health program of tremendous importance.

Another significant project was the establishment of a retirement plan for Andover teachers. Although we were in the midst of the Depression, the trustees were still under the hypnotic influence of Tom Cochran and inclined to believe, with him, that any feat was possible when backed by enthusiasm and persistence. At a period when other similar campaigns languished or failed, a small group of alumni, headed by Lansing P. Reed, John W. Prentiss and F. Abbot Goodhue, actually raised more than $500,000, and we were able to put our project into operation on July 1, 1937 — a truly remarkable feat under the circumstances. The plan, worked out with the Teachers Insurance and Annuity Corporation, was contributory on the part of both teacher and school, but special arrangements were made for the older men.

My sponsorship of what was called the Teachers' Fund lost me the friendship of three or four of the older instructors who felt that it was unjust to insist on their quitting at the age of sixty-five. One of them, I recall, said to me angrily, "I'm really in my prime — far better than any young fellow could be!" Nevertheless the idea still seems to me essentially sound and fits with the broad philosophy of caring for the elderly. Once in a while in the Good Old Days a teacher who lived on into his seventies became a valuable decorative tradition, around whom legends were clustered and perpetuated. But the teaching of most older men in schools is likely to become rutted, and routine unconsciously supersedes inspiration. The system which Phillips Academy was one of the first private schools to adopt has since then been established by dozens of others. The problem has been, with rising costs, to keep the pensions adequate; but every effort is being made to preserve financial security for those who, having labored valiantly through the noontide, are approaching the evening of life.

The faculty at Andover was strong, and several of the men were at the top of their profession. In such a community a bachelor teacher is at a premium because of his value as a housemaster, for he takes up less space for quarters than a married man with a family. On the other hand, a married man with children is likely to understand boys better and to be more settled in his mind. The faculty on which I had served for twenty-five years included Freeman in American history, Benner in Greek, and Graham in chemistry, all of them bachelors of more than middle age, authors of books and scholars of distinction, with great prestige among their former students. Among the married instructors of high quality were Lynde, Tower, and Sides in mathematics, Leonard, Blackmer, and Paradise in English, Poynter and Benton in Latin, Stone in French, Barss and Dake in science, Pfatteicher in music, and others. Two able bachelors who later mended their ways and took wives were Shields, in biology, and James, in history. These were stalwarts, upon whom I knew I could rely. Heely, one of the best of the younger men, left in 1934 to become Headmaster of Lawrenceville, Eccles, whom I shortly appointed registrar, later withdrew to accept the Headmastership of St. George's. Charles H. Sawyer, the first Director of the Addison Gallery, is now Dean of the School of Fine Arts at Yale.

I am very proud of the group of younger men who joined the faculty during my regime. Several of them were Andover graduates, representing many colleges and universities, and a few were former students of mine. Darling, who succeeded Freeman in American history, came to us from Yale and had several books to his credit, and Miles Malone came from Hill and Hotchkiss. Bender, also an American history teacher, is now the able Director of Admissions at Harvard College. James H. Grew arrived as instructor in French, and shortly was promoted to be head of that department. Dudley Fitts, formerly at Choate, is not only a fine teacher but also a poet and critic of distinction. Chase, once on the Harvard staff and a teacher of Greek, has also made a name for himself as a translator and essayist. Bartlett H. Hayes, Jr., succeeded Sawyer as Director of the Addison Gallery and is one of the most influential men in his field. It is good for a school to have on its faculty men who are productive scholars and authors. The number of books for which the Andover faculty has been responsible would fill a long shelf. Among the others whom I lured to Andover were Pen Hallowell and Walter Gierasch in English, Dick Pieters and Bob Sides in mathematics, George and Harper Follansbee in biology, and Fritz Allis in English.

In our efforts to enlarge and strengthen the teaching staff we were aided greatly by the late Edward S. Harkness. I first met Mr. Harkness at Yeamans' Hall, a private club near Charleston, South Carolina, and later followed with intense and somewhat envious interest his munificent gifts to the Phillips Exeter Academy. When we started to think about reducing the size of our classroom sections, it occurred to me that Mr. Harkness, who had a keen and perceptive acquaintance with education on all levels and who had already given to Andover in 1928 the sum of $320,000 for the establishment of two "professorships," might conceivably look with favor on our plan. With this hope in mind I wrote asking him for an appointment and shortly received a courteous invitation to call on him in New York.

In his office on Madison Avenue I was greeted by Malcolm P. Aldrich, his executive secretary. After he and I had chatted a while, a door opened, and I was escorted in to Mr. Harkness, who was sitting in front of a blazing wood fire, evidently at leisure. He inquired about my plans, and I explained that I wanted to establish five new instructorships, each paying the income on $100,000 — that is, a salary of approximately $4000. He listened intently, asked some searching questions, and then moved on to general conversation about people whom we knew. As I shook his hand at departure, I felt very pessimistic — and Mac Aldrich was completely noncommittal. About three days later, when I had lapsed into despondency, my secretary came in waving a letter in her hand. "I haven't dared to open it," she cried, almost as excited as I was. As I slit the envelope, I caught a glimpse of a long piece of green paper, and looked at it with my heart beating at the rate of a hundred to the minute. "Five hundred thousand dollars!" Needless to add, it was the largest check I had ever received — or seen!

In my agitation I believe that I called up every member of the Board of Trustees by telephone. It was a period when the country as a whole was trying desperately to pull itself out of the depression, and this magnificent gift arrived at precisely the right moment to boost our morale. But when I began to reflect, I quickly saw that if we were to have five new instructors, we must have homes in which to put them. Mr. Platt had died in the autumn of 1933, just after his final building on the campus had been dedicated, and we had to engage another architect. I talked with Mr. William G. Perry, of Perry, Shaw & Hepburn, and asked him for advice. When his drawings and figures were ready, I called again on Mr. Harkness and explained my problem. "How much can you put up a modest house for?" he asked. I was prepared with the answer. "We can do it for about $15,000." "All right," he said at once, "I'll give you $75,000 for the five houses — but what about the classrooms?" I then told Mr. Harkness about the beautiful Bulfinch Hall, erected in 1819 and used for many years as the chief school building, but which during the late nineteenth century had been allowed to deteriorate, and after having been used as a gymnasium and then as a dining hall, had finally become a refuge for boxing, bowling, wrestling, and fencing, and even for the school band.

Mr. Harkness was apparently absorbed in my historical narrative. Then I added that I had consulted architects who had drawn tentative plans for putting a steel framework inside the brick shell and remodeling the interior to provide classrooms and conference rooms for the Department of English, together with an attractive small debating room. The cost, I explained, would be about $150,000. Mr. Harkness studied the drawings carefully and then remarked, "Mr. Fuess, you are certainly very farsighted. Did you have these plans made especially for me?" "I thought that I would be ready for anybody, Mr. Harkness," was all I could say. "Well," he commented, "it wasn't accidental that you had them with you." When I was forced to admit that I had him and his generosity in mind, he smiled and said, "All right, you go ahead with the five houses and the building. I'll take care of it."

Thus it came about that at commencement in June 1936, I was able to announce not only the Retirement Plan but also the establishment of the five new teaching foundations, the construction of five faculty houses, and the arrangements for the renovation of Bulfinch Hall. It is not strange that I said, "My heart is very full over these gifts from Mr. Harkness." A few, at least, of my dreams were coming true.

The new houses were put up in an area on the West Campus locally known as Little Siberia, because of its exposure to winter blizzards, and were shortly assigned to married teachers who, after years of dormitory duty, were entitled in middle life to some respite from the wearing responsibility. Bulfinch Hall, when rehabilitated, was as beautiful inside as it had always been outside, and the English teachers rejoiced in small sections of not over fifteen and in their personal attractive conference rooms. From being a structure of which we had all been a little ashamed it now became one of the show places on the campus.

The sequel to these interesting events ought not to be left untold, perhaps as a warning to other younger headmasters. The other Bulfinch building on the Hill was Pearson Hall, purchased by the Academy from the Theological Seminary and later moved by Mr. Cochran in the 1920's from its central position in Seminary Row to a site on the south side of the Great Quadrangle. There on the ground floor I had taught English for many years, in a classroom eighteen feet high, with old-fashioned desks and antediluvian lighting. In a mood of optimism I thought how fine it would be if Pearson Hall could be reconstructed as Bulfinch Hall had been and devoted to the study of foreign languages. Again I consulted Mr. Perry, who made some sketches, and when all was ready I paid a visit to Mr. Harkness.

His response was just as gracious as it previously had been, and he chatted with me as usual in front of the grate fire, pipe in hand. He had never been able to visit Andover, but when I described to him the visible results of his philanthropy he seemed much pleased. Then, as the conversation lagged, I drew out of my brief case a photograph of Pearson Hall and described in my most eloquent and appealing voice what I had in mind. He listened without comment until I had finished my story and then said, "Mr. Fuess, I think I have done quite a little for Andover and for you, and I'm afraid I shall have to stop now." I perceived that, in my ardor to get a large number of things done in a hurry, I had pushed the matter too far. I rose and said, "Mr. Harkness, you have done for Phillips what amount to miracles. You have enabled me as headmaster to do things which I could never otherwise have accomplished. I am deeply grateful, and sorry that I troubled you at all on this final matter." With that I shook his hand and went out. Unfortunately the school has never since been able to make the interior of Pearson Hall what it properly should be.

Bulfinch Hall was dedicated on May 15, 1937, on which occasion I attempted to point out that it was a symbol of the process through which a school like Phillips Academy should advance, by making the past contribute to the present and the future:

> The sturdy granite, the strong brick walls, still stand as firm as ever, but the building itself is modified to meet changed conditions. . . . The intellectual standard is as high as it ever was — I believe even higher. But the method of instruction, the technique of teaching, have unquestionably altered. Rigidity is giving way to flexibility. Restriction is yielding to reasonable freedom. . . . Here the old Andover and the new Andover are joined, one merging with the other, and not averse to perhaps even greater transformations in the future. For education can never stand still, but must evolve in orderly growth, using the best of the old as a basis for the new.

The period of the 1930's was as difficult in education as it was in economics. New types of tests were being experimented with by the College Entrance Examination Board. The advocates of progressive education were zealous in spreading their ideas, some of which were indeed major reforms. Nobody could be quite sure what direction trends would take. The problem was to keep Phillips Academy true to the best of its traditions and yet not to allow it to be cramped by theories rapidly becoming obsolete. Our policy had almost necessarily to be that laid down by Alexander Pope:

Be not the first by whom the new are tried,
Nor yet the last to lay the old aside.

We were not, however, afraid of new projects. A program of adult education in the town of Andover was started in 1934, at the instigation and through the co-operation of the faculty, and is still in operation. It has done an incalculable amount of good in the community. In 1939 we secured from the Carnegie Corporation a grant of $10,000 a year for five years to enable Dr. Gallagher and his staff to test a group of adolescents in every conceivable way through the four years of their Andover course. Exchanges of students with foreign countries, especially England, were arranged and carried through with much success.

Meanwhile the Academy, even in a period of financial depression, had been prospering. In 1936, for the first time in its history, the enrollment passed the seven hundred mark, and the number on the faculty had risen to over seventy. We were deliberately trying to enroll a larger first-year, or junior, class, on the theory that the longer a boy stayed at the school, the more we could accomplish with him. The building of Rockwell House gave us more and better accommodations for lads of thirteen and fourteen, and we aimed to provide the special treatment which they obviously needed.

Rather amazingly we succeeded each year in balancing the budget. Costs of heat, food, and wages were relatively low, and the gifts to the school did not perceptibly fall off. Not until the Second World War disrupted our national economy did Phillips Academy face a deficit. Even then, the situation was never so serious that it could not readily be mended.

For me personally those were pleasant years. My wife and I went to Europe nearly every summer, usually spending some time with English headmasters whom I knew. I was not so busy that I could not write, and I did my full share of speaking at schools and colleges, with trips each year to visit the alumni. Our vacations at Christmas and in the spring were spent usually at Palm Beach, where we found relief from the strain of school administration.

Then in 1938 came the shock of Munich and the unrest and fear from which the United States and the world have never since been free.

XII

Boys as Human Beings

AT a conservative estimate, I must have known during my four decades at Andover six thousand boys. They march before me in my memory like a panorama of the generations, a procession of American life, with its brilliance and folly, its accomplishments and failures. I can see now the fledglings who later became a Mayor of Denver, a Governor of Wisconsin, a Bishop of Minnesota, author of *The White Tower,* the producer of *Oklahoma!,* the President of Oberlin College, the Director of the Detroit Symphony Orchestra, the Director of the Yale Art School, the President of Boston's largest bank, the Headmaster of Lawrenceville School, the Managing Editor of *Fortune,* the Sports Editor of *Newsweek,* a foreign correspondent of the *New York Times,* the Chairman of the New York Federal Reserve Board, two of the greatest of American surgeons, the toughest of motion picture actors and the most benign of clergymen, as well as heroes, alive and dead, on many a battlefield around the world.

They are scattered now from Maine to Oregon, from Duluth to New Orleans. When my wife and I were taking a motor trip across the continent in 1949, we had been greeted and entertained in every city where we had stopped, and Mrs. Fuess had reached the point where she would not have been astonished if an old Andover boy had stepped from behind an isolated cactus plant in the Arizona desert. We had reached San Antonio on our way back from Los

Angeles to Hobe Sound. It was rainy, and we stayed most of the time in the hotel resting. As we stepped into the garage to pick up our Buick and push along to Houston, she remarked, "Well, this is one place where you don't know anybody." Within fifteen seconds a voice called out from one of the stalls, "Why, Claudie, what are you doing down here?" It was one of my former pupils whom I had not seen for thirty years!

In his delightful and authoritative book, *Understanding Your Son's Adolescence,* my former school physician, Dr. Gallagher, has a chapter headed "There Is No Average Boy." With this dictum I fully concur. Each boy, like each man or woman, is an individual, with his own personal traits, emotions, ambitions, hopes, and whimsies. Each is a male, with all which that implies, and likely to be in some moods rough, predatory, and obscene. Furthermore boys have their mob movements, resembling hysteria, when they are swept as a group by uncontrollable impulses. But the variations among seven hundred youngsters from fourteen to eighteen are immense. They are usually co-operative but often unpredictable, sophisticated but also childish, idealistic but also vulgar, lovable but also exasperating, noble but also degraded — in short, just like children of a larger growth.

Andover was in no sense an exclusive school, except in the sense that it was not easy to meet the scholastic requirements for admission. Nearly one third of the students were either being aided by financial grants or working their way, but that made no difference in the treatment which they received from the faculty and their mates. It seemed to me to be a completely democratic society, in which each member made his way on his own merits, regardless of the social position or financial status of his family. It was highly, sometimes ruthlessly, competitive, not only in studies but in athletics and all the other alluring phases of undergraduate activity;

but in this respect it was like life. Indeed the school was a microcosm, a miniature world, with most of the problems of human relations to be found in its larger counterpart. Perhaps this is why the "type" was rugged, resourceful, and self-reliant.

As a corollary, we displayed a cross section of American life — the opulent and the indigent, boys from farms and from city apartments, representatives of almost every state in the union. If there was any discrimination on the basis of race or color, I was not aware of it. In a school established by rather bigoted Calvinistic Congregationalists, we had nearly 10 per cent of Jews and about the same proportion of Roman Catholics, who attended assembly and sang the Protestant hymns without protest. We usually had two or three Negroes and would have accepted more if they could have met the stiff entrance requirements. They told me afterwards that they never felt themselves at any disadvantage.

Treated as they were like men, the Andover undergraduates met the challenge amazingly well. Many of them had traveled in foreign lands or possessed exceptional proficiency in languages, art, and music. They had seen interesting people in their homes and had talked with writers and statesmen. Among my pupils I recall an authority on firearms, a specialist on snakes, several competent airplane pilots, the owner of more than a hundred motion picture theaters, two Quiz Kids, a race handicapper, a pomologist, a steam-shovel operator, a professional xylophonist, and one expert tap dancer. We had representatives of all religions, including Buddhism, Confucianism, and Mohammedanism. One unbeliever who madly craved martyrdom refused to bow his head in prayer during the church services, but sat defiantly staring into space. The school minister spoke to him briefly on the matter — without effect. Finally one day the boy met me on the street and announced, "You know, Mr. Fuess, I'm an agnostic." I merely replied, "What of it?" He was so much disconcerted that he continued, "Well, I thought you might be disturbed when I didn't pray with the others, and perhaps I ought to explain." All I said was, "David, I only thought your conduct was a remarkable exhibition of bad manners by a fellow who is supposed to be a gentleman!" He flushed and walked off in silence; but within a few weeks he was bowing his head lower and lower while the Lord's Prayer was being recited, although I must confess that I never saw his lips move. He is probably now a pillar of the Second Presbyterian Church in Kansas City.

Some boys are blessed by their ancestors or by the fickle gods with every attribute making for social success. With sound bodies, they are capable if not outstanding sportsmen; they have the mesmeric quality of making friends easily; they do their class assignments without strain and possess the precious knack of passing examinations; they are emotionally well balanced, responding normally to the violent stimuli of adolescence; and they have an instinct for avoiding serious blunders. These are the "naturals," the delight of parents' hearts, who advance uninhibited and undismayed through the ordeals of school and college, captaining the teams and making the "right" fraternities, evading disaster and claiming leadership as their privilege. I have known many such, and have thanked God for them.

But side by side with these Olympians are the less conspicuous who are glad for modest honors and occasionally slip sadly into failure, who bear uncomplainingly the inevitable disappointments of group living, whose progress is often slow and painful, and who are content to serve in the ranks while others win letters and other decorations. One never knows, however, what the end will be. Often the campus favorites weaken early, perhaps because they are not toughened by adversity; while some lad relatively obscure on commencement morning turns up forty years later as an eminent surgeon or judge. I liked to feel that Phillips Academy was a good training ground for both types. I hope I was right.

The boys sorted themselves out with bewildering rapidity through a process seldom understood by their elders. As the new youngsters of fourteen and fifteen appeared each September at the headmaster's tea, they seemed superficially to be all equally well-mannered, shy, and undistinguished. By Thanksgiving, however, some were standing out above their mates for qualities which gave them prestige. Neither too aggressive nor too diffident, they had aroused the admiration of those around them. We on the faculty often deplored the choices, but they were the consequences of a pure democracy functioning freely. The boys would have resisted any attempt by the faculty to select their leaders. They wanted their own.

Allowing again for the inevitable exceptions, the students were basically well-intentioned and serious-minded. The reprobates won a good deal of publicity, just as hoodlums make the headlines in the newspapers; and the faculty knew them all. Indeed these offenders took up an inordinate amount of our time at meetings. But the large proportion of the undergraduates, day in and day out, worked reasonably hard, tried to obey the rules, and kept out of trouble. Like any other body of isolated males on a battleship, in an army camp, or in prison, they had their gripes, especially over the food and the minor regulations. But I found them pleasant in manner, amenable to argument, and in an emergency very reliable. However they may have behaved on their vacations, their conduct in public places was as impeccable as that of the teaching staff.

Dr. Stearns more than once quoted to me with approval the advice which he received from his predecessor, Dr. Bancroft, "Alfred, a lot of things go on all over the campus that a school principal ought never to see!" If a headmaster spends his time looking for little infractions of the rules, he will soon find himself with shattered nerves. Having been no angel myself in my childhood, I was often tempted to laugh when a frightened lad was brought before me for some offense like chewing gum in chapel or indulging in mild profanity. But I suppose that no teacher in a school can avoid occasional irritation. When I first went to live in Tucker House, I raked and seeded a neat bit of ground for my lawn and then put up signs: NO CROSSING! The land was on a corner, and the temptation to cut across was almost irresistible. One spring when I had been particularly vigorous in my denunciation of depraved young men who trampled down my grass, a diminutive offender squeaked, "Mr. Fuess, do you know who walked across there just before me?" "No," said I, "I guess I didn't see him." "It was Mr. Wilkins, the physics teacher — did you bawl him out?" The situation was a trifle difficult to explain, and I am sure that I was inconsistent in meeting it. In the following June the *Pot-pourri,* the Academy yearbook, devoted an entire page to a drawing of my house, with my face at each one of the twenty or more front windows glaring with baleful eyes at my newly seeded lawn. After that, I tried to keep my irritation under control. I eventually concluded that the proper place to make paths on a campus is where boys — and men — naturally go. Having been taught that a straight line is the shortest distance between two points, they put that knowledge into practise.

Each boy is an individual, but collectively they have their lapses, when they are swept by uncontrollable impulses. Phillips Academy traditionally has no faculty supervision in the dining hall. Week after week everything would go smoothly as it does in the average restaurant. Then during the week before an Andover-Exeter game some excited lad would throw a bun, and soon there would be an outburst of bun throwing, with the accompanying clamor. The student head-waiters could do little to quell the riot. Inevitably the bachelor teachers sitting by themselves in their own dining room would be disturbed, some of the chief offenders would be reported to the Discipline Committee, and we would have penalties to inflict. Because some of the best boys in school were often involved, the problem of suitable punishments was difficult. The attitudes of faculty members would range from the savage to the gentle, with all the emotional variations in between. Some of the instructors whom I most respected felt that we should tolerate no nonsense, but should act promptly and severely. Others merely murmured, "Boys will be boys," and were inclined to forget the episode. The final votes usually reflected both the violence of the provocation and the weariness of the staff.

Through experience I learned that heavy penalties do not prevent violations of the rules. When we were "firing" boys for many offenses, we had much more disorder than we did later when we became more reasonable. Expelling undergraduates for smoking does not stop the use of tobacco any more than prohibition shut off drinking in the 1920's. A cigarette addict can always be tempted by a convenient grove or fireplace. Even when smoking is allowed under specified conditions, as it is at Andover, it is a perennial problem; but it should not be treated like drunkenness or stealing.

A few responsible school leaders with good instincts and a feeling for law and order can do more than any number of irate faculty members. If the students, guided by their elected officers, reach the conclusion that certain things just "aren't done," the headmaster can cease to worry. Here again boys are extraordinarily like sheep in their proneness to ape the sartorial habits of the Big Men on campus and to co-operate when co-operation becomes fashionable. Ian Hay was right when he wrote, "The god that schoolboys dread most is Public Opinion."

I made plenty of mistakes in administering discipline. Being temperamentally quick-tempered, I sometimes burst out angrily, thus losing whatever advantage I claimed over the offender. Occasionally I took matters into my own hands and exercised my constitutional right of pardon, only to learn that my soft-heartedness was regarded as weakness, even by the beneficiary.

The saddest sequence was when, after I had pleaded for an offender and he had been let off lightly, he was shortly detected in an even more heinous breach of regulations. Then my associates cried, "We told you so!" and I was left with the awareness that I was regarded as an "easy mark." I was obliged reluctantly to reach the conclusion that, in spite of what the psychologists maintain, there are some "incorrigibles," on whom kindness or sympathy is wasted and who insist on going wrong, no matter how decently they are treated. More times than I like to admit, my confidence in the essential goodness of human nature was shattered by a gross violation of my trust.

I soon came to perceive a kind of pulse beat or rhythm for the school year. The hubbub and adjustment of the opening days in September were followed by a period of relative quiet, when the correspondence was light and I could relax and play golf and pass untroubled evenings. After the first marks were given out in late October, the scholastic goats were separated from the sheep, letters of warning multiplied, and I had to meet with disappointed parents. During the two weeks before the Andover-Exeter football game, tension mounted, and the entire school was on edge. Then came the letdown of the Thanksgiving recess and the studious weeks before the Christmas vacation, when the boys were too busy preparing for examinations to engage in many illicit activities. As the holidays opened, I was busy for three or four days, dictating more than seven hundred personal letters to parents in an attempt to present a brief description of their sons' successes or failures. After that heavy pressure, Florida for a few days was always a welcome relief.

With the return at the opening of the winter term even the drones settled down to hard work, broken by the Winter Promenade, which stirred the boys who were susceptible to female charms. At the end of the term came another period of intense application to books. I always felt that in our American educational system we gave too many set examinations; and as a teacher I deliberately tried using only short tests — unannounced. I still believe that this procedure is a more accurate way of finding out what a pupil really knows than any formal examination can be. Here again, however, there is a difference of opinion, and I was never able to marshal enough convincing arguments to influence some of my colleagues. The examinations, mostly informal, which we have to face as adults are usually unexpected, and we are allowed little time for getting ready.

Spring was a delightful season at Andover. Most farsighted teachers completed the hardest part of their assignments during the winter, when conditions were favorable for study. The dullards in the student body were by that time pretty well sorted out. Some of them had left, unable to meet the competition, and others had undergone enough of a reform to meet the minimum requirements. Hence the atmosphere in May and June was pleasant, except for those borderline seniors who were worried about getting into college. The tempo slowed down, the boys could lie around on the grass on warm afternoons, and life seemed again worth living after the New England winter. It is true that the faculty had to keep prodding the delinquents into action, and then more action, so that the lights in certain rooms burned far into the night. Moreover the first humid winds of spring stirred the blood and inspired some undergraduates with a desire for a little deviltry. But for the most of us the days passed altogether too quickly, and commencement, with its absorbing busyness, was upon us before we knew it. After that came hurried faculty meetings, the "Good-by" greetings, and then the almost oppressive calm which envelops school campuses when the life force has gone and "all that mighty heart is lying still."

Placing myself in the confessional, I must admit that I sometimes took terrifying chances. After one close football contest with Exeter, a gang of adventurous students tore down two Exeter banners from the dormitories where they had been hanging. When the news spread on Sunday morning, I was much concerned, for Bill Saltonstall and I had an informal understanding that no such high jinks would be permitted. On Monday morning, after spending a restless night, I rose in assembly and explained that while this in some respects was only a childish prank, it did involve me in an embarrassing situation with the Exeter authorities. "I should greatly appreciate it," I continued, "if the fellows who have those stolen banners would return them to my office this morning. I shall be out from eleven to twelve and would like to find them there when I come back. No questions will be asked."

This was one of those speeches which either succeed — or fail miserably! As I walked back to my office after assembly, not quite sure whether or not I had made a tactical blunder, two boys — members of the Student Council — asked to see me for a moment. One of them announced rather sheepishly, "Mr. Fuess, Bill and I have those banners, and we'll bring them in to you right away. To tell the truth we didn't realize that there would be so much fuss about the matter. We just wanted to pep things up a bit!" I could only thank them warmly, and before night the banners were on their way to Exeter, with my apologies. But suppose they hadn't been returned!

The schoolboy code of honor, no matter how absurd it may seem to an adult, can never be ignored in dealing with undergraduates. Only when one of their mates has become positively vicious will they testify against him. He may copy his neighbor's answers, he may have liquor in his room, he may filch magazines from the newsstand, he may sneak out of his dormitory on nefarious missions — but nobody will "squeal" on him. This is the chief reason why honor systems, however successful they may be in some colleges, seldom work in secondary schools.

On the other hand, the code is subject to strange interpretations. When I was busy with the alumni fund and with money-raising campaigns, I often had to desert my class to keep an engagement. I would then explain, "I'm sorry, but I am called away for the rest of the hour, and I'm leaving an examination for you to take. Please put your papers on the desk when you have finished and leave quietly." In after years several of my former pupils told me that on such occasions nobody did any cribbing. One of them remarked, "You did a smart thing in just going out and never warning us not to cheat. The way you left us completely to our own devices made it impossible for anybody to pull anything crooked!" That is one interesting aspect of boy psychology.

To "visiting firemen," boys are not only tolerant — they are courteously demonstrative. They may complain bitterly of the monotony of talks by the headmaster or the school minister, but when anybody from the outside speaks, no matter how platitudinously or tediously, they will applaud until their palms are sore. In church, they suffered patiently the dullest of sermons. When Dr. Stearns was principal, one expected clergyman was taken ill, and a preacher had to be secured on short notice from a neighboring city. When the moment arrived for his discourse, the minister leaned over the pulpit, smiled expansively, and began, "I love boys!" The situation was critical. Al put on his fiercest expression and glared at the seniors in the two or three front rows as if to say, "If you start anything, there'll be trouble!" But nothing happened, and afterwards one of the school leaders came up to the principal and asked, "Didn't we do well, Mr. Stearns?" He replied, "John, you're a credit to the school and to your family's training."

The patience of a schoolboy congregation is often sorely tried. One winter three successive clergymen took as their theme the parable of the Prodigal Son. Again three visiting clergymen in a row ended their sermons with a stereotyped quotation from Sir Henry Newbolt, beginning, "There's a breathless hush in the close tonight," and concluding dramatically, "Play up! Play up! and play the game!" There was a hush all right as number three started on his peroration, and I could see the lips of many undergraduates forming the familiar words. Indeed I almost expected to have the whole congregation burst out simultaneously, in accord with their leader, "Play up! Play up! and play the game!" But again some deep-seated respect for the church as an institution repressed any demonstration.

On one painful morning a clergyman of national reputation preached a sermon identical in text and argument with that used by an eminent divine the week before. A little Sherlock Holmes investigation disclosed the unfortunate fact that both were "canned" sermons, evidently from the same source. At another tense moment a Yale dean suddenly stopped in the middle of his remarks and said, "If the man who is moving about in the gallery will only keep still, I shall be grateful. I am speaking extemporaneously and can't keep my mind on my theme." The "man" thus admonished was one of the faculty proctors who were moving cautiously about, checking the attendance below. A lady present in the congregation told me afterwards that she had heard the dean deliver precisely the same "extemporaneous" talk the week before at Vassar College. Such are some of the weaknesses of members of "the cloth."

Boys are diabolically clever at discerning, mimicking, and ridiculing the eccentricities of their teachers. Often at commencement the seniors would prepare and present a skit of some kind, "taking off" on the peculiarities of the faculty. I was cured forever of rubbing the bare top of my bald head by an imitation of me given by a clever student. When in assembly I announced that most of the trouble in the school was caused by a disorderly "5 per cent" of the undergraduate body, I was haunted by ironic references to that unfortunate phrase. A boy caught in an indiscretion would grin and say, "Well, sir, I guess I'm one of the disreputable 5 per cent!" At first I laughed, but as time went on I smiled only as if I mocked myself, and I was soon sick of the expression.

During one recitation a young instructor talked for some time about a trip to the British Isles which he had taken the previous summer. After class a very small lad looking as innocent as one of Murillo's cherubs came up to the master's desk and asked, "You've been a good deal in England, haven't you, Mr. Odell?" "Well, yes, I think I might say I have." "I guess you know a lot about their customs, don't you?" "Yes, I probably do," was the reply. Then the tiny youngster looked up and, his eyes twinkling, said, "Well, Cheerio, Old Top, Cheerio!" What could be done about that?

I had one most regrettable weakness as a headmaster. It was difficult for me to remember faces and to associate names with them. I was not quite so bad as the headmaster of a neighboring school who on one occasion after a baseball game shook hands with all the members of his own team as if they were visitors and invited them to spend the night. But I frequently, when meeting a group, forgot the names of my own boys; and once I resolved to address each one as Pete, thinking that the law of averages would make me more often right than wrong. In this case they all turned out to be Bobs or Bills.

On the other hand, probably because I have dealt so much with the printed word, if I am given a name I remember everything associated with it. Thus if an old Andover boy meets me on Boston Common, I may not recognize him until he says politely, "I'm Bullwinkle, class of 1921." Then all sorts of facts rush to my mind, and I can recall his record in his class, his family relationships, and even the time when he was put on probation for overcutting.

Boys in these days have a genuine respect for rules, especially when the reason for them is explained. When a mother would plead for some exceptional privilege for her son, he would frequently come to me privately and say, "I knew perfectly well that I couldn't have my Christmas vacation extended, but Mom simply wouldn't listen to me." A youngster deprived of some of his precious week ends because of his poor scholastic record told me, "I got exactly what I deserved, and Dad should never have come up here to kick about it to you." Boys understand all the recognized conventions of the school much better than their parents do, and this is the chief reason why they don't like to have them too much around on the campus. Their elders simply do not comprehend the principles by which the lives of their sons are governed.

In dealing with boys it is imperative that a headmaster should have two important qualities — a sense of relative values and a sense of humor. He should perceive the difference between a sin and an indiscretion, between a calculated defiance of law and order and a careless neglect of a rule. He should understand that laughter is a great solvent of confusion, often clearing completely an atmosphere fraught with tragedy.

As I have suggested, differentiations in temperament and ambition appear very early and are readily recognizable. Some boys are visibly nervous; others are lethargic. Some are conscientious; others are excruciatingly careless. I once escorted a bishop through a senior dormitory where two rooms were side by side on the second floor. One was neat and orderly, with every necktie smoothed out and each article in its proper place. The other was strewn with shirts and shoes and crowded with miscellaneous and unattractive junk. Both boys were members of the Student Council, and each was a reliable citizen. But they were entirely opposite in personal habits and modes of living, and probably neither has changed to this day.

Living in my house at one period we had a most extraordinary aggregation of undergraduate types. Ned was shy, methodical, reserved, and studious. Pete was a muscular and gregarious extrovert, interested chiefly in games and regarding classes as a sideshow to the main tent. Horace wanted to spend all his time in the biological laboratory nursing snakes. Oscar had a passion for stage carpentry and could be found at almost any hour designing and constructing scenery. Bill was a born trader who made a profit on every financial transaction. Hank was constantly writing editorials for the school paper although he loathed his English class on general principles. Each had his own private interests; yet they dwelt together in amity.

I do not mean to imply that these boys were static. Their special interests sometimes shifted almost overnight, and after a summer vacation they came back physically bigger and intellectually more mature. Sometimes what might be called Lady Luck operated in an unpredictable way. A boy whom everybody called Mac had been in school for three years and one term, faithful, reliable, but relatively obscure. By sheer hard work he had made the board of the *Phillipian*, the undergraduate newspaper, and had moved up automatically until he was the first assistant editor. Nevertheless he was inconspicuous and certainly had little influence. In early January of his senior year the editor in chief of the *Phillipian* unexpectedly had to leave school. The next person available for the position was Mac. He took over, and within two weeks the paper, which had been following a conventional and tame course, took on new life. The editorials were sprightly and entertaining, and even the changed make-up reflected the personality of the editor. Mac was then elected to a vacancy on the Student Council and within a few weeks was a power on the campus. By the close of the year he was recognized by both boys and faculty as one of the three or four outstanding members of the graduating class. Throughout this experience Mac was calm and self-possessed, confronting prosperity as if he had been accustomed to it all his days. His rise from insignificance to prominence was so rapid as to be startling, and made me wonder how many other "mute inglorious Miltons" might be waiting for their opportunity.

People often ask me what I think of the "younger generation." This is a difficult question to answer, for the boys of the 1950's are as varied as any group which preceded them, and no generalizations can be more than approximately accurate. Furthermore I have been in contact only with a rather carefully selected group, which included very few perverts or "hot-rods" or amateur holdup men. The teen-agers who set fire to school buildings, chop up grand pianos, and overturn tombstones in cemeteries do not often seek admission to a school like Andover.

The boys whom I know in this generation give the impression of competence and self-reliance. They are not communicative, even with their parents; consequently it is difficult to find out what their real reactions are. But they have an amazing capacity for meeting crises without quailing — and they have already had plenty of them to face. These youngsters born in the 1930's know little from personal knowledge of an orderly world. No one could blame them very much for crying simultaneously and with anguish:

The time is out of joint; O cursed spite,
That ever I was born to set it right!

This, however, they do not do. About them is little of the notorious Lost Generation of the 1920's. Although they manifestly do not relish the confusion in the midst of which, without their desire, they have been thrown, they make few complaints. They accept military service, even when it interrupts their cherished plans, as if it were as inevitable as birth or death. Because they wish to snatch what happiness they can before their universe dissolves, they plan to marry early. But they do not quit! It may be resignation which keeps them going, but it more closely resembles pride. Pity in any form is what they least desire.

Perhaps because of bitter family experience they care less about making money than their fathers and more about doing good. More and more they are choosing the missionary professions, such as teaching, medicine, the Christian ministry, and public service. They have a very real concept of which satisfactions are durable and which are transitory. They do plenty of thinking about such perennial and intrusive problems as labor relations, racial discrimination, censorship, poverty, disease, crime, and education. In many cases they have, as adolescents, evolved for themselves a pattern for living. They are aware that they have to fight for the freedoms which then enjoy, but they are ready — not enthusiastic or glory-seeking, but prepared to face whatever comes.

If we haven't confidence in these boys, we may as well abandon hope for the world. For these will be the men who must carry its burden, twenty and thirty and forty years on. What they are thinking now in their hearts will determine the course which the evolution of the race will take. If they are early disheartened, if they view themselves as the unhappy victims of an irrational society, if they cannot make sacrifices willingly, then humanity is doomed. But if they are, as I believe them to be, aware of their responsibility and equipped to meet it, conscious of our internal weaknesses but confident in our latent strength, endowed by nature and training with patience and vision, then we can leave the scene without crying: *Après nous la déluge!* I wish to put myself on record as feeling, after living long with youth, that the newer generation is better, more to be trusted, than the old.

XIII

Men of the Profession

TEACHERS, like clergymen, are sensitive regarding the stigmata of their occupation, and indeed the general public once did place the two professions in a class by themselves. Even now the impression cannot be entirely eradicated that schoolmasters are less robust and virile than industrialists; and they themselves are still afraid of being treated as if they belonged to a third sex, not forceful enough to be masculine and certainly not delicate and alluring enough to be feminine. But no impression of educators I have known could be more mistaken. My acquaintances among teachers have not needed to yield to any group — bankers or lawyers or engineers — in what are considered to be the rugged virtues. The caricature of the pedagogue, with his trousers above his ankles and his sleeves halfway up his wrists, his emaciated and bony body, his oversized horn spectacles, and his hairless, shining dome, in no respect corresponds to reality. As they chat in the lobby of the Statler or the Biltmore, headmasters are as well groomed as the members of the National Association of Manufacturers, and unquestionably more articulate.

Naturally teachers, like clergymen, do not want to be classified as epicene or even peculiar. The Reverend Nehemiah Boynton, one of the most eloquent preachers of his day, was often annoyed by the too ebullient adulation of admiring ladies. Once when he was idling in his bathing suit on the beach at Nantucket, he was approached by two simpering spinsters, one of whom inquired, "Is this the Reverend Nehemiah Boynton?" Back snapped the reply, "Not in July and August, madam!" In the summer he wished to have the immunity of any other vacationer.

No apology is needed for American educators of the last half century. One of them, Woodrow Wilson, belongs with the world's Very Great. Others, like Charles William Eliot and Nicholas Murray Butler, Bliss Perry and William Lyon Phelps, have had an influence extending far beyond their own campuses. Among secondary-school leaders, several have left their stamp not only upon their own boys but also upon American culture and civilization in the broadest sense.

The first headmaster whom I knew well was, of course, Alfred E. Stearns, of Phillips Academy. Nobody could have been less of a dry-as-dust pedant or cloistered dreamer. He had a magnetism which attracted old and young. Even before the development of modern psychology, he was aware of the complicated motives which lead students into indiscretions and he never magnified a youthful peccadillo into a crime. Yet he did not hesitate to punish severely any meanness or viciousness of mind.

No one could come within Al Stearns's range without being impressed by his sincerity, his kindliness, and his simplicity. He had no subtleties or hidden schemes. He seldom disguised his emotions, but went straight to the point, without evasion. At times he displayed a fiery temper, and on at least two occasions peremptorily "fired" an instructor in anger, only to repent and apologize before sunset. Sometimes he made enemies by the stout fashion in which he spoke out, but the boys liked his positiveness and strong convictions. Without being in any sense a prig, he continually stressed the importance of moral issues; and like Thomas Arnold he was more interested in forming character than in producing scholars. Down in his heart he preferred men who do things to men who think things.

In the Headmasters Association, of which he was president in 1914, Stearns was a leader on the conservative side. An undismayed advocate of the Greek and Roman classics because of their value as cultural subjects, he was a believer in intellectual discipline and a critic of "progressive" theories in education. When these issues were introduced in the Association, he, with Endicott Peabody and Horace Taft to back him up, staunchly upheld the traditional program, and it took an audacious "modernist" to stand up against their wit and raillery. The trio loved to poke fun at the professional jargon of psychologists, and they hated Teachers' College at Columbia and all its works.

Great though his public success had been, Stearns underwent tragic family experiences, and his retirement at the age of sixty was due to illness both of body and of nerves. But he made a glorious recovery, became President of the Board of Trustees of Amherst College, wrote some excellent books, and kept himself very much alive. He made up his mind to live away from Andover, feeling that his presence there might embarrass his successor. But whenever he did come back at my urgent invitation, he gave much pleasure to all of us, his friends.

Endicott Peabody, who founded Groton School in 1884, was twenty-eight years older than I, and I did not begin really to know him until 1934, when he was nearing eighty. To me then he was awesome, very definitely an Olympian. When the Headmasters Association once met at Amherst, I was housed at President King's residence, with Al Stearns, Horace Taft, and Peabody. One evening he said to me, "I understand that although your real name is Claude, everybody calls you Jack. My name is Endicott, but my friends call me Cottie. Why don't you try it?" I did "try it," but it was difficult for me not to think of him as "Dr. Peabody" or the "Rector."

When at the Headmasters Association we instituted a memorial service for the dead, it was inevitable that we should ask Dr. Peabody to conduct it. The occasion being formal, he wore his full clerical regalia. After paying an impressive tribute to the deceased brethren, he proceeded to the reading of the names. Unluckily, however, his eye fell by mistake on the list of the newly elected members, and when he continued solemnly to read it one by one, the faces of the novitiates presented a study in bewilderment. It is my impression that Dr. Peabody never realized what consternation he was spreading, but some of us found it difficult not to smile.

Dr. Peabody conveyed a human grandeur such as few people I have known. He was a magnificent specimen of the Grand Old Man, still erect and towering in his eighties and looking like the embodiment of rectitude and moral force. He had built a great school by his own personality. Many people thought him austere and unbending, but he was very gracious to a younger and inexperienced headmaster. It was good for us to have him around as an example to follow.

Horace Taft, who had also created an important school, was outstanding too, but in a different way. Like Stearns and Peabody, he was well over six feet tall and dominated any gathering. He was, however, far more of a humorist, and a twinkle always lurked in his tolerant eyes. No one in the Association knew more good stories or told them better. No one was quicker with the retort courteous and witty at just the right time. Once Dr. Peabody rose to protest that the name of his school had been misprinted in our little catalogue so that it appeared as "ROTON" with the initial "G" left out. Mr. Taft promptly remarked that it was not an important matter — only a mistake in spelling.

At one meeting the genial Frank S. Hackett, of Riverdale School, was describing his recent campaign for the school committee in a New York City district. He was saying how amazing it was that he polled so many votes in spite of the fact that he had previously been almost completely unknown. "But I went out," he continued, "and talked and talked and talked. I must have spoken all in all to more than ten thousand people!" Taft, who had been listening keenly, inquired, "Do I understand, Frank, that by talking you managed *almost* to get elected?" "That's right," replied Hackett. "Suppose you hadn't talked!" commented Taft, with his broad smile.

In *Memories and Opinions,* his autobiography published in 1942, Mr. Taft wrote delightfully of his experiences and recounted some of his best stories. He liked particularly to quote what was once told to him by Headmaster William S. Thayer, of St. Mark's School. After Dr. Thayer resigned he made the mistake of criticizing some of the changes which were being made by his successor in the curriculum. "Ah!" commented one of the teaching staff, "you fellows who have served your term and retired are like rovers in croquet. You have been through all the wickets yourselves and now have nothing to do except to go around and knock the other balls out of position."

"Uncle Horace" could make comments which nobody else in the Association would have dared to speak out loud. Two distinguished and very well-known clerical members were engaging in a heated discussion on some minor matter of undergraduate discipline. After listening a few minutes, Mr. Taft left the room, and I followed him outside for some fresh air. "How's that debate coming out?" I asked. "There won't much come of it," he replied, "one of them never was a boy, and the other never grew up!" This brief characterization was so perfect that it was ludicrous.

In recent years the meetings of the Association have been

held in midwinter, at the Westchester Country Club in Rye, New York; and the members, isolated, often penned in by the weather, and with no outside recreations to tempt them, find themselves thrown much in one another's company. The atmosphere is informal, the addresses are above average, the conversation is stimulating, and everybody has a good time. Since the proceedings receive no publicity and the group never commit themselves to any educational policy or program, the members feel free to speak out their minds; and here and there in smoke-filled rooms or in corners of the lobby all the current problems of schools and colleges get discussed. The fact that nothing is ever really settled does not discourage the disputants.

During the early stages of the progressive movement, when it had the aspect of a crusade, the liberals in the Association were headed by the "Three Smiths" — Perry D., of the North Shore Country Day School in Winnetka; Herbert W., of the Francis W. Parker School, in Chicago; and Eugene R., of the Beaver Country Day School, in Chestnut Hill. When one of this famous triumvirate rose to his feet, the conservatives, headed by Peabody, Taft, and Stearns, prepared for the fray, and the younger members sat back to watch and listen to the battle of words. The debate was carried on with the rapier, not with the bludgeon, and one could almost hear the audience murmuring, "A hit — a very palpable hit!" Every shade of opinion was represented, from the cautiously reactionary to the audaciously radical. Some members were loquacious; a few never said a word unless called upon. Some were scholars; others were clearly good fellows and men of the world. Some were convivial; others were on the ascetic side. Very few were dull.

Among the members have been some of my closest friends — those whom I admire most in the procession. It would be difficult and perhaps unjust to discriminate among so many choice spirits, but I cannot help mentioning Wilson Farrand, of Newark Academy, neat in body and mind, master of the crisp and cutting phrase, and Spencer McCallie, of Chattanooga, hard-fisted, jovial, and resilient, who was equally at home making stump speeches and carrying on a revival meeting and who became the Voice of Dixie to his fellow members. Among those who have retired from active school administration but who are still welcomed as honorary members are William C. Hill, formerly of the Springfield Classical High School, whose occasional addresses sparkle with epigrams and glow with erudition; Charles C. Tillinghast, once the Head of the Horace Mann School, a brilliant and entertaining public speaker with a gift for clarification and summarization; Norman Nash, translated from St. Paul's School to a bishopric, who has adorned two kindred professions; the talented Archibald C. Galbraith, of Williston, long Secretary of the Headmasters Association; William L. W. Field, of Milton Academy, a fine example of the dynamic liberal mind; N. Horton Batchelder, a grand old stalwart, who built Loomis School into a distinguished institution; Walter F. Downey, formerly Headmaster of the English High School in Boston and for a time Commissioner of Education in Massachusetts; John Briggs, of St. Paul Academy, with his robust and penetrating wit; and Richard M. Gummere, formerly of Penn Charter School and until recently Director of Admissions at Harvard, the model of the courtly and cultured gentleman.

Believing as I do in the motto *Ad Juniores Labores,* I feel no regret that the conduct of the Association has fallen on younger but equally capable shoulders: George Van Santwoord, Greville Haslam, Allan V. Heely, Frank D. Ashburn, Edward W. Eames, John Crocker, James W. Wickenden, Howard Rubendall, Arthur Milliken, Lester W. Nelson, Paul Cruikshank, Seymour St. John, and many others who represent the best in schoolmastering. These very active brethren welcome the "old-timers" with a courtesy which we greatly appreciate and which makes us still, in our retirement, feel at home.

Of two Olympians I must speak with rather special affection. Lewis Perry became Principal of the Phillips Exeter Academy in 1914, and I first met him and heard him speak on October 10 of that year, at an Andover Founders' Day. His address on that afternoon was a masterpiece of relevancy and humor, and it was there that I became aware of his genius as a raconteur. One of his anecdotes seemed to me perfectly conceived to illustrate the point that teachers must be human as well as scholarly. Let him relate it in his own words:

> I remember very well a college professor of great erudition, of profound learning, but whose common sense if it appeared at all appeared but rarely and was usually in eclipse, who one day was taking his afternoon stroll and came to a colored man who was putting his dog through some tricks. The professor stopped and then after a moment said, with a condescension which no man, black or white, who lives in a New England village will tolerate, "How do you teach your dog those tricks? I can't teach my dog any tricks." And the colored man without raising his eyes from his task said, "You've gotta know more than the dog—you've gotta know more than the dog, or you can't learn him nothing!

Under Lewis Perry, Exeter prospered as never before in its history, and the friendship between him and Dr. Stearns brought the two Phillips Academies closer and closer together. In each institution were faculty members who in the old days almost hated the other school. Shortly after settling at Andover, I became acquainted with Professor James A. Tufts, the Head of Exeter's English Department and a very dignified gentleman. In the early autumn we met by chance on Stratham Hill near Exeter and chatted pleasantly about things in general. As we parted, Tuffie, as he was universally called, said to me, "Professor Fuess, you are the only decent Andover man I ever met." "But Professor Tufts," I protested, "you know I didn't go to Andover." "Ah!" he exclaimed, "Professor Fuess, that explains a lot!" I have always regarded that as the almost-perfect tribute.

Al Stearns and Lew Perry, as the heads of the two Phillips Schools, had many common interests. Both were thorough sportsmen, both were fond of people, and both believed in the development of character as the culmination of secondary education. They worked together as friendly competitors until Al's retirement in 1932; and when I suddenly took over in 1933 I found in Lew a counsellor who helped me over many an obstacle. We realized that the origins and objectives of Andover and Exeter are identical and that the success of one is tied up with that of the other. In June, 1946, when Dr. Perry closed his distinguished official career, I said of our two schools:

> We are indigenous, not exotic, as thoroughly American as grapefruit or chewing gum. We came into being, with similar aims and ideals, as the consequence of the same philanthropic impulse. We have never ceased to be liberal, democratic, and national, concerned with the production of good citizenship and sterling character. Never have we lowered our standards in response to an ephemeral wave of mediocrity. I venture to think that we stand for something important in an age when isolationism, intolerance, and materialism are increasingly prevalent.

This was doubtless highly prejudiced testimony, and I quote it mainly to show that the schools are part of one family, united by intangible but unbreakable ties. Their rivalry has been a stimulus to both institutions, and they have regularly stood together in crises against the preachers of false doctrine.

Frank L. Boyden was a senior at Amherst when I was a freshman, and I did not see him again for many years after graduation, when the news gradually began to spread of an unusual school at Deerfield under an unusual headmaster. But I really did not come into close contact with Frank — or Bill as he was known in college — until the 1930's. Then we became intimate friends; and of recent years I have probably seen more of him than of any other school head.

Once when Frank, Harold Dodds, and I were spending a spring vacation at the Hillsborough Club near Pompano, in Florida, Harold and I had been taking a nap on a rainy afternoon. As we woke up, Harold asked, "Where's Frank?" We looked around in our little cottage and finally discovered him sitting on the side of his bed, one foot tucked under him, looking through the pictures of his boys in the Deerfield yearbook. He was fifteen hundred miles away from the school, supposed to be taking a rest, and yet it was his students who were always on his mind. It was the perfect unconscious pose for the portrait of a great headmaster.

My admiration for the achievements of Helen and Frank Boyden is unbounded. In 1902, just after his graduation from Amherst, he took over a local academy with only eleven pupils and one small schoolhouse. Fifty years later, it had become one of the foremost independent schools in this country, with nearly five hundred students and a score of beautiful buildings. Originally unique in its methods, it has sent out teachers who have carried on Boyden's policies in other schools, including Governor Dummer, Tabor, Hebron, Fountain Valley, and Holderness.

Some American headmasters have possessed great talent, but Frank Boyden has genius. Indeed his personal touch has made Deerfield what it is. With his love for horses and antiques, his Yankee shrewdness, his aversion for public speaking, his passion for telephoning and automobiling, his unaffected simplicity combined with benevolent despotism, his complete absorption in the life of his school, Dr. Boyden is a fascinating phenomenon, but he is also a powerful influence on our secondary education. I have long enjoyed talking each year at the Deerfield vesper service, and I was proud to be a speaker in 1949 at its huge sesquicentennial celebration as well as at dinners in 1952 to observe Frank's fiftieth anniversary as headmaster.

The New England Association of Colleges and Secondary Schools, of which I was president in 1942–1943, includes many of the headmasters whom I have already named, but also a strong group of college presidents. I suspect that I may be the only man who ever breakfasted with President A. Lawrence Lowell, of Harvard, in full evening dress. In the winter of 1931, when I was working on a biography of the late Senator Henry Cabot Lodge (a project subsequently abandoned), I went to a dinner given by Dr. and Mrs. Frederick Winslow at the Club of Odd Volumes at which President Lowell was a guest. It was a very frigid February evening, and as we left in our silk hats and tails, I said to him, "Let me take you back to Cambridge." But when I turned the key in the lock of my ancient Dodge, it broke off, and I was left with no means of opening the door. Much chagrined, I said to Mr. Lowell, "You'd better find a taxicab." But he replied, "No — I want to see how resourceful you are!"

My only thought was to walk down Mount Vernon Street to the Charles Street Garage, and we slid down the slippery slope together. There we mounted to the front seat of a wrecking car and returned to the scene of the disaster, where my automobile was lifted and towed back to the garage. Again I urged Mr. Lowell to go back to his home, but he seemed to enjoy the situation and declined to leave. The proprietor sidled up to me and whispered, "Who is that guy?

I've seen his picture somewheres!" "That," I answered nonchalantly, "is President Lowell of Harvard." "Oh, my God!" he almost shouted, and then went out and returned with a box of the longest, noblest cigars I ever saw. Mr. Lowell carefully selected one, lighted it, and then settled back in his chair to await developments. The mechanics had to remove the door of my car, and the job must have consumed at least an hour. Finally, well after midnight, the repairs were completed, and soon I deposited the president at the door of his residence on Quincy Street in Cambridge. I started to say "good night" and drive off, but he asked, "Where are you going now?" "Out to Andover," was my natural reply. "Oh, no, you're not," he responded. "You leave the automobile right there in the driveway and come in. I'll supply you with pajamas and a razor, and you'll be perfectly comfortable." He was so graciously insistent that I had to accept his hospitality. The next morning, after a comfortable sleep, I appeared in my white tie and evening clothes for breakfast. I watched his spaniel, Phantom, perform his tricks and then stepped into my Dodge and drove back to Andover, where I changed my outer garments and appeared just in time for my morning class in English literature.

When President Lowell was very much occupied with the construction of the Appleton Chapel, at Harvard, he came out one day to inspect our Cochran Chapel, at Andover, one of the finest of Charles Platt's buildings. Looking up at the elaborately carved oak capitals of the interior pillars, he remarked whimsically, "There you have it, Fuess, the symbols of the difference between Andover and Harvard — you have cherubs, we have lions!"

In 1937, when James Phinney Baxter, III, was drawn from the mastership of Adams House, at Harvard, to become President of Williams College, I sat next to Mr. Lowell on the platform in Williamstown when Baxter was being inaugurated. He had evidently been through an exhausting period and as the ceremonies began fell quite peacefully asleep. When the presiding officer introduced Mr. Lowell, I reached over and nudged him in the ribs. He aroused himself at once, stepped to the speakers' desk, and delivered a most felicitous address, beginning, "What can an Old Bird like me say to those who rob its nest?" At his conclusion, he returned to his chair and without embarrassment resumed his slumbers during the remainder of the proceedings.

My connection with the New England Association has been made even more pleasant by my intimacy with two of its executive secretaries, George S. Miller, of Tufts College, and his successor, Dana M. Cotton, of the Harvard School of Education — men who have carried the routine burden with ease and have made the association influential. Their contribution to education in New England has been great.

The College Entrance Examination Board, with which I have been associated in many capacities since the 1920's, has been for me a source of pleasure and stimulation. I have served at one time or another on nearly every one of its committees. Twice I helped to rewrite its constitution, and I was a member of the group that in 1947 made the arrangements for setting up the Educational Testing Service, which took over some functions of the Board. For several years I have been the Board's chief custodian, responsible for the investment of its considerable reserve fund. Something of my regard and respect for the organization I tried to incorporate in my book, *The College Board — Its First Fifty Years,* published in the autumn of 1950 in commemoration of its founding in 1900.

The Board was in its early days operated effectively, if somewhat parochially, by an Inner Ring of keenly interested persons identified with Eastern colleges and schools, especially Harvard, Yale, Princeton, Columbia, and the seven women's colleges. In 1930 Professor Carl C. Brigham, of Princeton, became the Board's Associate Secretary and through his adventurous aggressiveness persuaded his colleagues to experiment with what were first called "psychological tests." For its present position of leadership, however, the man chiefly accountable is Professor George W. Mullins, who became secretary in 1936. It is far from being my intention to reiterate here what has been said more at length in my *History;* but I cannot leave the topic without paying a deserved tribute to George Mullins, who quietly but persistently put Brigham's rather iconoclastic ideas into operation and thus led American education along a new and different track. Mistakes were made, of course, and often the fascinating new theories were ridden too hard and too far; but Mullins had vision — a rare quality in scholars — and could see far enough ahead to disregard temporary difficulties. Furthermore he had the skill to win his point without antagonizing those who disagreed with him. I might add that he possesses to an unusual degree the priceless gift of friendship.

Before his death in 1942, at the ripe age of eighty, Wilson Farrand, formerly Head of Newark Academy and one of the founders of the Board, had been accustomed to invite a group of six or seven of his associates to dine with him twice a year, on the nights before the New York meetings in spring and fall. After he died, the survivors continued the custom, calling themselves in his memory the "Farrand Cabinet," and the informal dinners are still held, usually at the Century or the University Clubs. Here ideas were tossed about, often before they had reached even the nebulous stage, and the exploratory discussions sometimes led to permanent policies. The Nestor of these dinners in recent years has been Dr. Frederick C. Ferry, formerly President of Hamilton College, to whose wisdom the Board is deeply obligated.

In another connection I have suggested that George Mullins might be compared to D'Artagnan, in his relationship to what could be styled the Board's "Three Musketeers" — Radcliffe Heermance, of Princeton; Richard M. Gummere, of Harvard; and Edward S. Noyes, of Yale — each of whom has been at one time Chairman of the Board. Rad Heermance undoubtedly has some of the physical characteristics of Porthos, but unlike that rather gullible guardsman, he is not easily taken in and his common sense is equal to his intelligence. Again and again in Board meetings his calm and witty arguments have won the majority over to his side. Dick Gummere, whom I have mentioned before, is well cast as Athos, with his happy balance between conservatism and exploration as well as his native aristocratic dignity. Ned Noyes, the youngest of the three, must be the Aramis, cool and farsighted, one of those

> *Whose blood and judgment are so well commingled*
> *That they are not a pipe for Fortune's finger*
> *To sound what stop she please.*

It would be easy to make a long catalogue of College Entrance Board leaders who have affected and determined its philosophy. This would include, of course, the two chief founders, Presidents Eliot and Butler. Among the others not already mentioned would be William Allan Neilson, long the President of Smith College; Professor Robert M. Corwin, of Yale, for eighteen years on the Board's Executive Committee, a man of sound Yankee humor and mental robustness; Miss Mary E. Woolley, of Mount Holyoke, the first woman to be chosen chairman; Miss Marion E. Park, of Bryn Mawr, who became chairman in 1939; and Miss Katharine E. McBride, also of Bryn Mawr, who heads the organization at this date of writing. Although the Board in a mood of extraordinary self-sacrifice transferred its test-making skills and facilities in 1949 to the Educational Testing Service, it still has a rich future ahead of it. I said in my *History,* "Its job is certainly not finished, and the enticing vistas that lie ahead encourage it to go forward with faith and hope."

In this hurried survey of educators within whose range I have been fortunate enough to be drawn, I have omitted some of the most eminent and interesting. President Ernest M. Hopkins, of Dartmouth, was on the Andover Board of Trustees for several years and at the meetings never failed to make some salty contribution to the discussions. Once I conceived the bright idea of awarding each June at commencement a Phillips Medal to some outstanding alumnus. The members of the Board listened with patience and apparently with approval to my explanation of the plan. Finally when the motion was about to be passed, Hopkins said, "Well, Jack, I suppose you've thought it all out. But have you considered that every time you present one of those medals there will be fifty alumni who think they deserve one — and the forty-nine who don't get it are sure to be sore?" I did some quick meditation myself and then replied, "Hoppy, you're right as usual; let's forget my suggestion." Yankee common sense triumphed in this case, and it was not the only one.

As President of Dartmouth, Hoppy would with great regularity and mild humor protest against the power of the Yale influence at Andover. He felt, as I often did, that it was a mistake for the school to send such a disproportionate number of its graduates to one college, no matter how good. There was nothing that he or I could do about it, however, and he eventually abandoned the battle. When he resigned from the Board, it was not on that issue.

The presidents of my own college, Amherst, I have of course known well. Of President Alexander Meiklejohn I recall chiefly his famous reply to an observer of educational procedures who, commenting on the average American college undergraduate, said, "Well, you can lead a student to water but you can't make him drink." "Ah," observed Meiklejohn, "but you can make him thirsty!" Just how this could be done Dr. Meiklejohn did not fully specify, but the theory was sound.

President George D. Olds, able though he was, took office in 1924 when he was in his seventy-second year, too late to formulate and carry through any important changes in policy. President Arthur S. Pease, who succeeded him, was a learned classical scholar who once, when he was harassed by administrative duties, said, "How I hate to make decisions so rapidly and on so little evidence." He it was who reminded me of the Vermont farmer who engaged a hired man to help him with his chores. On one blistering July day the farmer found the hired man complaining of the sun and sent him to the cool cellar to sort out potatoes. A little later he paid a visit to the fellow and found him in an ugly temper. "What's the matter now?" asked the farmer. "You were sore about the hot weather, and then I put you down where everything is comfortable. What are you grousing about now?" The man pointed to the pile of potatoes and answered, "Too damned many decisions!"

Nevertheless Stanley Pease was a good president, in spite of his protestations, and the trustees, in accepting his resignation, rightly declared, "He has fulfilled the high hopes attending his election." His successor, Stanley King, was the ideal college executive, imaginative, efficient, and decisive. As I have explained, he wanted me to join the college faculty, and I should have been very happy in that atmosphere. With the selection of Charles W. Cole, in 1946, following King's resignation, I had something to do, for we had worked together on the Executive Committee of the Alumni, and I was only too well aware not only of his scholarship but of his gifts as an administrator. Amherst has been indeed fortunate in King and Cole, two different but extraordinarly effective leaders through a critical period.

Of all contemporary college presidents I suppose that I have known best Harold W. Dodds, of Princeton. For many vacations we have been together, first at Summerville, South Carolina, then in Florida — at Palm Beach and the Hillsborough Club — and finally at Yeamans' Hall, near Charleston, South Carolina. Often Frank Boyden would come with us, and the three of us, each one a different personality, got along perfectly. Wherever we could, Harold and I played golf, neither one of us being a star performer. When I was awarded the honorary degree of Doctor of Letters at Princeton in June 1938, President Dodds, after reading the citation and watching the hood placed over my shoulders, shook my hand and with an impassive congratulatory face muttered, "I'll beat the life out of you at golf next time we meet!" It is my recollection that the threat was fulfilled.

I received an honorary degree at Yale in 1934, when President Franklin D. Roosevelt was the most distinguished guest. Billy Phelps, in his *Autobiography with Letters,* has described vividly what happened on that occasion. All the degrees had been given out but two — those for President Conant and President Roosevelt — and Phelps was about to proceed with his presentations when Governor Wilbur L. Cross, from his place among the members of the Corporation, rose and addressed the President of Yale, James Rowland Angell. Much embarrassed, Phelps retreated and sat down, only to be called up and awarded by Angell the degree which he had so well earned. "I think," wrote Phelps, "that it was the most stunning surprise of my life." Certainly it was a highly dramatic incident to those of us who were the observers.

In 1925, just as Ernest M. Hopkins, of Dartmouth, was being cited for an honorary degree by President James R. Angell, a man in the front row fainted and had to be carried out. Hoppy turned to Angell and asked, "Is this a regular part of your Yale ceremonies?" Angell came back with his customary felicity, "Well, we have had protests, but I don't recall any as immediate as this!"

Education in America can boast of a body of men and women who in public spirit, good citizenship, and devotion to duty can hold their own with the representatives of any profession. Many of them are not inferior to bankers and industrialists in their ability to read and analyze budgets, to institute efficient practices, and to carry on human relations. This country has had no wittier speakers than President Angell and Principal Perry, President Baxter and Headmaster Tillinghast, and no more competent wartime leaders than Presidents Conant, Carmichael, and Compton. Educators have a habit, especially in national emergencies, of roaming beyond their local range into national and international affairs. As I said at the opening of this chapter, the time has long since passed when any teacher needs to present any apology for his occupation. It is one to which anybody may dedicate himself with the consciousness that the rewards and opportunities are both great.

XIV

Diverse Recreations

MORE than most professional people, teachers require relief and diversion, both physical and mental. Their occupation, largely sedentary, demands the reinvigoration of outdoor exercise. Furthermore their daily routine is spent so largely with less mature and often subservient minds that they ought, if only for the sake of avoiding dogmatism, to rub up against superior intelligences. A boarding school is actually a tiny but mainly self-sufficient world, the inmates of which are always in danger of smugness or parochialism. It does a schoolmaster good to be propelled, even against his will, into a society which never heard of his institution and doesn't want to learn about it. Bankers and businessmen, doctors and lawyers, can teach him a great deal that he ought to know. It is salutary, moreover, to have companions who do not acquiesce tamely or timidly with all that one says. Whenever I was tempted to think that Andover affairs were going well, I tried to escape into gatherings of persons who didn't really care whether the place was functioning or not and who, after the preliminary polite inquiries, turned to other topics of conversation. Because it is difficult for a provincial not to be assertive, especially after he recovers from his initial fright, a teacher can profit by a little robust opposition.

Recreation of the right sort sends a harassed teacher back refreshed for his routine tasks. Nerves get frayed, feelings grow sensitive, and energy diminishes as the term moves on. Dr. Bancroft, in the 1890's, seeking peace, used to take a Boston & Maine train to Boston and then ride back again. For him it was like unstringing a taut bow. Problems which are oppressive in the office become less difficult when one is walking along a woodland trail. "Take your puzzles out into the open," said Colonel Stimson to me, when we were talking about a faculty mix-up. "Let's go out and breathe some uncontaminated air." And then we would set off through the Cochran Sanctuary to stretch our legs and see the laurel and the rhododendrons.

When I was a boy in the Mohawk Valley, not even the most tireless local angler had ever heard of a dry fly. Plenty of hopeful fishermen waded down the brooks on April fifteenth each spring, but they used worms. On the first promising day of the season my father invariably took a spade and dug carefully around the asparagus roots in the garden, hunting for what were called "night-walkers." These were placed in an old tomato can, with holes punched through the top. My father's rod — called by him a "fish pole" — was certainly not manufactured by Hardy or by his American equal, Orvis, of Manchester, Vermont, but it was serviceable and durable. It was made up of two sections, quite different from my own, which was merely a length of bamboo without a reel.

My father's costume consisted of his winter galoshes, a flannel shirt, an ancient pair of pants, and one of his shapeless old hats, so that he looked like one of the scarecrows set up by farmers to keep off predatory birds. The day was usually Saturday — the only time when my father felt justified in leaving his law office. His route was never altered — up Madison Street, over to Tower Avenue, down the lane to Tower's Pond, and from there along a narrow branch of the Big Creek. More than once after I was ten years old I was invited to accompany him. Even I, inexperienced though I was, could tell that his technique was unorthodox. Assuming, in the first place, that fish have neither ears nor eyes, he splashed around in the water and then dangled his worm in the muddied pool which he had just left. Of course his hook caught on countless alder bushes, and his progress was marked by intermittent but sulphurous "damns." For him to have lured even the least sophisticated trout under such conditions would have been miraculous.

Yet he did sometimes accomplish that miracle and bring home two or three speckled fish a trifle over the legal six inches in length. These my father cleaned on the back porch, while I watched the process with delight; and my mother fried them in corn meal. When each one of us — my mother, my brother, and I — had consumed his tiny morsel and praised its delicacy, my father's holiday was complete. He could rest on his laurels till another spring.

My father's example inspired me to efforts of my own, at which I was moderately successful. My most notable exploit occurred when I was about fifteen, at Lake Woodhull, in the "North Woods," when I was camping there with some friends for the summer. One afternoon I started off by myself for some fishing and, after wandering two or three miles up a stream without much luck, took a trail back to our cabin. Soon I came upon an attractive pool, in which countless fish seemed to be leaping; and adjusting my tackle I dropped in my bait and instantly hauled out a good-sized "square tail" or brook trout. I had five or six in my creel and was preparing for one final cast when a tall, bearded figure, vociferously irate, rushed up and cried, "What in hell are you at?" "Just doing a little fishing," I answered, and then the man asked, "Don't you know a fish hatchery when you see one?" I had been trying, naturally with some success, to catch fish in the hatchery of the Adirondack League Club. My age and size and terror and obvious ignorance must have operated in my favor, for the guide, after a few comments about "damn-fool-kids," released me and allowed me to return to camp.

Later in the Temagami country of northern Ontario I enjoyed such fishing for small-mouth black bass as I have never had since. For practical reasons I was using a plebeian tubular steel rod, with a heavy nine-foot leader and three streamer flies. Once in a remote spot called Wilson Lake I had three bass on hooks at the same time and had to fight them while they floundered here and there in grotesque confusion. Eventually all three were netted by my companion, Warner Taylor, and weighed in the aggregate a trifle over nine pounds. A photograph of this bass trio in the net is one of my most cherished treasures. But this, too, was clumsy angling. The fish were so hungry that any lure would have sufficed, and no skill or deception was required. Only under such circumstances could I have been so successful.

In my early days at Andover I frequently, with Al Stearns or Larry Shields, waded the brooks in northern New Hampshire, especially Perry Stream and the Diamonds. Here I experimented with the wet fly, with only indifferent success. I also did some fishing in the vicinity of Dublin, New Hampshire, my summer home for twenty years. But not until late middle life did it become a ruling passion — and then chance determined my destiny.

My surgeon friend, Dr. Arthur W. (Jimmy) Allen, of Boston, suggested in 1943 that I accompany him and some of his professional colleagues on a fisherman's holiday, in early September, to Lake Mitchell, north of Woodstock, Vermont. At that time I had no equipment of which I was not ashamed — no decent rod, no good reel, and certainly no flies. "Never mind," said the genial Dr. Allen, "we'll fit you out with what you need on this trip. You'll get your own quickly enough later — if you really like the sport." And so our party of eight, including three doctors and their wives and Mrs. Kenneth D. Blackfan, the lady who was eventually to become my second wife, set out for northern Vermont. As we drove into the camp, Dr. Allen commented, "This will be an easy start for you. Even a dub can kill his limit in this pond!"

Thus opened a new and altogether delightful phase of my education. That evening on the club veranda I watched the process of unpacking and assembling the tackle. I saw the other surgeons — E. Granville Crabtree and Horace Sowles — join with Dr. Allen in actually caressing the delicate rods as they put them together. They oiled their lines with scrupulous care, smoothed the feathers on countless colored flies, tested their leaders, and even tried a few casts from the porch into the twilight.

Then said Dr. Crabtree to me, "You and I will be up tomorrow at four and out on the lake."

Each of my three generous companions wanted a share in my training, and each believed that his piscatorial pedagogy was the best. Before daybreak I was out in a leaky flat-bottomed boat with Dr. Crabtree, who showed me tactfully how to cast a fly and then offered further advice when my preliminary movements showed that I was indeed a novice, measured by his standards. By sheer luck my first fly that actually lighted on the water deceived a small rainbow trout, and I promptly convinced myself that I was already the American Izaak Walton. But I was unable to strike the tiny fish properly, and he escaped, to the poorly concealed disgust of my instructor, on whom it was rapidly beginning to dawn that his pupil would require a long period of guidance. "Now," he said, after a pause, "Allen and Sowles aren't bad fishermen, but if you'll just let me give you a few private pointers, we may make a respectable fly caster out of you yet." So, with incredible patience, he toiled with me through the morning, until I discovered something of the correct technique. What was even more important at that stage, I learned how basically ignorant I really was.

I came in at noon, having landed three fish while Dr. Crabtree was securing his limit for the day. I did feel, however, as if I had made a little progress. Towards evening, Jimmy Allen came along and said, "Come on, Jack, and let me see how good you are!" On the pond I made a few puny casts, after which my new teacher commented, "Well, I have seen worse attempts, but you need a little coaching. Granville and Horace are all right — equal to most situations. But just let me show you some things that they may have overlooked." And so my Crabtree style, such as it was, was changed, and using the Allen methods I brought in two or three more trout — while Jimmy, incidentally, was filling his creel.

The next morning it was Dr. Sowles who was to take me out. He began by remarking, "You've certainly had some good sound training from Crabtree and Allen. There aren't any fishermen better than those two. But if you'll only just follow out one or two of my theories, you may be able to show them something!" For the next three hours I did my level best to imitate the special tricks of my third master, who, like the other two, seemed to have no difficulty in making the fish jump all around his flies. When I returned to the dock, I should have been a glorious combination of three highly successful piscatorial procedures; but my mind and hands were confused, and I had reached that unhappy stage of evolution, so familiar to novices in any sport, when I was painfully nervous and awkward. I then and there resolved that, whatever the consequence, I would be my own individual self — a disciple of neither Allen nor Crabtree nor Sowles, but a blend of all three. Each one adhered to certain fundamental principles, essential to even mediocre success in fly casting. But each one had also his personal and peculiar devices, which he had developed to suit his mental and physical traits. At whatever cost I decided to be a Fuessian, and I have remained such ever since, often to the despair of my far more competent companions.

Furthermore I have been forced to admit that I shall always be a "dub." It fills me with envy when I see a slight woman like Mrs. Allen cast her line out fifty feet directly into the wind while mine flops miserably just beyond the oars. I still watch with unbounded admiration my friends who aim at a ripple far in the distance and hit it at every attempt. Once at Round Pond, on the Megantic Club Reservation, the conditions as twilight fell seemed ideal, but the trout were lethargic, rising only languidly and without any apparent intention of feeding. Suddenly from a leafy circle of green weeds a leviathan leaped high in the air, described a graceful curve, and returned to the ripples with a splash. Dr. Crabtree, although he was facing in the other direction, heard the slight noise behind him. With amazing speed and agility he whirled about and shot his line far out over the water until the gray hackle was directly above the area from which the fish had emerged. Then, as the monster jumped, Crabtree struck with perfect timing and played him skillfully until he was netted. He weighed on our scales rather more than three pounds, and we returned him almost undamaged to his native element.

It would be a proper ending if I could honestly assert that I eventually became the equal of my masters. Unfortunately I never did. But I am an illustration of the important truth that even a mediocre performer can have plenty of fun if he does not expect too much. The Megantic Club, already mentioned, controls property in both Maine and Canada. The two largest lakes are Big Island and Chain-of-Ponds (locally pronounced *Chenapun*), but there are numerous smaller bodies of water, some of them difficult to reach except by a walk over a rough and rocky trail, and here the fishing is unexcelled. To these ponds my wife and I, with our old French-Canadian guide, Joe Arsenault, have gone on several occasions and have had as much pleasure as the Allens, who surpass us at every point. One does not have to be an expert to enjoy fishing as a pastime — or to write about it! More than most recreations, it offers both relaxation and excitement, even when the luck is bad.

Golf is another diversion which I took up relatively late in life, too late to acquire a professional stance or style. After some cow-pasture experiments in my childhood, I tried the game again in college with my classmate, John G. Anderson, later a player of national reputation, but quickly found that I could not compete with him. I did not become an addict until 1914, when my family began spending the long summer vacation at Little Boar's Head, New Hampshire. Within easy reach by trolley was the flat course of the Abenaqui Golf Club, and I was soon devoting all my spare time and most of my money to the sport. There in 1915, on the old twelfth hole — about 135 yards long — I made my first hole-in-one, using what was called in those days a "mashie" — the equivalent, I suppose, of a present Number 7. I have since had three other holes-in-one, all on the second hole (145 yards) of the short North Andover Country Club course, the exact dates being August 12, 1942, May 10, 1944, and September 13, 1945. The cards, attested (in two instances by a minister of the gospel) and framed, hang on the walls of my study, and I try to make sure that no visitor will miss seeing them.

On one broiling August day I came out from Boston in the mid-afternoon to the Abenaqui Club to find the New Hampshire State Amateur Golf Tournament in progress. As I entered the golf shop, a very countrified-looking fellow stepped up and asked whether I would join him for the qualifying round. I had not expected to participate, but learning that he was badly in need of a partner to confirm his score,

I changed my clothes and appeared at the first tee. The man looked as if he had never seen a driver or even a putting green, and I resigned myself to an unhappy experience. On the first hole I drove my customary 170 yards, and then he stepped up with a heavy iron and without even a preliminary "waggle" smote the ball and landed hole high on a hole about 240 yards in length. He got an easy three and I my usual four. On the second hole, 190 yards long, he took a midiron and made the green about four feet from the pin. My curiosity then got the better of me, and I said, "Would you mind telling me your name?" "Surely not — my name's Guildford!" And so I played eighteen holes with the great "Siege Gun," who on that day, as I remember it, was the medalist with a snappy 65.

The time arrived when golf became for me my major recreation. It was easily accessible, not too strenuous, and offered the maximum of social gratification. On Wednesday and Saturday afternoons in spring and fall four of us — an artist, a manufacturer, a banker, and I — would motor to courses all through eastern New England — to Myopia and Essex County, the Country Club and Braeburn, Belmont Springs and Charles River, Vesper and Nashua. Sometimes we would take even longer excursions, as far as Kitansett and Oyster Harbors and Wiano, and on one memorable trip our quartet went to Long Island and on ten consecutive days played ten different courses, including such championship links as the National, the Engineers, the Links, the Lido, and Piping Rock. Considering the lessons which I have paid for and the divots I have dug up, I should be a par performer. As a matter of fact, my best rounds were 86 at the Country Club, and 89 at Myopia; the only courses on which I have broken 80 have been notoriously easy. But having early made up my mind that I could never be Walter Hagen, I have not been disturbed by failure.

Over the years I have played many of the great courses in the country, including Pine Valley, Seminole and Gulf Stream, Ekwanok, Pebble Beach and Cypress Point, the Bobby Jones course at Augusta, the three courses at Pinehurst, Eastward Ho! (at Chatham) and Yeamans' Hall. I have an excellent memory for topography, and even today I can put myself to sleep by playing in my imagination a favorite course hole by hole — the long drive straight down the fairway, the well-placed brassie, the accurate approach, and the one long accurate putt. In these dream games I never dub a shot from the tee or slice into the woods; and usually by the time I have reached the tenth green I am fast asleep.

I have probably had as much genuine fun playing the level and uninteresting course at Rye Beach or the very short nine holes at Dublin, New Hampshire, or at North Andover as I have had at St. Andrews or Sandwich. Indeed I am an illustration of the fact that a player may be mediocre and yet derive immense satisfaction from trying to break 90. When President Taft was spending the summer of 1909 at Beverly, on the Massachusetts North Shore, great discussion arose among the members as to whether he could go around the very sporty Myopia course in less than 100. On August 24, when he started out, heavy bets were placed as to how he would come out, and his progress was reported almost from hole to hole by relays of caddies. When he emerged from the ordeal with a score of 98, several thousand dollars changed hands, and he felt, as he said, "like a king." I know exactly how pleased he must have been.

Having arrived at the period when my golf is best described as a "form of low cunning," I can look back in reminiscence and forward with only tepid hope. Furthermore advancing age and signs of decrepitude have given me a new sense of proportion. Billy Phelps once wrote, in all sincerity:

> If I were now given an opportunity to spend every day for the next five hundred years in an invariable program of work all the morning, golf all the afternoon, and social enjoyment all the evening, I should accept with alacrity, making only one stipulation — that at the end of the five hundred years I should have the privilege of renewal. And that's that!

Fond though I was of Billy, I should find such an existence, with one day patterned after another, insupportably monotonous. There is a mood for golf as there is for fishing or billiards. There are mornings when it is delightful to start out, with ax and clippers, cutting out trails through the woods or to stroll with one's dog as a companion along woodland paths. The main thing is to escape for a while from work and find relief in play.

As a schoolmaster I have necessarily had to be interested in all forms of competitive sport, and I recognize their value as part of the educative process. It is important for teachers to put athletics, like social activities, in their proper place, as contributing their share to a boy's development but not as usurping the position of supreme importance. Matthew Arnold declared that "Conduct is three-fourths of life"; but I have known instructors who would have subscribed to the dogma that "Athletics are three-fourths of education." It is the especial business of coaches and trainers to watch over the bodies of the students and turn out teams as good as the material permits. But I know of no figure more pathetic than that of a middle-aged teacher of mathematics who spends most of his spare time gossiping with the students about games. Naturally a headmaster has to remember always that to the average youngster football and baseball, hockey and basketball are tremendously exciting and that proficiency in these muscular activities is a campus asset. The head must never forget that in the dormitories sports rival sex as a subject of conversation. It is his business to encourage and cheer, and behave at the moment as if the Great Game were a crucial test of supremacy. At rallies he must invariably postulate victory, assuming a virtue though he have it not. My variable popularity at Andover never reached a higher point than when I luckily and accurately predicted the score of one football contest with Exeter exactly as it turned out — 27 to 6. After a game was all over and if we had won, the undergraduates, clad in pajamas, carrying torches, and led by the band, paraded to the headmaster's house, and there from the back terrace I listened to the raucous cries of "We want Claudie!" and then, with rather ostentatious modesty, appeared and congratulated the team and the school. On such occasions I was always really happy, for an athletic triumph may actually revive a deteriorating student morale.

For years I played for the faculty against the school golf team. One May the captain, Jim Brown, a fine boy and a good friend of mine, was slated to be my opponent. The North Andover fairways are very narrow, and Jim, who was not only very nervous but was also an erratic driver, sliced or pulled his ball out of bounds on each of the first six holes. With that handicap I was able to hold my own and finally defeated him one up. The school paper, of course, made the most of my victory, and Jim was obviously discomfited. The following spring Jim, still on the team, asked especially to be matched against me. On the first tee he carefully selected an iron, even then outdriving me by fifty yards. He played every shot with the greatest care, and it is my recollection that he defeated me ten up and eight to go. Not even the Pope's mule had a sweeter revenge!

Of athletics, organized and unorganized, as a part of education in our independent schools, much has been written, often by people who know very little about existing conditions. One desirable aim, of course, is to develop in each boy a physique which will withstand the demands of vigorous and rigorous living and enable him to carry on the intellectual and nervous activity of mature life. The prescribed physical exercise of the school program should be planned to produce and maintain good health and show the adolescent how properly to care for his body.

But there is more to it than just body building. The impulse to engage in competitive games is one which requires guidance rather than stimulation. Furthermore rivalry in sports helps to build morale in the participants and, if wisely controlled and placed in its right relationship to other school activities, is a most important factor in a lad's growth. What I liked best about the Andover system was that all the boys had not only an outlet for their pent-up physical energy but also an opportunity to excel. We had contests not only with outside schools but also between classes and houses on the campus. In the evening informal games of touch football or softball would spring up spontaneously, out of sheer delight in exercise. Furthermore the types of sport were so numerous that nearly everybody's ambition could be gratified. If a boy was too light for football, he could play tennis or golf, or skate or swim.

At Andover I detected no overemphasis on athletics, such as pessimists today deplore. The coaches of the teams, both at Exeter and Andover, were fine sportsmen who would tolerate no trickery or evasion of the rules. They liked to have their teams win, of course, and trained them frankly to that end. But they did not want victory at any cost. And the spirit of the players as well as of the performers always seemed to me extraordinarily healthy. We had no Hessians in our football army.

Furthermore, except in rare instances, even the most prominent Andover athletes were not victims of the proselytizing tactics of college coaches or overardent alumni. Our top performers did not choose their college because of inducements offered them by graduates of Harvard, Yale, and Princeton. Sports writers, in their desire to gain space and attract attention, have done much harm in this country; but most Andover boys had developed a sound sense of values and were not deceived by the temptation of newspaper publicity. Some of our best players have confessed to me that they were disgusted with the only half-concealed subsidization of athletes so widespread in the Middle West and South. Indeed the national overemphasis on football and basketball is repugnant to most of the independent school boys who play those games.

The relationship between Exeter and Andover was almost ideal for the inculcation of good sportsmanship. The teams were usually well matched, and the contests were seldom one-sided. Neither school admitted athletes merely for their prowess in games or relaxed the rules in order to favor them. The boys played hard, of course, but did not brood over defeats, and with most of them it was their studies which counted most. I used to like to quote to them Oliver Wendell Holmes's remark in his *Autocrat:*

> To brag little — to show well — to crow gently if in luck — to pay up, to own up, and to shut up, if beaten, are the virtues of the sporting man.

The saddest young men that I knew were those who, because of some extraordinary athletic ability, reached the height of their achievement when they were school or college undergraduates and were more lauded at eighteen or twenty than they ever were later. But many of the finest athletes, while I was at Andover, were among the best students and never tried to capitalize on their skill in games. On the Board of Trustees at Phillips Academy were three great school and college sportsmen — Fred T. Murphy, Robert A. Gardner, and William E. Stevenson — who had made their mark in later life in other vocations.

I have suggested that it is salutary for a schoolmaster to break loose occasionally from his routine and mingle with men of other occupations. For me this was done in part by visits to the alumni, but also through the geniality of clubs. Dr. Samuel Johnson, who certainly knew what he was talking about, defined a club as "an assembly of good fellows, meeting under certain conditions." The Tavern Club, in Boston, answers this description perfectly, and the "conditions" are altogether agreeable. I never knew how or why I was elected, and the first time I went to the clubhouse by myself I was so much frightened that I actually paused for a minute or two on the threshold and contemplated running away. Hidden away on Boylston Place — which is really an alley — it looks like nothing better than a place of ill repute; but within, all is calculated to warm the heart. At the round table, where we gather for luncheon, takes place some of the most provocative conversation in America, and any rash participant making a pronouncement must be prepared to defend it. I recall one argument over the word "categorical" which consumed more than an hour and ranged from Milton to President Eliot, from sermons to sardines. Such an intellectual climate is blighting to dogmatism or conceit, and therefore particularly healthful to teachers. The dinners, presided over by the inimitable Lewis Perry, are perfect in their spontaneous conviviality. On one especially merry evening a member who had dined too well shouted at Lewis, "Too few and too late," to which he, without a pause, replied, "No, too many and too early!" One sits down with specialists in literature, journalism, music, and painting, and with polite amateurs who seem to know everything without making their learning offensive. The Tavern was a wonderful refuge for a troubled headmaster; and even now, when perplexed by some complicated research problem I have found in it a very present help in time of trouble.

For many years I belonged to both the Century Association and the University Club in New York, but I found myself using the former so seldom that, with deep regret, I gave it up as an extravagance. The University Club, however, with its bedrooms and private dining rooms, has long been for me a base of operations in New York City. Woodrow Wilson, while President of Princeton, often came to the club library to write his speeches in an alcove where he could not be interrupted. I know of no more agreeable place for an hour of quiet reading, or even an inconspicuous nap after lunch. The chairs are deep and seductive, the ashtrays are in precisely the right spot, and the librarian, Mark Kiley, is always ready to help when needed — but never obtrusive.

Dining clubs have long flourished in New England, and I have belonged to several. The one which I have enjoyed most is the Examiner, which is more than a century old and meets at the Parker House on the first Monday of each month. There from fifteen to twenty-five members gather to eat a simple dinner and listen afterwards to the reading of a paper by one of their number. The variety of subjects discussed has been amazing. I can recall reading papers on "Calvin Coolidge," "Mysterious Islands," "The Lure of the Whodunit," "Congressional Immunity," and "Tom Brown and His Successors"; and I have listened over the years to many brilliant articles by such gentlemen as architect Charles D. Maginnis, astronomer Harlow Shapley, philosopher Ralph Barton Perry, Judge Charles E. Wyzanski, journalists Frank W. Buxton and Lucien Price, President Leonard Carmichael, ex-Governor Robert F. Bradford, clergyman Charles E. Park, diplomatist Sir Herbert Ames, and many others.

* * *

The Fuess family first began going to Dublin, New Hampshire, in 1920, when we were looking for a permanent summer home. This we never acquired. Spring after spring came around and we discussed the situation, only to end by renting the most convenient available cottage we could afford. Thus we had houses of all descriptions. For three years we occupied a huge stone edifice which had once been the British Embassy in the days when Lord Bryce was a Dublinite. Usually, however, we had less pretentious quarters, but the pleasures of the place were not dependent on the size of one's residence.

Dublin is located at the foot of Mount Monadnock, on one of the loveliest lakes in America. It has to offer good swimming, excellent tennis and horseback riding, and mediocre golf, together with brisk upland air and delightful people. In its old days it had Mark Twain, Thomas Wentworth Higginson, and Amy Lowell; and later came a magnificent triumvirate of octogenarians — Raphael Pumpelly, Henry Holt, and George Haven Putnam. Abbot Thayer, the artist, had died, but George de Forest Brush, the most carefree and absent-minded of men, was still painting. It was a legend in Dublin that when he sold a canvas the money, in bills and coins, was placed in a bowl on the mantelpiece, and any member of the household was permitted to help himself — until the cash was gone. I was in a group in 1924 the first time he heard a radio broadcast, and he did an impromptu war dance around the instrument to indicate his elation.

The king and queen of the Dublin I knew were, by common consent, Joseph Lindon Smith and his wife, Corinna. They lived in a rambling house on Loon Point, the most desirable location on the lake, with lovely gardens, a picturesque outdoor theater, and facilities of every kind for the production of pageants. Joe Smith loved children, and each summer on Independence Day and Labor Day he gathered all of them in the vicinity for a "show" in which each one had a share.

He was not only an artist and an archaeologist of distinction, but also an actor and an incomparable raconteur. He really was at heart a child, in the simplicity of his nature, and he always reminded me of an adult Peter Pan. His wife, Corinna, more practical but no less charming, was always there to complement and sustain him.

I have never seen a place where more talent was available in so many different fields. Alexander James and Richard S. Meryman were younger artists, pupils at one time of Abbot Thayer and very much contrasted personalities. Alec was shy, sensitive, and retiring, very much withdrawn within himself but with a refreshing sense of humor; "Wig" was gregarious and practical, with good Yankee common sense. In other fields we had Irving Babbitt, the Harvard humanist; John Lawrence Mauran, the St. Louis architect; George L. Foote, the musician and composer; Miss Amy Peabody, the sculptress; and Robb Sagendorph, who edited the *Yankee* from a tiny office on his place. There were patrons of the arts, like Daniel K. Catlin, President of the Board of the St. Louis Art Museum, and Frank C. Smith, who held a similar position in Worcester. For public figures we had Franklin MacVeagh, formerly Secretary of the Treasury; Mrs. Charles MacVeagh, wife of the Ambassador to Italy and Japan; Grenville Clark, the lawyer with such a fine record of public service; and many other persons of high intelligence and cultural interests.

It would be difficult to overemphasize the part which Dublin played in my own education. The spirit of the place was very stimulating to a young man eager to develop whatever potentialities he might possess. Among people who talked about books, it was easy to try to write or at least to think of writing. Older men were there to give advice and encouragement. Each Saturday afternoon the Dublin Lake Club sponsored an informal talk, with Joe Smith presiding, and everybody, old and young, attended. I can remember well my apprehension when I first appeared before that critical audience. The time came when I spoke every summer, on a most astounding range of topics from "Universal Military Training" to "The Poetry of T. S. Eliot," but always with the consciousness that I was among friends who would condone my shortcomings and applaud even my oldest jokes.

Squam Lake, also in New Hampshire, where my wife, Lulie, and I have lately been spending our summers, is very different from Dublin — rather plain by comparison, with none of the visible signs of wealth, and much more intimate. Mrs. Armstrong, whose genius has created the twin colonies of Rockywold and Deephaven, has bound together through her personality a group of people with varied interests and occupations, who live in small and simple cottages on the shores of a beautiful lake, gathering for their meals in a common dining hall where the food is self-served. The diversions are adequate — swimming, tennis, bass fishing, canoeing, and mountain climbing — but the people are more important. They are mostly of the intellectual type, many of them teachers, doctors, and clergymen.

The Sunday morning services on Church Island are unique in New England. Boats of every kind, from the *Queen Mary*, the Rockywold launch, to fragile canoes converge on the island on a pleasant Sunday. The services are held outdoors, with a rough granite boulder as a pulpit behind which is a large wooden cross, painted white. Music is supplied by an ancient organ which has to be pumped by an energetic youngster. The preachers are among the ablest in the country: Sidney Lovett, Ted and Guthrie Speers, Morgan Noyes, Paul Sargent, Richard Preston, Dean Henry Washburn, Bishop Charles Hall, Wallace Anderson, and many others. The scenery is glorious, and one may literally lift his eyes unto the hills and find help. Here in the midst of a confused and groping world is a place of peace and faith.

On December 8, 1919, Viscount Grey of Fallodon delivered at the Harvard Union an address, later published, on "Recreation," which had an immediate as well as a permanent influence on my attitude towards life — partly by confirming opinions which I had already codified. After pointing out that the three most important things making for happiness are some moral standard by which to guide our actions, a satisfactory home life, and a form of work which justifies our existence to our country and makes us good citizens, he speaks next of the desirability of making profitable use of our leisure. To him games, sports, and gardening are all worth while, but he continues with the statement that "books are the greatest and the most satisfactory of recreations," and he ends with the statement that "of all the joys of life which may fairly come under the head of recreation there is nothing more great, more refreshing, more beneficial in the widest sense of the word than a real love of the beauty of the world." By this, he explains, he means an appreciation of great music, beautiful pictures, splendid architecture, and "other things that stir us with an impression of everlasting greatness"; and he refers especially, as he closes, to "the enjoyment of the beauty of nature, because it costs nothing and is everywhere for everybody."

I am prepared to go along with this as a creed to follow. The pleasures of the body have their place, but it is delights of the mind and spirit which bring the durable satisfactions. If we teachers do not impress this fundamental truth upon our pupils, if we do not keep a nice sense of definition and proportion, we have failed with them and with ourselves. Thomas Hardy, in his charming poem, "Great Things," begins with the lines:

Sweet cyder is a great thing,
A great thing to me. . . .

and goes on, after mentioning the dance as another "great thing," to speak of love:

O love is, yes, a great thing,
Greatest thing to me!

I am sure that each one of us has his peculiar recreations, some pleasant but ephemeral, others more enduringly refreshing. But the best of them all must stir "thoughts beyond the reaches of our souls." It is this test which makes Chartres Cathedral or the "Fifth Symphony" or "Tintern Abbey" or the Matterhorn so significant in our lives. Fortunate are we if our tastes are so eclectic that we can enjoy them all.

XV

Colonel Henry L. Stimson

AS headmaster I first became intimately acquainted with the strongest, noblest older personality I have ever known, a man who, unconsciously on his part, contributed immeasurably to my education. Henry L. Stimson, of the class of 1883 at Phillips Academy, had been one of its trustees since June 8, 1905, but I had had little opportunity to know him well. My first recollection of him, however, is very vivid. On a visit to Andover in January 1912, during his term as President Taft's Secretary of War, he found the snow covering the ground to the depth of more than a foot, and at once said to Mark Stackpole, the school minister, "Can't we dig up a bobsled somewhere and coast down Phillips Street, the way I used to do?" I was present when the question was asked and suggested that we might borrow the massive sled belonging to the PAE society, of which Stimson had been a member. A little telephoning achieved the desired result. Soon four or five co-operative boys appeared at Mark's house dragging the huge double-runner, and we all pulled it to the top of Phillips Street. As there were few automobiles in those days, we could count on a comparatively unobstructed course.

Mr. Stimson lay down flat on his stomach, in the style vulgarly known as "belly-bump," having made up his mind to steer. I sat on his legs, and the others adjusted themselves, not knowing quite what to expect from what must have seemed to the students to be an ancient man. After all, he was fifty-five years old! The ride, however, was perfectly managed. We made the sharp curve to the left at top speed and finally landed, some of us breathless, at the railroad bridge, without mishap and to Stimson's ejaculated delight.

Occasionally in the succeeding years Mr. Stimson returned to Andover. On October 11, 1913, he and ex-President Taft were the two principal speakers at our first Founders' Day, when we dedicated a memorial tablet to mark the site of the original school building. Knowing that I was preparing a book on the Academy, he asked me for material which he could use in his historical address. In the autumn of 1915 Mr. Stimson brought General Leonard Wood to Andover to talk to the boys and faculty about the need for preparedness, in which both leaders were keenly interested. From then on for many years following his active military service in the First World War he was busy with the private practice of the law or on government missions.

In 1928, while he was Governor General of the Philippines, he cabled Al Stearns offering him the position of Commissioner of Schools in the islands. Dr. Stearns declined but suggested me for the post, and Colonel Stimson then wrote making the same proposal to me. I must admit that I was somewhat tempted at the prospect of what seemed likely to be a fascinating adventure, but my wife and I finally decided that we wanted to remain in Andover, where I had ahead of me the prospect of writing biographies as well as teaching.

During his years as Secretary of State under President Hoover, Colonel Stimson seldom visited Andover. In December 1934, however, he was my guest at the headmaster's house and spent four days speaking to various groups, sitting in classrooms, and making himself acquainted with what was going on at his old school. I recall vividly how much interested he was in my plans for the enlargement of the faculty and the raising of a Pension Fund. Now that his career of government service was apparently finished, he hoped to spend more time at Andover.

Judge Bishop died at the close of 1934, just after Colonel Stimson had paid his memorable visit to Phillips Academy. As soon as I returned from Florida, I talked with Alfred L. Ripley, a former President of the Board who had retired in 1931 from that office, but was still a member and lived conveniently nearby in Andover. Like Stimson, he was a Yale graduate, and the two were close friends. When I explained to Mr. Ripley how much I wanted Colonel Stimson to be President of the Board, he said, "You're flying high, young fellow, and don't be discouraged if you're turned down. My blessing on you!" After consulting three or four others, including President Hopkins, I went to New York and approached Stimson on the subject. He was very frank in answering, "Jack, I'm an old and tired man — but my public life is over, and maybe I could take the job on, if you'll promise me that I won't have to assume too much responsibility." To this I quickly agreed, and at the meeting in January 1935, he was elected, enthusiastically and unanimously. I felt that we had made a master stroke!

During the next few years he and Mrs. Stimson came at frequent intervals to Andover, staying usually at the headmaster's house, and he became well acquainted with the members of the faculty. Although he liked especially to visit the classes in Greek and Latin, he also turned up now and then in American history and was very willing to talk informally and "off the record" regarding his experiences in politics and diplomacy. An unusually handsome man with an attractive smile, he held himself erect and looked much less than his age. Even in his seventies he took long walks, rode horseback, and climbed mountains. Many people thought him cold, and he could be reserved, almost remote, when he was not among friends; but he was warmhearted and affectionate in his own circle. In discussions he had a one-track mind which refused to be diverted, even to interpose a little ease, from the main issue. "Wait, wait," he would say impatiently when one of his fellow trustees wandered from the subject, "one matter at a time, gentlemen." He particularly disliked being hurried, and his logic moved slowly but inevitably towards its conclusions. His reactions towards meanness, trickery, or evasion in government circles sometimes had torrential manifestations, and he hated malicious gossip. Archie Butt records that in 1911, at a private dinner, Vice-President Sherman told a "smutty" joke, and everybody laughed except Stimson, who remained "grimly silent"; yet he was no prude, and his personal habits, although temperate, were by no means ascetic. His temper was short, and his irascibility, familiar to all his associates, sometimes culminated in blasts of profanity. He was especially proud of his combat record in the army and was very sensitive to any omission of it in his record. His sense of duty dominated his every decision, and he was remarkably free from personal vanity or ambition. More than any man I have ever known, he was interested in serving rather than in getting.

Although he always seemed worn and tired when he arrived in Andover, he was resilient after a night's rest, and we often set out the following morning after breakfast for a hike through the countryside. On these walks we discussed the international crises which, in the 1930's, were recurring with discouraging frequency. Making no secret of his distrust of both Hitler and Mussolini, to say nothing of the Japanese militarists, he watched their aggression with troubled suspicion. When the Italians made their unwarranted attack on Ethiopia, he told the trustees, "We could have stopped all this in Manchuria if we had been willing to take the decisive step, but our country will support a war only when we are attacked." He often praised President Roosevelt's foreign policy and felt that he was in advance of public opinion in his recognition of the menace of Nazism. On June 14, 1940, at the Andover commencement, after warning me that he was planning to "speak out," he delivered in the Cochran Chapel one of the most important speeches of his life. Without mincing words, he said:

> Today our world is confronted by the clearest issue between right and wrong which has ever been presented to it on the scale in which we face it today. . . . The world today is divided into two necessarily opposed groups of governments. These governments are divided both by irreconcilable principles for international behavior without their borders as well as by irreconcilable principles of human rights and behavior within their borders. One group is striving for international justice and freedom, both without and within, while the other recognizes only the rule of force, both without and within. Over eighty years ago, Abraham Lincoln pointed out that a nation could not endure permanently half slave and half free. It would have to become all one thing or all the other. Today we are faced with that situation in the outside world, and the world has become so small that there can be no doubt of Lincoln's prophecy. The world today cannot endure permanently half slave and half free. . . . In this great crisis, and in the decisions which you will have to make, you will carry with you the confident hope and faith of us who have the welfare of this academy at heart.

In the following week at the Yale commencement, Colonel Stimson delivered much the same speech, which was reproduced, considerably enlarged, over a radio network. On Wednesday, June 19, in his New York law office, he received a telephone call from the President offering him the position of Secretary of War. Stimson had heard rumors that his name was under consideration but had given them little credence, believing that his lifelong association with the Republican Party was an insuperable barrier. After talking with Roosevelt, Stimson discussed the matter with his wife and two of his law partners and then accepted on condition that Robert P. Patterson be appointed Undersecretary of War. The public announcement that Stimson would join the cabinet was made on June 20, on the eve of the Republican National Convention in Philadelphia, and he became immediately a highly controversial figure. The Chairman of the Republican National Committee, John D. M. Hamilton, an Andover graduate in the class of 1913 and a member of Colonel Stimson's school secret society, promptly called the latter a "traitor to his party," along with Frank Knox, another Republican, who had accepted the post of Secretary of the Navy.

Everybody who knew Stimson was aware that he had reentered public life out of a sense of duty. He was in his seventy-fourth year and entitled to peace after stormy seas. He could gain absolutely nothing by taking again an office which he had held thirty years before. The attacks on him by unprincipled politicians, particularly when they belonged to his own party, annoyed him greatly. In the following autumn he came back to Andover for the football game against Exeter. At the buffet luncheon before the game Hamilton was also my guest. When the two men met in the hall, Stimson turned coldly away without even a nod.

At the commencement luncheon in 1940 I told the alumni that I had long abandoned my neutrality and declared that the school, like the nation, must be prepared to meet any emergency. That summer Mrs. Fuess and I went for some weeks to the Au Sable Club, in the Keene Valley in the heart of the Adirondack Mountains, where the Stimsons had spent their vacations for many years. There we walked over many of the woodland trails in that mountain paradise, played some very amateurish golf, bowled on the green, and sat at tea time on the veranda of the Stimson cottage while Colonel Stimson unburdened his mind. He was like an old war horse who, after a period of pasture, was now once more smelling powder and enjoying the sweep of action. For the moment his fatigue vanished, and he was full of plans for preparedness. "It's just the way it was back in 1915," he said. "History is repeating itself!"

In June 1941, he was too busy to return for commencement, but he urged me to tell the undergraduates that under existing conditions the sanest procedure for a youth of eighteen or nineteen, no matter how eager he might be to volunteer, was to remain in school and secure the best possible preliminary training of body and mind. This policy, with Stimson's reiterated support, we maintained throughout the war. When he could not appear at commencement or at the quarterly meetings of the Board of Trustees, his place was filled by Dr. Fred T. Murphy, of Detroit, the next oldest member, but we never took a decisive step without consulting him.

On the evening of Saturday, December 6, 1941, Mrs. Fuess and I were at dinner at a private home in Boston. Among the guests was a high-ranking officer in the navy who, as the men sat around smoking, declared with much emphasis, "It would be impossible for the Japanese to accomplish anything in the Pacific. Our air force and navy have complete control of the China Sea and could crush any attack within a few hours." This opinion was corroborated by a professor in Harvard Law School, a Boston industrialist, and our host, who was a well-informed attorney. On the next day, Sunday, at luncheon, I was called to the telephone by a member of my faculty, who cried, "Have you heard the news over the radio? The Japanese have bombed Pearl Harbor?" In my ignorance I demanded, "Where's that?" And then he told me the story, and like millions of other Americans I could almost feel a new era opening, not only for me but for thousands of boys like those on the Andover campus.

The American entrance into the war after Pearl Harbor naturally changed everything. What had for months seemed possible or probable was now a reality, and the independent schools, like Phillips Academy, had to make their plans. Fortunately we could get the best available advice direct from the Secretary of War, and all our arrangements had his approval. In the *Atlantic* for May 1942, I tried to summarize the program which we had set up during the preceding months. Disclaiming any intention of becoming a military school, we endeavored to "organize almost overnight the forms of specialized training required for armed combat between nations." We insisted, however, that it was desirable for every student to secure his diploma, if possible, and also his admission to college. While we had no interest in any "formal uniformed regiment," such as we had sponsored in World War I, we placed more emphasis on mathematics, physics, and chemistry, and even offered elementary courses in communications and radio. We allowed a small group of boys, with the permission of their parents, to take flying lessons at a nearby airport. One such, having mistaken the Shawsheen River for the Merrimack and having also run out of gas, made an emergency landing on the lawn in front of the Tewksbury Asylum and later received commendation from professional fliers for his skill and resourcefulness in a crisis.

Impromptu classes, requested by the students and conducted by co-operative masters, started up all over the campus as they had done in the medieval universities. Feeling that our huge plant ought not to lie idle during the long weeks of summer, I recommended the establishment of a summer session. This opened in July 1942, with Mr. Wilbur J. Bender (later the Dean of Harvard College) as its director and an enrollment of about 200. The teaching and administrative staff, drawn almost entirely from the academy faculty, agreed to share equally in the work to be done and to accept the same amount of pay, regardless of their age or previous salary. The undergraduate body consisted of three groups: Phillips students who wished to make up scholastic deficiencies; youngsters who, hoping to enter the regular session in the autumn, had come to test their abilities and learn whether they could meet the requirements; and some boys from other schools who wanted to take courses which would aid them when they entered military service. The general opinion was that the innovation was an unqualified success. Incidentally the policy of having the students make their own beds and serve themselves in the dining hall was so popular that it was shortly adopted by the regular session as part of the war program; and even with the return of peace it was retained as a measure of economy.

As a direct consequence of this experiment we undertook, with Colonel Stimson's approval, a form of "acceleration," which would allow upper-middlers to carry four major courses during the summer and thus save one full term. Eventually we gave to such students, if they were in good standing when they left, the regular school diploma, *honoris causa*. The second summer session, in 1943, under the direction of Alan R. Blackmer, had an enrollment of 260 and was a complex organization, with manifold activities. One fascinating feature was a program of "body building" based on army principles. On February 25, 1944, Phillips Academy held its first winter commencement, with a graduating class of thirty-one seniors. These boys had done their last two years' work with only very short Christmas and Easter holiday interruptions, and not one of those who started failed to win his diploma. It was a fine demonstration of what can be done when boys have a compelling motivation. Acceleration was given up when hostilities ceased, but the summer session had proved to be so valuable that it was continued and is still in operation.

With the outbreak of war we immediately expanded our adult education program so that hundreds of men and women from Andover and vicinity were able to get, at trifling cost, instruction in first aid, air-raid protection, navigation, communications, spoken German and Spanish, and other useful "war subjects." Prospective draftees were enabled to review their mathematics and science to their very great benefit. Some of this was quick improvisation, but the program as a whole was carefully planned and frequently revised to meet new needs.

At one point I conceived what I thought to be a brilliant idea — an orientation course, which would prepare our boys in a general way for entering the various branches of the service. The outline was drafted, mimeographed, and submitted to the trustees at one of their meetings. Colonel Stimson, who was presiding, turned the pages and then, with an assumed sternness, glared at me and said, "Jack, you have committed the unpardonable sin!" Naturally I was discomfited and stammered a very meek, "Sir, what have I done?" "Damn it!" he answered, "you've put the navy first. You ought to know that although the navy may be first in Great Britain, the army takes precedence in this country." Some of the trustees thought this was a joke, but it was not altogether a jesting matter with the Secretary of War.

At commencement in June 1942, Colonel Stimson was present and gave his blessing to our projects. He told the members of the senior class that although the desire to volunteer is noble and natural and volunteers have played an important part in American history, the draft law had been enacted to meet the needs of a complex situation by selecting citizens with the utmost care for service with the armed forces. He advised them to wait for the official call of duty and to let those in charge decide when they were needed. By this date seventeen members of the faculty were in uniform, and it was obvious that the burden on those who remained in their classrooms and dormitories would be heavy. When I was offered a post in Washington, Stimson quickly squelched me by saying, "You can't go. The place for you old fellows is right at home!" I didn't even dare to retaliate that he was eighteen years older than I!

In September 1941, I published in the *Atlantic* an article on Colonel Stimson and was delighted to receive from him a letter, dated September 1, reading as follows:

> I returned a few days ago from my trip to the Pacific Coast and found your article in the *Atlantic* awaiting me. It added a warm cheer to my homecoming to think that I had a friend who would write such an estimate of my personality. My wife and my sister, who would be the two most fierce critics of any debits in your account of me, say that it is perfect. That must mean that you have said everything that was possible in my favor. All I can say is that I am very proud and grateful to have had such a display of your friendship. Thank you very much.
>
> I am feeling a little stale and battered at the end of this long, hot, and straining summer. Also a little worried over some of the reactions in the country and anxious over what may lie before us. I had a stimulating but not restful trip to the Pacific Coast — nearly 6000 miles of flying in eight days. So I am taking a week off at Highhold trying to gather strength for the autumn. But with a plane standing by ready to take me at any moment to a restless Washington, it is not quite as restful as it would be at St. Huberts!
>
> With affectionate greetings to Mrs. Fuess, I am, as always, your friend.

In my *Atlantic* article I told two or three stories which threw light on Stimson's character. During the summer of 1939, when I was with him at the Au Sable Club, he climbed several mountains, moving slowly but steadily and holding his own with his younger companions. Once we went off on a short fishing trip to a camp on Upper Au Sable Lake. On our return he was, at his own insistence, rowing a guide boat — a very delicate, unstable craft — with a strong gale blowing us along in fitful gusts. The waves ran high on the narrow lake, and the intermittent squalls threatened to turn us into the trough, in which case nothing could have saved us from a bath in the icy water and a swim of at least a hundred yards to the shore. Stimson finally had to shift both hands to one oar in an effort to bring us about, and for a few seconds the struggle was indecisive. I was sure that we would founder and, in precaution, had removed my trousers and shoes. At last with one mighty tug he pulled the boat about, and we drifted to the nearest lee shore. Not for an instant did he betray any alarm, except to remark in a matter-of-fact manner, "I suppose you can swim."

One of his most notable traits was his passion for fair play. Believing that, unless an evil motive was involved, every man is entitled to a hearing, he was always watchful not to pronounce a judgment without hearing all the evidence. On one occasion when the trustees were sitting around quite comfortably after dinner, somebody uttered rather casually a half-slurring criticism of Mr. Justice Frankfurter. Stimson sat up a little straighter in his chair, attracted the attention of the others, and then began with a good-natured smile, "Gentlemen, perhaps you'll let me tell you what I know of Felix Frankfurter." He then proceeded to review Frankfurter's career from the time when, as a young graduate of Harvard Law School, he became Stimson's assistant as United States Attorney for the Southern New York District, to the period when he declined a nomination for the Massachusetts Supreme Judicial Court and finally, in 1939, became Associate Justice of the Supreme Court of the United States. It was a simple but thrilling story, punctuated by picturesque incidents and enlivened by intimate comments. Gradually Stimson built up the portrait of a keen-minded, farsighted, very honorable lawyer and jurist, and some of his audience found themselves modifying their preconceived and not very well-substantiated prejudices. "I do not agree with the Justice in all that he says," concluded Colonel Stimson, "but I regard him as a fine American citizen and an ornament to the bench." The incident had a lesson for us all.

Although he complained frequently of fatigue, Stimson was almost equal to Mr. Churchill in his energy and resiliency. In April 1942, he flew one morning from Washington to Long Island, leaving Mrs. Stimson at his country estate, Highhold. Continuing on to Camp Edwards, on Cape Cod, he examined the cantonment and troops and had luncheon and a conference with some divisional officers. He even had time to summon to him a Phillips Academy instructor, Philip K. Allen, who was having some trouble about his promotion to a first lieutenancy and whose case I had brought to his attention. In the late afternoon he boarded a plane for the Boston airport, where he was met and motored to Andover, twenty miles to the north. After a short rest and dinner, he insisted on inspecting the Academy Rifle Club and talking with those who had it in charge. Incidentally, although he had always shot left-handed because of an eye difficulty, he was still a first-class marksman and astonished the boys by his prowess. On the following morning he was up at seven o'clock and, after breakfast, strolled about the campus, revisiting his schoolboy haunts. As he looked around in his old room on the third story of Coy House, he said, "They used to call me 'Kid' Stimson because I was so small and wore knickerbockers. I never really grew up until I got to Yale." He lunched at his own request with about twenty undergraduates and answered their eager queries about the war. He presided from two until five o'clock at a meeting of the

Andover Trustees and then flew down from Boston to Long Island in time for a late dinner with his wife. Throughout the trip he was on the alert, remembering names without hesitation and never missing an appointment on his crowded schedule.

It was, of course, very exciting when the news spread over the campus, "Colonel Stimson's coming!" A delegation of excited seniors would call at my office to find out whether he would consent to speak in the morning assembly. When I rather reluctantly mentioned their request to him, he usually replied, "Jack, I just can't. You'll have to tell them I'm too tired." But after a night's rest, he would ask me at breakfast, "What do you think I ought to talk about?" Then he would appear at George Washington Hall, walk down the aisle with me to the platform amid thunderous applause, and address the boys in words of very moving eloquence. What impressed the students most was his burning sincerity and his simple directness. He was not in any sense a humorous or witty man; but he did once tell the story of Mrs. Murphy, who, thinking that a "jeep" was a female "Jap," was fearful of the damage to the morals of her son from associating with one.

Although ordinarily calm and self-controlled, he could at times be as excitable as any child. When he visited the headmaster's house, he was put in a bedroom on the second floor, without any telephone. One Sunday morning at six-thirty I was awakened by the insistent ringing of the telephone bell, and a voice from the Pentagon Building demanded to talk with the Secretary of War. Rather reluctantly, I knocked on his door, and he appeared in his pajamas, obviously aroused from a sound sleep. Although he grumbled a bit when I told him what had happened, he came down to my study, and I shut the door. When he emerged a few minutes later, he executed something resembling an Indian war dance, slapped me on the shoulder, and almost shouted, "Rickenbacker's safe!" He had left instructions at his office that he was to be called at any hour of day or night when news of the great airman reached Washington.

In late July 1943, after a brave fight against an incurable ailment, my wife, Elizabeth, died in the hospital, and I was left, lonely and desolate, in my Andover home. Almost at once, Colonel Stimson characteristically invited me to be his guest at the Au Sable Club. It was the period of stringent gasoline rationing, and I had almost to exhaust my supply driving my Dodge to St. Hubert's, a distance of 265 miles. After an all-day trip I arrived at the club about five o'clock in the afternoon and looking out of my second-story window, saw Colonel Stimson bowling on the green. A moment later he came rushing up to greet me and express his sympathy. For two weeks I was with him almost constantly, playing nine holes of golf a day and often rowing with Mrs. Stimson and him on the lovely lakes. In mid-August I saw him off for the Quebec Conference, at which Stimson came to the grapple with Churchill on the matter of the Normandy invasion — and won. It was at this meeting that the Chiefs of the Naval Staffs reported that victory was at last in sight in the war against the German U-boats. On his return, Stimson was especially pungent in his references to Churchill's personal habits — his sleeping all the morning and sitting up half the night, and his abnormal consumption of brandy without any impairment of his reasoning powers.

In the 1930's, when Colonel Stimson thought that his public career was over and that he would never again live in the capital, he deeded to the Phillips Academy Trustees his beautiful nineteen-acre estate of Woodley, located in the heart of the residential section of the city. When he accepted the appointment as Secretary of War in 1940, he at once requested me to ask the trustees for permission to occupy

Woodley during his incumbency. Needless to say, it took only a little telephoning to adjust that matter satisfactorily. When he became Secretary of State in Hoover's cabinet in 1929, Stimson had purchased the estate for more than $900,000, and it was indeed one of the showplaces of the capital, with a long history behind it. There Mrs. Stimson and he settled down again in 1940, and there he remained until he retired from office in 1945.

Stripped of its furnishings and draperies, Woodley today looks very much like a run-down Southern mansion, with the brick disintegrating and the woodwork in disrepair. But when the Stimsons lived there, the walls were lined with portraits and attractive paintings, and in the study were signed photographs of famous men all over the world with whom he had been associated. His huge flag as Governor-General of the Philippines covered one side of the living room; and the enormous crystal chandelier over the dining room table had been the gift of the Filipino Republic. A gigantic wistaria — the largest and thickest I ever saw — had almost crushed in the roof of the back veranda which overlooked the rolling terrain of the estate. Close by was the famous croquet ground where Colonel Stimson played with Cordell Hull and other elder statesmen. The house, which had sheltered so many great Americans, had about it a kind of melancholy charm. It should be preserved, if only for its historical associations.

There the Stimsons lived throughout the war — very quietly, for he had to conserve his physical resources. Although I tried to trouble him as little as possible about school affairs, he frequently urged me to come to Washington, if only for the night, so that he could keep informed. I planned to arrive by plane in the late afternoon, in time for the one rum cocktail which he regularly drank after returning from the Pentagon and putting on a dinner coat. Dinner was always a pleasant affair, with no other guests; and afterwards he and I would leave Mrs. Stimson and go to his study and talk about the academy. Once we started on a topic, he insisted on finding out all about it. He inquired about various members of the teaching staff, asked questions concerning boys in whom he was interested, and seemed to be in touch with countless details. About nine o'clock, however, he would show signs of weariness. Then I would simply declare that I had had a hard day and should like to go to bed. This fiction was always accepted graciously, and he would seek his rest. He told me once that there had not been a single night since he took over his duties as Secretary of War that he had not resorted to sleeping pills. The indomitable spirit of the man, his intense devotion to duty, were most inspiring.

On one occasion I engaged a taxicab to take me from the Shoreham Hotel to Woodley. The driver, a communicative young American of Italian antecedents, had been wounded in North Africa and sent home for discharge. Now he had a temporary job but, although he could drive perfectly, he had been told that his disability might cause him to lose it. At Woodley I asked him to return for me at nine-fifteen; and at dinner I told the Stimsons the story. The colonel said very little, but when the cab appeared he went out with me and had some conversation with the driver. It turned out that he made an appointment for the veteran to see him at the Pentagon the next morning and assigned him to a permanent position as army chauffeur. This is only one of several such incidents which I could relate as showing the thoughtfulness of the man.

In the winter of 1944–1945, when the war was in its critical and final phase, a request was issued by the Office of Defense Transportation that all nonessential travel be curtailed in view of the pressing military need. At once I called Colonel Stimson, who approved my suggestion that Phillips Academy abandon its customary spring vacation and hold its commencement in mid-May, thus avoiding the necessity of having some 700 or more undergraduates crowding the trains when troop movements were in progress. I next invited to my office the members of the Student Council and told them in confidence how matters stood. One of them, to my delight, asked, "Why do we go home at all? Can't we just stay here and attend classes as usual? Then we'll all get out that much earlier in the spring." The idea met with quick approval, and eventually the undergraduates, responding to an appeal from their own leaders, voted unanimously to comply with the government's request.

Within a few hours I asked several headmasters of independent schools in New England to meet in Boston to discuss possible united action on our part. To my amazement I found that many of them were opposed to altering their published schedules. I remember that one said, "How can we be sure there's any real need? It's probably all newspaper sensationalism." When I talked with Colonel Stimson over the telephone that evening, he only remarked, "It's just tragic that they won't help. If they only knew — if they only knew!"

Fortunately things broke just right. The weather throughout the usual spring vacation period was dry and sunny, so that the boys could be outdoors at their games. We held our commencement on May 13, after which the boys disappeared to their homes, glad to be free so early in the season. Often since then alumni have congratulated the school on putting the interests of the country first.

Meanwhile, on April 12, President Roosevelt had died. On May 1 the Hamburg radio announced that Adolph Hitler had committed suicide. On the following day the Russians captured Berlin, and two days later the German forces surrendered. I said on May 8, when we held a special V-Day service at the school:

> In this temporary hour of justifiable exuberance, let us be very humble. Now that this one foreign war is over, we have our own domestic responsibilities. We have fought for freedom. Let us keep ourselves free. We have fought against intolerance. Let us keep ourselves tolerant. We have fought against tyranny. Let us keep ourselves democratic. We have defeated a ruthless enemy. Let us be sure to keep our own house in order.

These were measured words in the hour of victory. I have often thought of them since and wondered at the change which took place in American public opinion within a few months after that hour of national dedication.

The summer session of 1945 opened with 252 enrolled students. On Tuesday, August 14, when President Truman announced the surrender of Japan, I was staying with my friend, Dr. Frank L. Boyden, at his summer home on Sunapee Lake, in New Hampshire. That night everything was quiet around us, but the radio told the story of celebrations in cities from coast to coast. The next morning I drove my automobile to the nearest filling station and said authoritatively — and successfully — "Fill her up!" The years of war at last were over — we thought for a long, long time.

Colonel Stimson flew to Potsdam in July, but returned to Washington in time to receive the dramatic news of the two atomic attacks on Japan. He was very weary, but remained in office as Secretary of War until his seventy-eighth birthday, on September 21, 1945, by which date our victory was presumably total and complete. He went back to his farm at Highhold for a well-earned rest and never again visited Phillips Academy. On the following April 25, however, in the Hotel Roosevelt in New York City, the Andover Alumni Association sponsored a dinner in his honor. It was his first public appearance since his resignation from the Cabinet; and Mrs. Stimson was fearful that the strain might be too much for him, especially since he was convalescing from an illness. But when he rose to address his four hundred fellow alumni, his voice rang out with its familiar resonance. His closing words seem now to have been particularly appropriate:

> Never has the world so needed the leadership of America and American principles. The United States is now the acknowledged leader upon whom the hope of that world rests. . . . I often shudder lest the restless and selfish symptoms which have been appearing among us today may lead to a failure similar to that which followed our Great War of thirty years ago. It is a time when only high leadership can save us, and that leadership must come from American youth. In such a situation I am happy to take encouragement in the example of steadfast courage and faith which I have found now manifesting themselves in the great school at Andover.

Shortly after hostilities ceased, my own life was brightened by my engagement and marriage, on December 15, 1945, to Mrs. Kenneth D. Blackfan, known to our friends as "Lulie." We went to Palm Beach, Florida, on our wedding trip, returning to be greeted by the faculty at a reception shortly after New Year's. Thus as I moved into my "sixties," I had happiness and an incentive for living.

At commencement in June 1946, we held a memorial service commemorating the one hundred twenty-six sons of Phillips Academy who gave their lives for their country in the Second World War. The new President of the Board of Trustees, Henry W. Hobson, Bishop of Southern Ohio, delivered the address, and the congregation then stood while I read the long list of the dead. I had known nearly every one of them, and to some of them had been very close. No one realizes more than a headmaster the cost of war in human lives — the best human lives! Every teacher on the Hill had seen his boys go out, sturdy, confident, blithe in spirit, to face terrible hazards in far-off places like Guadalcanal and

Okinawa and North Africa and Sicily, and later on the coast of Normandy. They represented about the finest the human race had to offer; yet they were so often cut down before they could reproduce their kind and certainly before they had a chance to rebuild a diseased society. The tragedy of those names carved on the Andover Memorial Tower or on the scroll in the Cochran Chapel is that they were so much better stuff than those who stayed at home, loafed on street corners, and went on strike for higher wages. When I had to read aloud the names of the dead, I sometimes could hardly lift my voice. It seemed as if I were seeing again friend after friend!

On October 14, as if to symbolize the end of an era, Colonel Stimson wrote me a letter tendering his resignation from the Board of Trustees. In it he said in part:

> It would be impossible for me to describe the wrench which the severance of the ties of forty-one years of service on the Board causes to me; so I shall not try to do it. I have come to the conclusion that Andover is a little too far from New York for a man of my age to perform the duties which I should be performing but am not able to discharge. I have seen the Academy grow until it seems a second home to me, and I have formed friendships among the Trustees and the faculty which I shall never forget.

From then on I saw Harry Stimson only intermittently and seldom for very long. He was occupied working with his young assistant, MacGeorge Bundy, on his great autobiography, *On Active Service in Peace and War,* and made no public appearances. I did, however, correspond with him from time to time, and asked his advice on school affairs. When he died in December 1950, I was one of those who attended his funeral services in his peaceful country home on Long Island. The great of the land were there to pay him tribute — Herbert Hoover, George C. Marshall, Felix Frankfurter, his military associates, his law partners, his school and college mates. The simplicity of the service accentuated the nobility of the man.

I am sure that Colonel Stimson, without realizing it, conveyed to those around him something of his own dignity and high-mindedness. He could be austere, but only in the presence of cheapness or vulgarity; he could be angry, but only with inefficiency or disloyalty or insincerity; he could be scornful, but only of little men or mean thoughts. Being within his range was a liberal education. He taught me not to fear to express my views when I thought I was right. He taught me to consider problems on the highest possible level. He taught me, I hope, in some degree the scorn of miserable aims that end with self.

XVI

English Interlude

ALTHOUGH verbal labels are usually to be distrusted, I have never been annoyed at being called an Anglophile. It may seem strange that, with an obviously German name and a Bavarian ancestry, I should have grown so fond of England and the English people. Possibly the long line of Moores and Kenyons and Pettibones and Matthewsons and Perkinses on my mother's side may have had something to do with it. But it is more likely that I discovered in England, first through reading and later through travel, an intellectual and spiritual kinship. As far back as 1906 I was thrilled by Kipling's *Puck of Pook's Hill,* with its glorious story "A Centurion of the Thirtieth" and the interspersed rhymes, especially Puck's songs ending:

Trackway and Camp and City lost,
Salt Marsh where now is corn;
Old Wars, old Peace, old Arts that cease.
And so was England born!

She is not any common Earth;
Water or wood or air,
But Merlin's Isle of Gramarye,
Where you and I will fare.

By good fortune I was able to "fare" there very often. My first visit in 1906 was intentionally a literary pilgrimage, during which I went to the conventional places — to the Scottish Lakes and Edinburgh, to the English Lake Country, to

Stratford-on-Avon and Warwick and Kenilworth, to Stonehenge and Salisbury Plain, to Windsor and Stoke Poges, and, of course, to Oxford and Cambridge. With keen delight my friend Sweeney and I bicycled between

These hedge-rows, hardly hedge-rows, little lines
Of sportive wood run wild.

With the diligence of an ambitious scholar I memorized long passages of poetical description and penetrated to the far corners of museums. At the home of the late Emery Walker, furthermore, I actually met Swinburne and Kipling in the flesh. My only conception of the physical Swinburne had been derived from the famous Watts portrait in the National Gallery showing him with a great shock of reddish hair like some strange-colored chrysanthemum; and when I was introduced to a diminutive man with a head as bare and white as an egg, I was horrified. He said very little, contenting himself with muttering some inaudible words, and it was hard to imagine him as the passionate bard who wrote:

In the greenest growth of the Maytime,
I rode where the woods were wet,
Between the dawn and the daytime,
The spring was glad that we met.

As for Kipling, I have a distinct recollection of a short very much bespectacled man who looked like a small edition of Theodore Roosevelt but who uttered outrageous things about America and Americans. I was much too frightened to make any reply and could only slink away defenseless to take refuge with one of my hostess's daughters.

On eleven later trips I learned to know rural England almost as well as I did New Hampshire. With my friend, Mark Stackpole, I walked over Exmoor and Cornwall and Dartmoor, where had roamed recently the hound of the Baskervilles; I climbed Helvellyn and the Peak of Derby;

I canoed with Cushing Goodhue down the Thames and the Wye; I covered by walking and bicycling and motoring almost every picturesque inch of the Cotswolds; I went, book in hand, to the Dorchester of Thomas Hardy, the Cornwall of Hugh Walpole, the Five Towns of Arnold Bennett, and the inns made famous by Charles Dickens. In London I took my Baedeker to the houses where Dr. Johnson and Thomas Carlyle and Robert Browning had lived and died. I even spent hours in Baker Street, visualizing the haunts of one of my heroes, Sherlock Holmes. I have been, I think, in every cathedral, from Durham down to Canterbury, and in countless parish churches. The time came when I could hire a small automobile and motor out of London on the Great North Road to Bedford and Sulgrave Manor and tiny villages with funny names tucked away in hollows among the hills.

In 1928, when we had our sesquicentennial celebration at Andover, I had as my house guest Mr. Frederick B. Malim, then Headmaster of Wellington College, in England, and we became well acquainted. Three years later, following my son's graduation from Phillips Academy, I took him on a short summer sightseeing trip to the British Isles, and we stopped to see some of the famous public schools, including Eton, Harrow, and Rugby, as well as Wellington. When shortly afterwards I became Headmaster of Andover, one of the first items on my program was the bringing about of some relationship, formal or informal, between English and American schools. Malim had been at Phillips Academy; I had been at Wellington. The two institutions were comparable in size and aims and prestige. Furthermore Malim and I had the authority to make arrangements without having to consult Boards about details. The first Andover boy to go to Wellington was Frederick W. Griffin, '35, who within a few weeks of his arrival broke every school record in swimming. Griffin returned from his adventure with a bastard English accent which certainly startled his friends but from which, under steady pressure, he eventually recovered. The first exchange student to arrive at Andover from Wellington was Richard Stoker, a fine representative both physically and intellectually of his country. Not only did he make the fifth hole on the North Andover Country Club in one; he was also elected to *cum laude* and won six senior honors in his studies — more than any other member of his class. After these initial experiments, Malim and I had no doubt that our project had the happy result of making boys from the two countries respect and like one another.

Before this, Father Sill of the Kent School, together with N. Horton Batchelder, of Loomis School, and W. Houston Lillard, of Tabor Academy, had organized the International Schoolboy Fellowship, through which several American students were sent annually to English schools on an exchange basis. The plan had worked very successfully, and in 1936 I agreed that Andover should become a member. In that year Lincoln Clark, '36, was selected in a vigorous competition to go to Malvern College, where he made an outstanding record.

Since that date, except for two or three of the war years, Andover has regularly received each autumn one English boy, and in return has sent as many as three students to various English schools in one year. I recollect with some amusement and much pride the three young men whom we sent successively to Harrow School, which I had grown to know well because of my friendship with its headmaster, Paul Vellacott. The first was Howard A. Reed, son of one of my Andover trustees, a fine student — otherwise he could not have been chosen — but also a rugged athlete who, to the amazement of the Harrovians, tossed a twelve-pound shot into the air as if it were a gooseberry and was promptly dubbed

"Rosebud." The next year the representative was Walter Aikman, not in any sense an athlete, but a lad with brilliant dramatic gifts who took the leading part in the Harrow dramatic performance of that year. The third was Donald Blackmer, son of one of our Andover masters, a first-rate scholar who actually won the speech contest at Harrow — a feat never accomplished before by a "foreigner." Mr. Moore, the present Headmaster of Harrow, said to me in 1950, "It would be impossible to find three boys more different, and yet each made an important contribution to some phase of Harrow life."

The number of American and British boys who have enjoyed this experience has grown now to large proportions. Those who have gone to England under the International Schoolboy Fellowship from various schools in this country must have reached considerably more than two hundred, and all have come back as ambassadors of good will. Eventually I was chosen chairman, and in that capacity arranged to have the correspondence and authority taken over by the English-Speaking Union, which now in its New York headquarters arranges all the details and has assumed full responsibility for the functioning of the fellowship.

For a time in the 1930's we had a similar exchange on a smaller scale with Germany, and at least three very carefully selected German youths came to Andover. One of them, Helmuth Scheid, acquired fame by winning, *solus et unus,* a soccer game with Exeter through an almost miraculous goal in the last few seconds of play. Unfortunately one of the Andover graduates who went to Germany returned a vociferous convert to Nazism, and it became obvious that this particular exchange was not accomplishing what we had expected. When it was evident what Hitler's designs really were, the plan was quickly abandoned.

The escapades of some of our guests were unusual, even

startling. One of them, after school was over in June, started out in an ancient Ford car with three American companions on a trip to the West Coast. They had limited funds but unlimited imagination. On a July evening at my summer home in Dublin, New Hampshire, I received a telephone call from New Orleans. The line was not clear, and all that I could understand was that some young Englishman was in jail and needed $300 immediately. Aware of possible international repercussions, I tried to take prompt action, but getting $300 from Dublin to New Orleans on a Sunday evening in summer was not the easiest business in the world. Finally I reached a high official of the New England Telephone and Telegraph Company who, perceiving the emergency, accomplished the necessary miracle. The next morning, when communications were better, I telephoned one of our well-known alumni in New Orleans and asked him to investigate the case. He reported shortly that the English boy had gone into the men's room in a motion picture theater, and as he was removing his coat a pistol dropped from his pocket and a bullet went off into the wall, barely missing a bystander. The police were summoned, and he was apprehended on three serious counts: carrying concealed weapons, impersonating a sheriff, and forgery. It seems that in Denver he had purchased a revolver in a pawnshop. Later in San Francisco he had bought a sheriff's badge in a similar store — how it got there is an unexplained mystery. Finally he had written a letter to himself purporting to be his appointment as sheriff. When he was arrested, the badge was pinned on his vest and the forged document was in his pocket. It took a judge with a considerable sense of humor to perceive the fun in these antics, and Meigs O. Frost, '07, although he was a well-known journalist in the city, was successful only in reducing the fine to fifty dollars. The young man later appeared at Andover, very much chagrined, and paid up. I regret to have to admit that his American companions apparently ducked out when the trouble began and left the lone Englishman to face the music by himself.

In the spring of 1935 I invited Mr. George C. Turner, then Master of Marlborough College, to deliver at Andover one of the lectures on the Alfred E. Stearns Foundation. He spoke brilliantly on the subject "The English Boarding School." He and his companion, Mr. Sumner Scott, spent two weeks on the Hill, meeting classes and exchanging ideas with faculty members. In 1938, on the same Foundation, came Mr. H. L. O. Flecker, Headmaster of Christ's Hospital, the "Blue Coat" school, who talked about its traditions, aims, and activities. Arrangements were made for both Mr. Turner and Mr. Flecker to visit other schools besides Andover, and they carried back with them personal impressions which helped greatly the whole exchange plan. The Headmaster of Rugby, Mr. Hugh Lyon, was also my guest for a few days in 1946.

In 1947, Mr. Flecker and I, by private arrangement, effected an exchange in instructors, with Mr. Edward Malin coming to Phillips Academy from Christ's Hospital and Mr. Alan R. Blackmer of our staff taking Mr. Malin's place at Horsham. Here the opportunity was offered for two first-rate teachers and observant commentators to learn something of the progress being made in other countries. Each one brought comparisons and contrasts back to his own institution.

In the spring of 1938 I was asked by the English-Speaking Union and the Carnegie Foundation, operating jointly, to go to England to speak at some twenty English public schools. This was a happy blending of duty and pleasure which I could not resist. Accordingly my wife and I persuaded our good friends, Dr. and Mrs. Arthur W. Allen, to accompany us, and we sailed on the *Queen Mary* in April, returning in time for commencement after a trip which was in every way a Great Adventure. I spoke at various English schools, discussing "The American Scene," in an address which was later published in my little volume, *Creed of a Schoolmaster.* I tried in my speeches to tell English schoolboys, without boasting or condescension, what the United States was really like. Naturally I had to vary the presentation according to the audience, and Dr. Allen who was compelled by circumstances to hear me early in the trip at Harrow and towards its close at Cheltenham declared that the second performance was very different from the first.

On our arrival at the Dorchester Hotel in London we found a magnificently ornate invitation to attend the dedication of a building at the King's School, in Canterbury, and were advised by Sir Frederick White not to miss it. Not having brought with me the necessary formal garb, I had to resort to the well-known firm of Moss Bros., and for one guinea was made resplendent in cutaway coat, striped trousers, and silk hat. We had already rented a small but brand-new Daimler which I was planning to drive myself; but we realized that on this occasion we had to be more "swank," and finally engaged a chauffeur who had once (so he said) been in the employ of the Queen of Norway. So, with a large placard on our windshield, we started off for Canterbury. As soon as we left Rochester, we began to meet long lines of boys who stood stiffly at attention, saluted, and sang "God Save the King!" with volume and vigor. Soon I was removing my "topper" every two or three hundred feet. "What's going on?" I asked the chauffeur. "I think, sir," he replied, "that they mistake you for the Duke and Duchess of Kent." Whatever their delusion, the crowds greeted us as if we were royalty, and we enjoyed the deception until we drove into the courtyard at Canterbury.

The dedication ceremonies were truly impressive. Both the

archbishop and the dean were present, with the genuine Duke of Kent presiding, and on the dais were sitting also Hugh Walpole and Somerset Maugham, both Old Boys of the King's School. The headmaster's name was Shirley, and virtually every speaker titillated the company by referring to the new building as "Shirley's Temple," until the joke was worn threadbare. Pages dressed in Elizabethan style, with ruffs and blue knickerbockers, escorted the guests to their places. When I was called upon as a "foreign" visitor to make a few remarks, I felt very commonplace in my conventional tails. Simply as a show, the dedication was packed with pageantry, and every detail was worked out to perfection. After this introduction to English pomp and circumstance, anything in the future was bound to seem an anticlimax.

My first formal address on my trip was scheduled for Harrow School, and when, after an excellent luncheon with the Headmaster, Paul Vellacott, I was presented in the famous Speech Hall to seven hundred or more young Englishmen, I was more frightened than I had ever been in my life. The room itself, semicircular in shape like an amphitheater, is beautiful and rich in historical associations; but I was thinking even more of the audience and what I could say to hold their attention. Like a similar group of schoolboys in America, however, they were not only attentive but generous in their applause. When I discovered that English-speaking boys everywhere laugh at the same jokes and respond to the same appeals, I felt more at ease, and the talk after that went uneventfully to the peroration. Once I had been initiated, I felt that I could talk, if necessary, in the Guild Hall without being too much perturbed. British courtesy and friendliness made me feel at ease wherever I went.

After Harrow, my wife and I moved by motor to Cambridge and Oxford and to some of the other public schools, not only to Wellington and Marlborough and Rugby, which

I had visited on previous trips but also to Stowe, Felsted, Leys, Radley, Clifton, Malvern, and others which were new to me and from which I learned much about English secondary education. I was at dinner with the Master of Emmanuel College, Cambridge, on that fateful week end when the Czechs decreed a partial mobilization of their army and it looked as if England might be at war before Monday dawned. The bright candles flickered on the ancient silver and the polished mahogany and the other symbols of British civilization — and there we were talking quietly about what might happen if Hitler did not cease his aggressive acts. The silence which followed the toast to the King was like many other such silences in English history, and each one present knew what was going through the mind of his neighbor.

I am an internationalist by philosophy, believing in the Brotherhood of Man and even in "the Federation of the World." Strongly and practically contributory to that end is the alliance between the United States of America and the British Commonwealth of Nations, and I was therefore pleased after my retirement to accept the Presidency of the Boston branch of the English-Speaking Union. Our similar backgrounds and cultural ideals make a stronger bond than any formal peace treaty. With common interests and aims we can help one another with the assurance that neither country will have a monopoly of giving. If this world is ever to resume its evolution towards a millennium, it will be because the English-speaking peoples have forgotten their petty jealousies and enmities and joined to create a new Renaissance of mind and spirit.

XVII

Human Relations

BECAUSE within his small world a headmaster is almost an absolute monarch, he has constantly to resist the temptation to be arbitrary and dogmatic. Moreover he must never forget that his decisions may involve the happiness or sorrow not only of students but also of faculty and employees. To a teacher's wife the assignment to a particular dormitory or the addition of a guest bathroom may mean the difference between relaxation and tension in the family. The imposition of extra tasks at unaccustomed hours may disturb a master's entire routine and peace of mind.

Having been a member of the faculty in my time, I knew well what courage it takes to approach the head on personal matters and how much fireside discussion occurs before the appeal is decided upon. My situation, furthermore, was complicated by the fact that so many of the staff were already my close friends from whom no secrets had been hidden.

At first I decided to leave my office door open and greet all callers in turn. Before long, however, I realized that people don't like to be hurried or to talk about their intimate concerns in the presence, actual or imminent, of others. Eventually I settled upon a program of appointments, like a physician, so that I could sit down with each visitor behind closed doors. This left each one free to open his heart with the assurance that he could not be overheard. I have listened to various theories on this subject, and doubtless circumstances alter cases; but I became convinced that a teacher should never be refused an opportunity of telling his troubles to the head in private conversation. Any headmaster, like a priest, is the repository of secrets — when babies are expected or bills are overdue — but he also learns to keep his tongue from wagging!

The weekly faculty meeting had long been an established institution at Andover, and every Tuesday afternoon we gathered in the beautiful room on the third floor of George Washington Hall to discuss current school problems. Theoretically anybody could bring up any undergraduate or any topic for discussion, and so far as I know this policy was carried out. It was sometimes hard for me, when the meetings became clogged with trivia, to conceal my impatience; but I am sure that in a school of any size such scheduled assemblies are desirable, if only to make each man realize that he is part of the show. As in any such group, a few wisecrackers could be relied upon to introduce comic relief, and the fanatics seldom failed to speak up, like automata, for their cherished doctrines. All this consumed time, but it was democratic and healthful.

With a faculty of seventy we inevitably did plenty of work through committees, and in this way each member had some part to play in operating the school. I inherited a smooth-running machine, organized on a departmental basis, which often functioned acceptably for weeks while the head was away on business. Each housemaster was in a sense responsible for his own small group of boys, and the deans, the excusing officer, the school physician, and the department heads, all had their own field of authority. I never worried about leaving the school, for I was aware that everything would be in competent hands.

The constitution of Phillips Academy provided for a body of self-perpetuating trustees, not more than thirteen or fewer than seven. For almost a century after 1808 the same Board operated both the Theological Seminary and the Academy, with the result that the minutes of many a meeting would end with the words, "No Academy business transacted." After the departure of the Seminary in 1908, however, the situation changed. The new, separate Board for the Academy was no longer predominantly clerical in its make-up. By 1933 its membership represented various occupations and for some years thereafter did not include even one Christian minister. The only nonalumnus, besides me, was President Ernest M. Hopkins, of Dartmouth, but his sagacity was of great value. At the time of my retirement the Board included one bishop, one lawyer, two college presidents, three industrialists, and four bankers, besides the headmaster. They were a fine group, faithful in their attendance, broad in their interests, and devoted to the school.

Necessarily the operation of a complicated organism like Andover had to be left largely with the headmaster, who was directly responsible to the trustees. I initiated the policy of submitting a somewhat detailed report to them at their quarterly meetings, commenting frankly on failures and successes and furnishing them with the relevant official news. In no case over a period of fifteen years did the trustees overrule any of my interim decisions. This was not the unanimity of "stooges," but of men who considered all phases of any current problem and were accustomed to compromise. The dinners when we gathered at the headmaster's house on the evening before the formal meetings were delightful, especially when Colonel Stimson or President Baxter or Bishop Hobson could be drawn into comments on men and events. Coming to Andover from New York, Washington, Chicago, Detroit, and other places, the members brought with them the atmosphere of the wider world.

The headmaster's duties involved serving on many national

committees and speaking before such groups as the President and Fellows of Harvard College, the New England Society of New York, the Holland Society, the College Entrance Examination Board, the Educational Records Bureau, the Southern Association of Private Schools, and many others. The number of addresses before colleges and schools ran up into the hundreds. The alumni were insistent that I should pay them regular visits in cities such as Syracuse, Rochester, Chicago, Louisville, St. Louis, Minneapolis, and even more remote places. All these trips had to be fitted into a schedule which was tight and exacting.

Despite the exhausting travel and more than ample entertainment, it was a rich and rewarding experience to get out among the alumni. Even before I was elected headmaster, I had met hundreds of them at Andover and on trips with Dr. Stearns; and as time went on I became acquainted with groups from nearly every city across the continent. On long tours I felt like a candidate for political office, with appointments for luncheon, dinner, and even breakfast, and sometimes speaking engagements at three or four local high schools. That I survived without acquiring chronic dyspepsia is a tribute to my physical inheritance.

The cordiality of the alumni took different forms, usually dignified but sometimes boisterous. My friends in St. Louis had a marked propensity for practical jokes. On one occasion I was driven to the entrance of a most imposing building. "Where are we now?", I inquired. "This is our principal radio station, and you are due to speak in five minutes!" "On what subject, if I may be permitted to ask?" "Oh, just something about education in the Middle West." Some one handed me a newspaper and, sure enough, there I was, photograph and all, with the statement that I would talk at three o'clock that afternoon for fifteen minutes. I was ushered into the room, without time to make even a brief note, and almost immediately introduced. Fortunately I had been speaking for the previous two weeks and could talk extemporaneously, while my tormentors, safe behind the glass partition, made obscene gestures of mockery as I went along.

Trustees, faculty, and alumni had their place for me in the Andover picture, but the most important element was always the boys. For them the academy was founded, and it was their interests that had first to be considered. A large majority of the undergraduates went quietly and normally about their business, perhaps resigned to their fate but certainly not resentful. A small coterie of active spirits, with the instinct of politicians, could stir up trouble far out of proportion to their numbers. Every October, for example, some of these would instigate an agitation for a "Long Thanksgiving Week End," with signed petitions and personal appeals to what was vaguely described as the "administration." This the faculty did not like, for it disrupted the continuity of the school term, sent students back with the germs of mumps, measles, and chicken pox, and even exhausted with revelry, and left a considerable number of boys from distant spots stranded for three or four days on the Andover campus with little to do, and therefore easy tools for Satan. No arguments existed for this long week end except that a little group of aggressive youngsters saw a possible opportunity for escaping from their studies. I may say parenthetically that I never at Phillips Academy saw any undergraduate become seriously ill from overwork. Once it was alleged that a brilliant Chinese student was sick from too much attention to his books, but it turned out that he was suffering from acute kidney trouble. The long week end was not needed as a respite — and anyhow the Christmas vacation of three weeks was close at hand.

The Student Council was constantly being urged to extort some concessions from the administration — the privilege for seniors of staying out of their dormitories until ten o'clock, the privilege of more day excuses for Boston, the privilege of wearing informal clothes more frequently. This pressure, as I look back on it, was part of the laxity of the times — the same trend which, at its worst, derided or demolished discipline and resulted in the uncontrolled outrages of teen-agers. Whether we liked it or not, a general relaxation in manners and morals did begin as early as the 1920's, and Phillips Academy, which drew its students from all sections of the country, could hardly escape its influence. But the traditions of law and order were powerful at Andover, and the faculty were not inclined to tolerate much nonsense. Within the school subversive movements were initiated by only a few boys, and the others who fell in line did so mainly because they did not wish to be ridiculed as peculiar. While the annual agitations for a longer Thanksgiving vacation were going on, many boys would seek my office and confide to me that they had no wish to leave the Hill for so long a period, but would much prefer to stay right on the campus. "My family don't really want me for that long," protested one lad. "They would like to rest up after Thanksgiving."

No one can be long in close association with boys at a school like Andover and despair of the republic. Although they were irresponsible, irrepressible, and exasperating, I have seldom known an appeal to their common sense and loyalty to fail, and the smart alecks and show-offs were not really popular. Furthermore the undergraduates were capable of extraordinary acts of generosity and helpfulness. During a terrific snowstorm in the Second World War period the tracks of the Boston & Maine Railroad were so blocked that all traffic was suspended. Some of the undergraduates heard about the crisis and asked me whether they could help. Soon groups of volunteers were on their way to Lawrence, where they were equipped with snow-shovels and set about clearing the rails. Many of them worked all night. When the job was completed, the railroad insisted on paying them union wages and sent me a check of considerable size. When I turned this over to the leaders of the enterprise, they held a short meeting and returned to say, "We don't want any money, Mr. Fuess. Please give it to the Red Cross or the Salvation Army."

Each autumn, on the night before the football game with Exeter, the Society of Inquiry conducted a Charities Drive, and with tremendous enthusiasm raised $4000 or $5000 for the support of worthy causes. More than once after a heavy blizzard which had piled deep drifts in front of my garage a troop of students, armed with shovels, would appear unexpectedly and "dig the Old Man out." Once a self-appointed committee of three boys brought me fifty dollars in small bills and requested me to give it, without mentioning its source, to a classmate who was clearly in need of a new overcoat. Incidents like this helped to restore my faith in human nature.

One of the criticisms which I would make of myself, and indeed of most teachers, is that we seem to be aiming to turn out citizens too much like ourselves. We are annoyed by roughness, noise, and independence, and place too much emphasis on mere receptivity and docility. The neat, well-dressed, and obedient lad is ordinarily the one who receives the faculty approval for being the "best all-round boy." Far more promising, in reality, is the imaginative, high-spirited fellow who sometimes gets into trouble through sheer exuberance but has what we call "drive." Give me for my money a robust nonconformist who has the courage of his convictions.

Sitting on the platform in chapel or church, I was again and again impressed by the immense vitality of the assembled group. Even in the silence of prayer, they almost exuded energy, like runners awaiting the starting gun. Although some of them were inarticulate, I knew that deep in their hearts they were conscious of the "burden of this unintelligible world" but were not dismayed by the prospect. Their potentialities for good were almost overwhelming.

A headmaster is often the repository of strange secrets and possesses information which he is pledged not to disclose. But except under unusual circumstances, boys find it difficult to treat him as a human being. He may try his best to be a boon companion, he may even play games with them, but he cannot in their eyes escape from his pedestal. I had within my control a small fund which I could use at my discretion to help students out of difficulties. Early in my administration I learned that a scholarship boy had only one rather threadbare coat, and I summoned him to my office with the intention of buying him a new one. He entered and sat down, his hands trembling, and evidently on the verge of tears, and asked immediately, "Mr. Fuess, what have I done?" He just couldn't believe that a request to come to the headmaster's office meant anything except a reprimand or punishment. I did everything I could think of to remove the barrier between them and me, but never could I make them feel completely at home in my presence.

One lad had been told by his father — one of my former English students — to come to see me if he got into any trouble. He appeared one morning to ask my counsel on a problem, spent a few minutes, and then left with a smile on his face. His father later sent me a paragraph in his son's next letter home, reading as follows — "You told me to go in and see the Old Man, and I did, and he was really very decent. What he said was all right. It all goes to show that you can learn something from anybody."

The headmaster's day at Andover was devoid of monotony. At eight o'clock I was in my office, ready to read the morning's mail. Then followed half an hour, perhaps more, with my secretary, answering correspondence. After that came a succession of appointments, with teachers and students and often with the parents of candidates for admission. At ten we held an assembly, over which I usually presided, with the Dean and the Registrar also on the platform. Often I had to deliver a short talk of admonition or praise. Bishop William Lawrence, to the end of his long life and after preaching hundreds of sermons, frequently had vertigo in the pulpit and was forced to grasp its sides tightly in order to pull himself together. No matter how many times I rose to address the Andover undergraduates I seldom stood up without some slight dizziness. As I became more experienced, I thought I could detect every mood of that audience, but I could never be quite sure. On some mornings they were chatty, restless, and noisy; on others they were preoccupied and subdued. The atmosphere before any athletic contest with Exeter was charged with electricity and any slight spark would produce an explosion. A headmaster has to keep his fingers on the pulse of the undergraduates and select the right moment for producing the right effect.

Later in the morning I held conferences with the school physician, the dean, and other administrative officers to find out what had happened overnight. Frequently I visited the infirmary to call on the patients. If a diagnosis of appendicitis had been made, we would have to get in touch with parents, who might be on a train between New York and Washington, or, as in one case, flying from Lima to Buenos Aires. Guests would arrive for luncheon, and my wife had to be notified of the number. In the afternoon I usually toured the grounds, pausing at the playing fields and the gymnasium to see what was going on in sports and ending at the Oliver Wendell Holmes Library for a chat with the librarian. Whenever I returned to my office telephone calls had to be made and visitors greeted. Seldom in the evening did I have leisure to pick up a book, for committee meetings were always being called and guests arriving. And after I had gone to bed, I often lay awake, wondering whether I had made a blunder in giving the troublesome Pete Jones a respite or approving the faculty action in putting Bill Johnson on probation. Ian Hay, describing the ideal headmaster, says:

> He is always tired, for he can never rest. His so-called hours of ease are clogged by correspondence, most of it quite superfluous, and the telephone has added a new terror to his life. But he is always cheerful, even when alone; and he loves his work. If he did not, it would kill him. . . . A man who can run a great public school can run an empire.

Even in my sixties my own education was astonishingly incomplete; and although my boys could never have suspected it, I was learning from them constantly, penetrating every day into the hidden recesses of some interesting adolescent minds. It was fascinating to speculate why this lad had responded in one way and that one in another, when confronted with the same problem. I learned gradually to keep my temper, to listen calmly to both sides of a dispute (and there usually were two sides!), to make allowances for moods and illnesses both mental and physical, to reserve judgment, to be dignified when I wanted to laugh and stern when I reproved a youngster for an indiscretion, to bear no grudges — and above all to remember my own youth. Boys are men in the making, and not too much should be expected of them. They often try to be more sophisticated than they really are and assume a maturity which they do not feel. The primary virtue of a teacher, after all, is patience — and then more patience!

When faculty, trustees, alumni, and students had been satisfied, the general public had still to be considered. Because the relationship of the academy to the town had always been close, I felt both as teacher and headmaster the importance of participating in local affairs. For ten years I was Chairman of the Andover Chapter of the American Red Cross, and I tried in other ways to do my share in a community which for me had exceptional attractiveness. As time passed, my circle gradually widened until responsibilities presented themselves in state and nation. Naturally I accepted invitations as Headmaster of Phillips Academy which I should have declined as a private citizen. It was important for the school that people should know what it stood for, and the business of interpretation through the spoken and written word fell to me.

My long experience as a schoolmaster has not left me cynical. On the contrary, and despite some disillusionment, I have found more good than bad in both boys and men. The evil is superficially more evident, and the good is more deep-seated, but it is there for emergencies. The liars, the cheats, the gangsters, and the exhibitionists all get publicity in our newspapers, which can never resist the temptation to sensationalism. But meanwhile quiet people go their unadvertised ways, attending to the sick, comforting the unhappy, and relieving the indigent, in the true spirit of the philosophy of Jesus of Nazareth.

I am old enough in years and experience to venture proffering advice to young, and even to prospective, headmasters — advice built on some of my own mistakes. And if this counsel finds expression in clichés, it can do no harm to reiterate the obvious. In reaching administrative decisions, it is very important to weigh all the evidence. Newton D. Baker once remarked that "the outstanding mark of an education is the ability of a person to hold his judgment in suspense on unsettled questions." Too often in the course of a debate over which I was presiding I expressed an opinion before all the testimony was presented and even impulsively announced my verdict before hearing the other side of the case.

Furthermore a headmaster must respect the views of others, especially of his associates on the faculty. He should never resent the disagreement of a teacher, if it is honestly voiced. As time went on, I deliberately resolved not to become irritated even when an instructor was straining for a wise-crack or seeking the academic limelight. It is easy for a headmaster, dressed in his authority, to become, almost without knowing it, pompous, dogmatic, and even tyrannical.

Again, any member of the staff who delivers a good speech or writes a forceful article deserves a note of applause. For some reason the members of the Andover faculty were chary in recognizing achievement by one of their own number. These omissions I attempted to rectify. I learned also that teachers, like other people, blossom under commendation, appreciate a casual compliment, and even enjoy having their birthdays remembered.

If a nasty job, like reproving a master or censuring a student, is on the docket, do it without hesitation. Some of my headmaster friends have told me that planned procrastination often automatically solved their problems, but this delay always seemed to me to be characteristic of a weak executive. I am sure that it is better to end each afternoon with all one's duties performed; and I will add, with some relevance, that prompt decision avoids many unnecessary catastrophes.

Through a crowded day it is essential to save energy by distinguishing quickly between what is vital and what is trivial, what is immediate and what can be postponed. A moral or ethical issue, for example, is far more important than a simple question of manners. Minor matters of discipline should be left to the discretion of the housemaster or the instructor, and never brought to the attention of the head. The administrator who has not learned how to delegate power is creating plenty of trouble for himself. It is his function to frame policies, not to wear himself out with details.

When once a question has been settled, worry must be left behind. Too many headmasters waste time by brooding over mistakes. The head should do his best to assemble the evidence, weigh it in his mind, and reach a just conclusion. Having done all this, he should proceed to the next problem. The congenital or chronic worrier will never be happy in the headmaster's office.

I wish that I could boast that I always practiced what I am here preaching. Some of what became my creed I learned gradually, as a consequence of bitter experience. Confronted with unexpected emergencies, I often lost my temper or had a rise in blood pressure. But the fact that we do not always keep the Great Commandments does not lessen their significance as a guide to conduct. And a headmaster as much as anybody should have a philosophy by which his decisions may be tested.

XVIII

World of Words

I CANNOT remember the time when I could not read; and everywhere I have gone, books have been around me. Thus it is hard for me to imagine a life spent without them. My private library at Andover contained twelve thousand volumes, most of them marked up. My taste is eclectic. I enjoy detective stories and still have a large collection of them stored on shelves in the basement. I read poetry, although my taste is old-fashioned and I prefer Tennyson to Auden and Swinburne to Robinson Jeffers. I like the novels of Dickens and George Eliot and Galsworthy and Somerset Maugham. But above all I like history and biography, literature that deals with real people.

With friends I have often speculated as to what books could be selected for a bedside shelf to furnish the maximum of variety and satisfaction. I should prefer, of course, to include the *Dictionary of American Biography,* Beveridge's *Marshall,* Sandburg's *Lincoln,* Churchill's magnificent volumes on both world wars, and all the novels of Thomas Hardy. But these take up space, and we were thinking in terms of single volumes. In preparation for a possible catastrophe I drew up a list of books I should like to have within easy reach while convalescing from, let us say, bronchial pneumonia or bursitis. It was a sincere choice, conservative but reflecting what I should like to turn to after enjoying a postbreakfast bout with solitaire. Here it is:

The English Bible (authorized version, of course)
The Complete Works of William Shakespeare (Students' Cambridge Edition)
The World Almanac (to settle factual arguments)
Who's Who in America (the biographer's treasure house)
Boswell's *Johnson* (for casual turning of pages)
Wordsworth's *Poems* (some as stimulants, some as sedatives)
The Complete Jane Austen (just because I like it)
The Oxford Book of English Verse (prescribed for memorization)
The Education of Henry Adams (to evoke a personality)
Alice in Wonderland (even though we know it by heart)
The Complete Sherlock Holmes (1323 pages of delight)
Gosse's *Father and Son* (one of the best in autobiography)
Galsworthy's *The Forsyte Saga* (reproduction of another age)
The Private Papers of Henry Ryecroft (to set one thinking)
Wells's *The Outline of History* (for ready reference)
Mark Twain's *Huckleberry Finn* (for sheer fun — and more!)
Barrie's *Courage* (to keep one's spirits up)
Osler's *A Way of Life* (tiny but tonical — and my wife likes it!)
Cabot's *What Men Live By* (good advice at little cost)
Bishop Lawrence's *Memories of a Happy Life* (to sustain cheerfulness)
Robinson's *The Mind in the Making* (to stir the logical processes)
Buchan's *Pilgrim's Way* (picture of a very gallant gentleman)
Cherry-Garrard's *The Worst Journey in the World* (the limits of human endurance)
Hardy's *The Return of the Native* (the novel at its best)
Sherwood's *Roosevelt and Hopkins* (a great experiment in biography)
Churchill's *A Roving Commission* (for its adventurous youth)

The number of volumes above cited is exactly twenty-six, and the space covered is less than three feet. Furthermore most of them are easily procurable. I have left out translations from foreign languages, thus arbitrarily eliminating Plato, Dante, Cervantes, Montaigne, Goethe, and other favorites of mine among the classics. Metaphysics, economics, scientific romances, and abnormal psychology are all omitted as unsuitable for bedside diversion. I have even reluctantly passed over such favorites of mine as Mitchell's *Amos Judd,* Doyle's *The Lost World,* and Hilton's *The Lost Horizon,* together with many yarns about mysterious islands. What I have attempted to provide is a judicious balance of information and pleasure. I make no claim that the selection represents the "greatest books in the world." Rather it is like Theodore Roosevelt's Pigskin Library which he took with him into the interior of Africa — his personal idea of what he would like to have close at hand for his own edification and satisfaction.

Once I read a paper before the Examiner Club on the broad and popular subject of detective stories. The group seemed to like what I said, and afterwards several members requested me to prepare a list of twenty varied Whodunits for summer reading. Sir Herbert Ames actually read at Murray Bay every one of my suggestions and confessed later that he enjoyed gratifying what he had always secretly regarded as a low taste. Since this list was made out in the 1940's thousands of mysteries have been published, some of them first rate. Indeed the avalanche of detective literature has now become so overwhelming that it is difficult even for addicts to keep up with what is being published. The practice of the Boston Athenæum of allowing readers to comment on the quality of the volumes which they take out leads to some amusing results. You pick up a book with an alluring title and read in the back:

Clever and fascinating A.R.B.
Absolute tommyrot F.A.G.

This is very instructive, particularly if one can guess who "A.R.B." and "F.A.G." really are in Boston literary circles. Fortunately detective stories still appear which grip the attention and force one to sit far into the silent night while some new sleuth on Cape Cod or in Whitechapel chases down the criminal. The writers whom I fancy are definitely the Old Masters in their genre, but they can hold their own, *me judice,* with most of their more modern imitators who write so copiously, anonymously, and pseudonymously for the various crime clubs. The list is now modestly presented for inspection:

Poe, *The Murders in the Rue Morgue,* 1841
Collins, *The Moonstone,* 1868
Doyle, *A Study in Scarlet,* 1887
Rinehart, *The Man in Lower Ten,* 1909
Freeman, *The Singing Bone,* 1912
Bentley, *Trent's Last Case,* 1913
Fletcher, *The Middle Temple Murder,* 1918
Crofts, *The Cask,* 1920
Wallace, *The Four Just Men,* 1920
Milne, *The Red House Mystery,* 1922
Biggers, *The House Without a Key,* 1925
Christie, *The Murder of Roger Ackroyd,* 1926
Van Dine, *The Canary Murder Case,* 1927
Queen, *The Roman Hat Mystery,* 1929
Hammett, *The Maltese Falcon,* 1930
Stout, *Fer-de-Lance,* 1934
Allingham, *Flowers for the Judge,* 1936
Innes, *Lament for a Maker,* 1938
Sayers, *Busman's Honeymoon,* 1937
Marsh, *Death of a Peer,* 1941

As I have said, my reading and writing have been chiefly in biography and history; but all scholars and schoolmasters have their cherished weaknesses, blanketed too often by their insistent daily routine. Mine include cornflowers, waffles, crimson neckties, mint juleps, wood smoke, and Chopin, but especially stories in the Scott-Stevenson-Anthony Hope-Rider Haggard-John Buchan tradition, dealing with lovely princesses in disguise, swordplay at dawn, meetings by moonlight, "hair-breadth scapes i' the imminent deadly breach," and all the paraphernalia of romance. When I weary of William Faulkner, Ernest Hemingway, John T. Farrell, and John O'Hara, I can escape to the woodland glades where neuroticism and degeneracy are unknown, and revel in plots which are unbelievable and heroes who never harden into reality. This is merely to say that, like all incurable romanticists, I cannot resist

Old, unhappy, far-off things
And battles long ago.

and the melodic songs which

Charmed magic casements, opening on the foam
Of perilous seas, in faery lands forlorn.

All through these early years at Andover I was writing — but certainly not romances. Editorials for the Phillips *Bulletin,* book reviews for the *Boston Transcript,* kept me out of mischief. The preparation of *An Old New England School,* published in 1917, had taught me much about the use of source material and about methods of research and organization. My duties as English teacher, editor of the *Bulletin,* and alumni secretary had to come first — by daylight. Consequently I formed habits then which long controlled my working hours. Often I would be up and dressed at five o'clock in the morning, drink a glass of orange juice, and settle down at my desk for two hours of uninterrupted labor.

My heart attack in the autumn of 1918, which forced me into meditation, led me to take stock of my career thus far and to realize that what I wished most to do was to be an author — not of plays or poetry or novels, for which I was unfitted — but of biography. Furthermore I had been so near death that I wanted to get busy before my allotted time was up. The problem was to find a fresh subject. What could I write about that would interest other people as well as myself?

Good fortune provided me with my initial opportunity. In my first wife's family the tribal god was Caleb Cushing, the Essex County orator, statesman, and diplomat, who had died in 1879, after a long and varied public career. All I knew about him was that he was a highly controversial figure who had been satirized by James Russell Lowell in the *Bigelow Papers* as "Gineral C." His extensive correspondence with most of the leading men of his time had been packed in wooden boxes which had been stored away for more than half a century in locked rooms on the Newburyport wharves. Mr. Lawrence B. Cushing, my wife's uncle and the legal custodian of the papers, had refused every investigator access to them, on the principle that he did not wish to be bothered.

The more I thought of that historical treasure trove gathering dust on the dock the more intrepid I grew. Finally I bearded the old gentleman in his lair and burst out, "Uncle Lawrence, I want to write the life of Uncle Caleb." "Well, why in hell don't you?" was the reply. "Because nobody will let me see the papers without your permission!" This startled him somewhat, and he growled, "Jack, you take those damned papers wherever you want to — only don't let me know anything about it." I interpreted this as a "free hand," and soon I was spending all my spare moments sorting out and reading the yellowed documents, learning much about the obscure areas of American history, and planning a full-length biography. During my summer vacation at Dublin, New Hampshire, I could devote ten or twelve hours a day to the project, and within a year it took shape in a manuscript which covered several hundred pages. When my friend, S. Spencer Scott, of

Harcourt, Brace, read it, he promptly wished to publish the book. It appeared in the autumn of 1923, in two volumes, and was reviewed favorably. By this time I was sure that it was my destiny to be a political biographer.

In this project I had the full co-operation of my wife's aunt, Miss Margaret Woodbridge Cushing, who is in her ninety-eighth year and still living in the family home on High Street in Newburyport. Even as a nonagenarian her eye is not dimmed nor her natural strength abated. She reads all the latest books and magazines without glasses, carries on a wide correspondence with her family, and maintains an active interest in politics. Her consistent and numerous kindnesses to me, I can never forget. She is a very great and gracious lady.

While I was convalescing from an illness in 1924, I plotted out a schoolboy story, which was later published by Lothrop, Lee & Stoddard in 1925, under the title *All for Andover*. As I read it now, it seems a stilted and oversentimentalized performance, but it was successful enough so that the publishers insisted on my writing a sequel, *The Andover Way* (1926), and I even ventured further with a boy's story, *Peter Had Courage* (1927), based on my childhood memories of Waterville. I am not precisely ashamed of these fictional indiscretions, but I knew that my talents — such as they were — lay along other lines. The three books have long been out of print, but I frequently receive letters even now asking where they may be obtained.

One evening in 1926 the doorbell rang and a young man entered who announced himself as Earl Balch, of Minton, Balch & Company. He shortly got down to business by asking whether I would be interested in doing a book in a series of biographies of unusual Americans. He mentioned several names, but the most appealing of them to me was Rufus Choate, another Essex County leader. When the arrangements had been virtually completed, he suddenly asked, "How much of an advance would you like?" Such a question had never been put to me before, and in my embarrassment I stammered something quite incoherent. Through a mental haze I heard his voice ask, "Would a thousand be enough?" And then he went to the desk in the corner and wrote out a check to me for $1000! It seemed at the moment like the easiest money I had ever made, but many months of research went by before my *Rufus Choate, the Wizard of the Law,* appeared in 1928. The final correction of proof came, I recall, in the very midst of Andover's Sesquicentennial celebration, and often I was up long before dawn, checking and rechecking references.

The time had now arrived, so I thought, for the major project at which I had been for some time aiming — a full-length biography of Daniel Webster, for which my *Cushing* and *Choate,* covering the same broad period, had furnished me with a background of knowledge. The trustees, presumably as a reward for my exhausting labor for the sesquicentennial celebration, generously offered me a year off on full pay, and for the first time in my life I could plan ahead to devote myself for several consecutive months entirely to writing. I had my own alcove on the fifth floor of the Boston Athenæum, overlooking the Granary Burying Ground, and there I dug in, as so many would-be authors had done before me. My wife and I during two summers at Dublin, New Hampshire, covered on foot and by motor almost every inch of ground in the area at the foot of Mount Kearsarge where Webster was born and brought up. We visited Dartmouth College and Fryeburg and Boscawen and Marshfield and the other spots in New England with which he was associated. We spent several weeks in Washington, getting acquainted with the Supreme Court Room and the old Senate Chamber and examining source material in the Library of Congress. For two months we were in Charleston, tracking Webster on a journey which he made to the South. Our wanderings carried us to out-of-the-way places and strange people, but it was all fascinating. When the book finally appeared from the Atlantic Monthly Press in the late autumn of 1930, it had a very favorable reception; and it is still, I believe, regarded as the authoritative volume on Webster. In the following June I was awarded honorary degrees from Columbia and Dartmouth.

In December 1945, just before my second marriage, Dr. and Mrs. J. Howard Means gave us a dinner at the Somerset Club. There with the famous Daniel Webster silver on the table and the sideboard, Marian Means presented me with the watch given by Daniel Webster on his deathbed, in October 1852, to her grandfather, Dr. John Jeffries, who was the statesman's personal physician. Some of the small parts of the mechanism were broken, and it had not run for many a year; but I had it reconditioned by an expert watchmaker and now wear it on very special occasions. It keeps perfect time, and is a tangible link with the great orator who died almost exactly a century ago.

Before I had completed the *Webster*, I had been asked by Dodd, Mead to write a life of Carl Schurz in its series of American Political Leaders. This I regarded in a sense as an act of filial piety, and I dedicated the book to my grandfather, Jacob Fuess, and his fellow revolutionists of 1848. This volume of more than 400 pages was started in January 1931, and I typed the last revised page on December 1 of the same year, throughout that period carrying on my routine work as a teacher. I have never done a job under greater pressure or with more satisfaction.

In 1932 I was commissioned by the magazine *Current History* to write articles on the three leading presidential candidates — Herbert Hoover, Franklin D. Roosevelt, and Norman Thomas. The article on Mr. Roosevelt, after I had interviewed him at Albany in early July, was written on the *Mauretania* while I was on my way to England and cabled back in time for the August issue. Most of what I said was inaccurate, but at the end I remarked:

> But Republicans will do well not to underestimate their adversary. He is no docile weakling or political nonentity. He will, I am sure, be a far stronger candidate than Cox, Davis, or Smith. He is a tireless campaigner, full of aggressiveness, and he knows the language of the common people, the people who, after all, cast a large majority of the votes. Finally, one must remember that he is a Roosevelt, and that the Roosevelts have a genius for doing the unexpected.

I am willing to base my reputation as a prophet on this one paragraph!

In view of my ventures into political biography I ought, perhaps, to say a word about my own political position. As an average American citizen, my political philosophy is based on the Declaration of Independence and the Constitution, with their emphasis on the freedom and the rights of the individual. With this pattern in mind, I have been resentful first against fascism and then against communism, which seem to me both to lead directly to totalitarianism. Beginning as a mild Hamiltonian, I have moved steadily in the direction of Thomas Jefferson, but I have gone through at least three periods of hero worship followed by disillusionment. In college, I thought that Theodore Roosevelt symbolized the dawn of a new idealistic era, until his egotism and personal ambition revealed his feet of clay. Then came Woodrow Wilson, who had the magnetism of the inspired crusader, especially when he evolved his concept of a League of Nations. The hour arrived when I perceived that his inability to compromise, as Lincoln would have done, did his countrymen a disservice — although to this day his seems the most forward-looking mind of my generation. For Franklin D. Roosevelt during the Hundred Days I had an immense respect, particularly because we were taking in one giant stride what might otherwise have demanded a century of political maneuvering. But I did not like many features of the New Deal, which threatened private enterprise, and it was not until 1940, when the full fervor of his internationalism became apparent, that I resumed my admiration. Although most of my presidential votes have been Republican — perhaps because I live in Massachusetts — I suppose that I am, strictly speaking, a "mugwump." Of the welfare state as now conceived I am both suspicious and fearful. All this is, of course, not important except in so far as it explains my day-by-day state of mind.

Meanwhile my friends at the Atlantic Monthly Press had been committing me to a new venture — a biography of Senator Henry Cabot Lodge, which would, they suggested, round out admirably the series of political leaders which already included Cushing, Choate, Webster, and Schurz. Members of the Lodge family were exceedingly kind in granting me permission to examine the large mass of unpublished letters and documents on deposit in the Massachusetts Historical Society. But as I studied Lodge's career and motives, and looked over his vitriolic private comments on his contemporaries, I could not view him sympathetically. I had no desire to repay the kindnesses of the Lodge family by producing what would necessarily have to be a critical biography. A Boston historian familiar with the facts once suggested that I might call my book "The Mean Little Cuss." At any rate, when the opportunity of writing the life of Calvin Coolidge presented itself very unexpectedly in 1933, I was apparently in the anomalous position of dealing simultaneously with two Bay State Republicans who never got along well together. A choice had to be made, and without any reluctance I abandoned my life of Lodge — then about one-quarter completed — and turned to a figure whom I could respect. Later Karl Schriftgiesser, in his book, *The Gentleman from Massachusetts,* dealt very thoroughly with Lodge — more frankly than I, under the circumstances, could possibly have done.

Once underway, I enjoyed writing the biography of Calvin Coolidge. Under no pressure from family or publishers, I could move leisurely from chapter to chapter, accepting the enterprise as a diversion from the less alluring duties of the headmastership. Furthermore, as I read his utterances, I liked Coolidge more and more as a person; and while I was not in accord with some of his political philosophy, I found him more enlightened in purpose and action than the apostles of the New Deal had conceived him to be. The biography was published in 1940, by the Atlantic Monthly Press, under the title, *Calvin Coolidge, the Man from Vermont.* It appeared shortly after William Allen White's *A Puritan in Babylon, the Story of Calvin Coolidge* (1938), with which it was naturally contrasted and compared. Mr. White and I, however, were attempting to do different things, and the two books, in my judgment, do not contradict but rather complement one another.

Robert M. Washburn, then a clever but caustic and indiscreet columnist on the *Boston Transcript,* habitually referred to Calvin Coolidge as "Count Citron" and to Frank W. Stearns as "Lord Lingerie"; and he had some legitimate fun at my expense during the period when I was apparently trying to write the lives of two very different statesmen at the same time. When I definitely turned towards Coolidge, with the approval of my publishers, he did everything within his power to assist me with stories and personal reminiscences.

Amherst men constitute one huge family in which the younger members are treated by the older ones like brothers and everybody knows everybody else by his first name. The first time I ever saw Mr. Coolidge — who was ten years ahead of me at college — was in 1915, when as Lieutenant Governor of the Commonwealth he was the principal speaker at a dinner in his honor at the Copley Plaza Hotel. More than a thousand alumni were present at the largest gathering Amherst had ever had; and Mrs. Coolidge had come down from Northampton, as the guest of Mr. and Mrs. Frank W. Stearns, to hear her husband speak for the first time. Indeed he did not even know that she was seated in the gallery. Towards the close of his address, which dealt chiefly with business but ended on an idealistic note, Coolidge quoted a familiar quatrain from Josiah G. Holland's "Gradatim":

Heaven is not reached at a single bound,
But we build the ladder by which we rise
From the lowly earth to the vaulted skies,
And we mount to its summit round by round.

On paper it is impossible to reproduce the extraordinary nasal tones in which he recited these lines. I can only say that "mount" from his lips became something like "mauount" and "round" was reproduced as "rauound," as if it had four syllables. The effect on me was irresistibly ludicrous; and Mrs. Coolidge has since told me that she almost choked with laughter.

Later I formed a slight acquaintance with Coolidge when he was governor and President, and I talked with him, of course, at the Andover Sesquicentennial. While I was gathering material on Lodge, I saw Mr. Coolidge — then in retirement — at Plymouth, Vermont, and found him most generously communicative, not at all the Sphinx of the legends. On my last visit with him in the summer of 1932, he remarked, "Mr. Fuess, you tell the truth about Mr. Lodge. That's what he would want, and that's what he's entitled to." On this occasion, when I suggested that I might like to write his biography, he replied laconically, "Better wait till I'm dead!" and turned the subject.

In preparing the *Coolidge* I naturally leaned greatly on Frank W. Stearns. On Sunday afternoons he would motor out from Boston or Swampscott to Andover, sit down in my study, and smoke a fat Havana cigar right through the paper band, oblivious to the pungent odor which quickly permeated the house. A man of simple habits and ideas, he had reached some startling conclusions regarding American history. He once said to me very seriously, "Mr. Fuess, the more you study American affairs the more you will be convinced that the greatest President we have ever had, leaving out Washington and Lincoln, was Benjamin Harrison." Mr. Stearns was slow-moving, physically lethargic, but very shrewd in practical affairs. His regard for Calvin Coolidge stopped only a little short of complete idolatry; and he often paused as he reminisced to say, "I can't be trusted in what I say about Mr. Coolidge. I admired him too much."

Mrs. Coolidge, a very gracious lady, gave me an absolutely free hand with the biography, turning over all her papers and letters and making no restrictions. The only request that she ever made of me was that I would not publish the size of her husband's estate. She did not wish to be made the victim of countless begging letters.

Of the many Coolidge stories which have made the rounds the best, in my judgment, dealt with the occasion when in the executive offices in the White House a group of journalists with time hanging heavy on their hands were talking about great orators, while the President was sitting in his revolving chair, gazing out the window and outwardly oblivious to what was being said. One of the newspapermen continued, "I heard Jim Watson last week out in Indiana speaking to his constituents. He was just magnificent. He ended up, 'And now, my fellow citizens, I have told you the facts, and you can vote for me or go to Hell!' Everybody laughed, and then Mr. Coolidge, swinging around, remarked in his dry tones, "It was a difficult alternative!"

In the 1920's I began writing short biographical sketches for the *Dictionary of American Biography,* then edited by Professor Allan Johnson, and over several years produced fifty-six articles on various figures, major and minor, in American history. Many of them were connected with Andover and Essex County, but the list also included Justin S. Morrill, William Lloyd Garrison, Henry L. Dawes, Henry Knox, Rufus King, and others who had a wider range. The research required was often extensive, and the pay was ridiculously low. I can recall once spending all my spare time for two weeks on an article for which I was paid twelve dollars. But I did acquire a considerable fund of miscellaneous knowledge which was to be useful later, and I learned the importance of accuracy, fairness, and sound judgment in estimating a man's significance for his contemporaries and for posterity. I made other contributions to the field in articles published in the *Atlantic* — one on "The Biographer and His Victims" in the issue for January 1932, and another on "Debunkery and Biography," in March 1933, the month when I became acting headmaster. In September 1941, I had published, also in the *Atlantic,* a character sketch of Henry L. Stimson. From then until my retirement as headmaster in 1948 I was too much occupied with war and education to undertake any further experiments with biography.

Circumstances have forced me into a kind of "vest-pocket" biography — the writing of commemorative inscriptions for tablets dedicated to my deceased friends. At this form of condensed appreciation President Charles W. Eliot was a master, and I tried to study, understand, and follow something of his technique. The summary of a useful life in a few words obviously should not be attempted in haste. In avoiding the reiteration of the obvious it is easy to miss the truth. At any rate the walls of the Cochran Chapel at Andover are lined with plaques for which I am responsible. One has to be very careful about words which take shape in bronze.

Like everybody who enjoys putting words together, I experimented from time to time with verses, although with indifferent results, particularly when I foolishly tried to be serious. At my summer home in Dublin the climax of the season was the Horse Show, with the dinner its principal feature. It was very decorative, with the riders in their pink coats and the ladies gorgeously gowned. Beginning in 1933 I was asked for several successive years to prepare a "poem" for the occasion; and thus, so to speak, "to order," I produced certain rhymes — on horses, on riders, even on dogs and sailboats. Then the war came along and the quaint custom had to be abandoned, much to my relief. The verses composed for the Horse Show in 1933 were printed later in *House Beautiful* and quoted extensively in the newspapers. If I repeat them here, it is not because of egotism but merely to demonstrate what a prosaic mind can accomplish as a tour de force:

I've been asked to speak for horses — and if I had my way,
I'd voice their equine feelings by crying out "Neigh! Neigh!"
But I am sure if I expect to keep my equinenimity,
This verse of mine must rise to heights of erudite sublimity.
It's tough for one who doesn't know a fetlock from a mane,
Or heeves from epizootic, or a spavin from a rein,
To think of all the quadrupeds for whom he ought to speak:
Bucephalus, who whinnied in a kind of nasal Greek;
The wooden horse Ulysses built to break the walls of Troy;
And Pegasus and Centaur — half pony and half boy;
The horse of Johnny Gilpin, of credit and renown;
The one King Richard called for when his fortunes tumbled down;
The horses of Apollo on their progress through the sky;

And that strange beast, the Unicorn, with fierce and fiery eye;
The nag that carried Paul Revere upon his midnight ride;
The mare that dashed from Ghent to Aix, and then just up and died;
The ass that Balaam owned — also the vengeful mule
Belonging to the Pope, who turned and kicked his master's fool;
The off horse and the cock horse, whatever they may be;
The pedigreed Arabian, and the jade of low degree;
The horse that grew horse feathers, and the mare that built a nest;
The morgan horse, the calico, the skeebald, and the rest;
The horse that bore Godiva in all her naked pride;
The magic steed of Persia which through the air could glide;
The dummy horse of Coolidge, the wild horse of the plain;
The steady-going Dobbin that the girls drove down the lane;
The sea horse and the saw-horse, and Absalom's grey mare,
Who left her master hanging from an oak tree by the hair;
Just think of every gelding, of chestnut, roan, and grey,
And all the gallant stallions that ever munched on hay;
"B.G.'s," "G.M.'s," "R.S.'s," from home and foreign stud,
The horse that won a ribbon and the horse that was a "dud."
The mustangs, percherons, and colts, the hunters and the idle,
Are represented here by me, who never held a bridle.
There are many I've omitted, but perhaps you'll let that pass —
I've spoken for the horses, but I fear I'm just an Ass.

Words may be spoken as well as typed and carved, and I have done my full share as a speaker. Even at Andover much talking had to be undertaken, and as time went on my schedule was enlarged. Dixon Ryan Fox, President of Union College, used to tell a story which, he said, might well apply to college and school heads. After having been away on a speaking tour for some weeks, he returned to Schenectady late one evening and stopped at a night lunch cart for a cup of coffee before going home. As he looked in the window, he saw a large lithograph of himself as chairman of the local Community Chest, and opposite his mouth were the words, "Open Day and Night!" Very few headmasters will miss the somewhat grim implications of this story.

Although I had done some debating and public speaking in Amherst, I was busy during the years which followed with study and received no invitations to address audiences. After I had settled in Andover, however, the situation changed. When my first invitation came to lecture at the local November Club before an audience chiefly of women, I was much excited. Fresh as I was from my study of Byron and the English Romantic Poets, I had selected as my subject, "Edward John Trelawny — the Friend of Keats and Shelley." I thought in advance that my paper was impressively profound and thorough, but I certainly got off to a bad start when the presiding officer, a lady as much embarrassed as I was, introduced me as talking on "Trelawny — the Friend of Sheets and Kelly!" My debut in the intellectual circles of Andover thus began to the accompaniment of shouts of laughter, especially from some of my rowdy colleagues on the Phillips faculty who had assembled in the rear of the hall.

Although I have done in my lifetime an inordinate amount of public speaking, I have never found it easy. Billy Phelps always maintained that talking had the same stimulating effect on him as a cocktail did for some of his friends, but I have not found it so. The preparation of a speech has been a careful, sometimes a painful, process; and when now and then I have been praised for my calmness of manner, I have been glad that my outward appearance did not betray the long hours of travail and trepidation before I ventured to my feet. So much has to be learned — the modulation of the voice, the importance of the pause, the timely introduction of the relevant anecdote, the casual variety of tone and gesture, and the need for watching constantly the reactions of the audience and recognizing the first symptoms of fatigue. Experience taught me that I would do better on occasions of some significance to write out what I had to say, paying attention to lucidity of expression, vividness of phrase, and continuity of thought. Surely it is preferable to read a fairly good speech than to stumble through a bad one without notes. On the other hand, I discovered that if I could memorize a few key phrases and then talk without a manuscript, I was less likely to bore my audience. The best counsel I can give to novices is (1) to err always on the side of brevity; (2) to give your listeners the very best you have; and (3) to remember that an ounce of sincerity and simplicity is worth a pound of bombast.

Platform speaking is not so long-winded as it used to be in the days of Webster, Everett, and Phillips; and radio and television have introduced new elements into the art of beguiling the public. But the orator still has his place and his influence. Many of us have not forgotten the presidential campaign of 1936, when it was said that if Landon had made two more speeches, Roosevelt would have carried Canada. As I write, the country is seeking a leader with a voice, who can magnetize people with a phrase and make them both feel and think.

The man who does much public speaking is bound to have his disappointments. The reporter for the *Herald* will neglect all that you have worked out with sweat and tears and fasten on some inconsequential phrase. I once delivered in New York an address on which I had literally spent weeks. Very little attention was given to my basic ideas, but across the country in nearly every newspaper was printed my trivial story of the small boy who when asked to name two ancient sports, answered, "Antony and Cleopatra!"

When I became headmaster, I was invited to occupy the pulpit at many schools and colleges, among them Yale, Amherst, Brown, Mount Holyoke, Bowdoin, Exeter, Milton, Deerfield, Bradford, Abbot, Governor Dummer, Tabor, Girard (which was always exceptionally interesting), and Hebron. At Phillips Academy itself, as I have said earlier, I settled on three church talks a year — one at the opening service of the fall term, one at Christmas, and one on Baccalaureate Sunday, and sometimes, after hours of preliminary mental and spiritual struggle, received the doubtful compliment that I was "improving." In the pulpit, however, I have never been able to escape the consciousness of my own inadequacies, and frankly I did not enjoy the responsibility of telling others how they should behave. Talks before educational associations belong, of course, in a different category, for here I was on familiar ground. After-dinner speaking is even more to my taste, for it leaves one free to express himself without any restrictions except those one chooses to impose upon himself, and the mood of the audience, comfortable after their food, is more responsive. Nor have I been unhappy with so-called "occasional addresses," at school or college anniversaries or the commemoration of special events. I find on the list of places where I have spoken such varied institutions as Harvard, Columbia, Dartmouth, Colgate, Simmons, Massachusetts Institute of Technology, St. Paul's, Choate, Williston, Taft, Groton, St. Mark's, Middlesex, Hotchkiss, Trinity, Baldwin, Beaver, McCallie, Thetford, Hackley, Holderness, Rivers, and Monson, besides those already mentioned. For many years I have presided with pleasure at the commencement dinner at Governor Dummer Academy, and I still have similar standing engagements from year to year at other institutions.

Many of these speeches have been reprinted in newspapers and periodicals. If I were to record a few to which I devoted the maximum of concentration, I should mention an address on January 10, 1939, at the Harvard Club of Boston before the Governing Boards of Harvard College: "The Vanishing Yankee," given at the 135th anniversary dinner of the New England Society in the City of New York on December 19, 1940; "The Responsibility of the Independent School," delivered on November 27, 1942, before the Middle States Association of Colleges and Secondary Schools; "Man and His Machines," a commencement address at the Massachusetts Institute of Technology in April 1944; "Yankee Individualism," read before the National Council for Social Studies in 1947; an address at the Sesquicentennial of Deerfield Academy on May 21, 1949; and "As Others See You," delivered before the Massachusetts Medical Society, May 17, 1950.

It is indeed difficult to weigh the potency of the spoken word. Some of Dr. Johnson's obiter dicta are, thanks to James Boswell, still quoted, with more appreciation of their humor (often unconscious) than of their dogmatism. I have listened to as many speeches as any man of my time and am aware how jejune, how interminable, and how solemn they can be. But public speaking is still an art, as practiced magnificently on the world stage by Winston Churchill. As used by such friends of mine as Lewis Perry, Robert Cutler, and J. Edgar Park, it can still delight the soul of man. For what I have in my humble way contributed to it, I am neither sorry nor ashamed.

XIX

Finishing the Course

AT A meeting of the Headmasters Association I sat down at a table for luncheon between two of my associates, both from Pennsylvania. Somebody asked them how things were going. "Never better," one of them replied. "We've got a long waiting list for next fall, our graduates are doing wonderfully at college, we're going to put up two new buildings, and the morale of the campus is perfect!" "And how are you getting along?" I inquired of the other. "Couldn't possibly be worse," he answered gloomily. "We had to fire four boys last week for cribbing. I don't believe we'll be able to fill our dormitories next year. Our records on the College Board are rotten. I wish I were in some other job." As a matter of fact, both men were good headmasters, but their temperaments were different. I experienced both moods during my fifteen years in office.

When I accepted the position, I was well acquainted with Oliver Wendell Holmes's poem, "The School-Boy," read at the Phillips Academy centennial celebration in 1878, in which he described his impression of his own principal, John Adams:

Grave is the Master's look, his forehead wears
Thick rows of wrinkles, prints of worrying cares.
Uneasy lie the heads of all that rule,
He most of all whose kingdom is a school.

Strictly speaking, my term as headmaster began on May 17, 1933. I had had nine predecessors with administrations varying in length from two to thirty-four years. Starting as I did at the age of forty-seven, I had clearly no chance of breaking any records; but I was unwilling to go down in history as the headmaster with the shortest period of service. I admit that I counted the months, and when in 1935 I had lasted longer than at least one of them, Frederic W. Tilton (1871–1873), I was much relieved. When I retired in 1948, at the close of fifteen years, I stood about in the middle, the average being seventeen years. It was a trivial matter, and one about which I could personally do very little, for disability and death come in due season to all men. But it was interesting that when I did retire, I was the second oldest person ever to have been the head of Phillips Academy. Clearly the job was not one for oldsters.

Like all headmasters, I had my honeymoon era while the enthusiasm over my accession was still high. I took office at a moment when several deaths in high places had left the faculty uncertain about the future. My frailties were well known to my associates — and generously discounted. Furthermore I seemed to be in reasonably robust health and not likely to fall apart too quickly. What the school community wanted most was some assurance of security and continuity. They were aware that I had been identified with the academy for over a quarter of a century, had written its history, and would probably not do violence to its tradition.

Having been very close to Al Stearns, my predecessor, I had learned from him some of the pitfalls and temptations of the position. He warned me of the five groups which a headmaster has to placate — the trustees, the faculty, the students, the parents, and the alumni — to which might be added the general public. A great English headmaster once observed, "Boys are always reasonable; masters sometimes; parents never!" For my part I found all of them ready to co-operate — even the parents! Often the interests of one group ran counter to those of another, as in cases where the faculty had ideas which were opposed to those of devoted mothers. Some of the teachers tried occasionally to make me feel that the academy ought to be run to suit their convenience; but it was, and is, my conviction that a school must be operated with the welfare of the boys chiefly in mind.

When things were functioning smoothly, it was exhilarating to be close to so much male vitality and fervor. The cheers could be so lustily wholehearted when the undergraduates were pleased, and their singing in assembly had the thrill arising from energy transmuted into action. The large majority of the boys went conscientiously about their business — with their gripes, of course, as with any body of segregated males, but with serious purpose. The proportion of those who were idle or recalcitrant or depraved was very small. Most of them, even when they made mistakes, had good intentions and in emergencies they were capable of real sacrifices. The human race as I saw it at Andover is in no immediate danger of physical or moral deterioration.

During my administration we tried several experiments in student government intended to give the older undergraduates more responsibility and thus to strengthen their self-reliance. In theory this seemed sound; indeed for short and favorable periods the system worked fairly well. But adolescents, except in rare instances, are not fitted to judge one another. It proved to be almost impossible to get them to act wisely in cases of stealing or cribbing or evasion of the rules. The schoolboy code which condemns tale-bearing was in itself difficult to overcome. Conceded a degree of freedom, smart-aleck undergraduates would publish irresponsible editorials in the school paper and thus give a wrong impression to the alumni. The truth is that boys of that age need and respect guidance. That is what teachers are for. So-called student participation in discussions of school problems is profitable, if only as a means of education, but student government is another matter. Most boys prefer to have discipline administered by some outside power. They do not object to arbitrary and even brutal measures provided they are just. All this I learned by the method of trial and error.

Out of seven hundred or more boys some are bound to be uncontrollable. As I stayed on at Andover, we expelled fewer and fewer students for disciplinary reasons — largely because we gave each case more careful consideration. The long-established system had been to bring each infraction of the rules up before the full meeting of the faculty, but this often resulted in hasty action dominated by an aggressive teacher. Soon we established a so-called Discipline Committee, of which I was chairman, which investigated lawless acts, summoned witnesses, and made the final decision. I am sure that this system resulted in a more satisfactory meeting of the ends of justice.

Perhaps the most discouraging aspect of the matter was the frequency with which well-intentioned leniency produced no improvement. Some full-blooded and undisciplined youngsters need a jolt to make them law-abiding members of society. In my first year as headmaster a fine athlete and natural leader who had constantly been in hot water finally reached the day before his graduation. I had had many interviews with him, admonishing and encouraging and threatening, and on that afternoon, as I met him in the corridor, I said, "Now Bill, we've gotten you along this far without your being dropped. For heaven's sake, watch your step for the next twenty-four hours!" On the next morning he was reported for an offense which could not possibly be tolerated in any self-respecting school, and we had to send him away without his diploma. The lad was not a criminal. He merely felt that he could get away with anything. It would have been better in his case to have facilitated his departure earlier in the year. As it was, the parents blamed all his delinquencies on me!

Contributory to law and order, but especially to the wise treatment of each pupil, were the efforts made through various channels to study the individual boy. The school physician, Dr. Gallagher, began with a very thorough physical examination of each entering undergraduate — an examination which often revealed hitherto undiscovered weaknesses such as diabetes or hernia or even defective eyesight. This was supplemented by intelligence tests administered in the dean's office, and later by a continuous succession of reports from teachers, housemasters, coaches, and others. This information, together with a small photograph, was placed on a card designed by the Registrar, Dr. Willet L. Eccles. From time to time through his course various people contributed their estimates of the lad's personality, achievement, and potentialities; and before long we often had more knowledge of the youngster than his family possessed. It was possible for me at a glance to determine in a rough way what the boy had done and was likely to do, and the files were extraordinarily useful when I was writing letters to parents at the end of each term. All this machinery was instituted within a short period as part of the business of understanding the boy. It would not be an exaggeration to say that more progress was made in five years in this field than had been accomplished in the preceding century and a half.

Necessarily some warning had to be given that this information should be used with caution. A few unimaginative or literal-minded teachers tended to overemphasize the importance of the psychological tests. It was most essential that an undergraduate should not be branded for life at a period when he was changing almost from month to month. Furthermore we had no objective means of testing what might be called the "moral" qualities, such as determination, and although we had grades for what we vaguely called "effort," we were only just beginning to comprehend the influence of "motivation." What we did have was a fairly complete picture of the boy as those who dealt with him thought he was at one stage of his development. What he became has often been surprising to those of us who knew him.

The medical program started in a modest way by Dr. Gallagher in the 1930's became eventually my pride and joy as headmaster and brought great prestige to the school. Through an annual grant of $10,000 over a period of five years from the Carnegie Corporation, followed by a similar award from the Grant Foundation, we were able to institute and carry on a very significant program of research and experimentation. One thing led to another. When we uncovered a case of mirror vision, we clearly had to do something about it, and soon we were forced to set up small courses in remedial reading. Strange new instruments appeared in the infirmary for testing reading speeds or brain waves or muscular reactions. We tried out the value of various preventive sera, with gratifying results. Especially important was the work done with athletic injuries, which were within a short period considerably reduced in number. Almost perforce the school physician and his staff had to enter the field of what might be called practical psychiatry — which at Andover was usually a manifestation of "common sense." We set up shortly an advisory board of specialists who could be called upon in emergencies. During my fifteen years as headmaster not one undergraduate died of disease, and only one of accident.

Some features of the record gave me deep satisfaction. In the examinations for the V–12 and A–12 program during the Second World War Andover won special commendation from both the army and navy for the quality of its candidates. This, of course, delighted Colonel Stimson. The development of our unique courses in the appreciation of art and music and in creative art had shown that a so-called "traditional" school could be interested in unconventional subjects. I was especially pleased with our attempts to teach modern languages — German, French, and Spanish — through auditory as well as visual channels. For generations these subjects had been taught in the same manner as Greek and Latin, with much memorization of forms and irregular verbs and much vain repetition of grammatical rules and exceptions to rules. Our experimentation in this field had a considerable influence on the instruction in modern languages in other independent schools. One highly original project was a regular evening radio program over the Lawrence station WLAW, which allowed us to provide symposiums on current topics for a wider public. The members of the faculty may not always have been "the first by whom the new are tried," but they were alert, imaginative, and open-minded.

Phillips Academy, as I have suggested, was far from being an autocracy. The faculty included strong, intelligent, and independent men, proud of their freedom, and only a very foolish headmaster would have disregarded their expressed wishes without good reason. I had been a member of the teaching staff for a quarter of a century and could understand the attitude of its members. The staff of now almost ninety men represented many shades of temperament and opinion. Among them were instinctive conservatives who questioned any hint of change, and a few radicals who were all for toppling the towers of privilege. Some were cautious; others were adventurous; a few of the less experienced were naturally uncertain. Some were inclined to a rigid philosophy which emphasized the letter of the law; others were disposed to be more flexible. It was the familiar contrast between the strict and the loose constructionists. But discussion was uninhibited, and views were frankly and courageously expressed.

So far as I am aware, no member of the teaching staff was ever hindered in expressing his views or suffered in any way when he opposed the headmaster's ideas. Nor, indeed, was any teacher ever questioned for what he honestly said in the classroom or on any public platform. Some of my best friends on the faculty were men with whose educational opinions I could not possibly agree.

Andover's faculty represented secondary education at its best. Many of them had outside interests which carried them into the broader world. They joined scholarly associations, contributed greatly to community welfare, wrote significant articles and books. But they never forgot that classroom teaching was their main business. I am not maintaining that they were all educational leaders. Like bankers or manufacturers or physicians they had their idiosyncrasies and sensitivities and prejudices. But I have never seen in academic or collegiate circles men more devoted to their jobs. They were eager for their pupils to do well and made many personal sacrifices in order to help them. On their enthusiasm, their patience, and their loyalty the reputation of the school largely depended.

Not for long was I free from criticism. As every administrator knows, any executive is bound to lose popularity when he makes promotions. One of the few serious mistakes made by Mr. Cochran in his philanthropies was the establishment of several "name foundations," with salaries disproportionately higher than those allotted to other members of the teaching staff. When I myself was appointed to one of them, I naturally rejoiced, but I quickly discovered that the attendant publicity was not relished by some of my colleagues. When, as headmaster, I had to fill a vacancy in these foundations, I was obliged to choose among seven or eight men, all friends of mine and all well qualified. After some long deliberation, I announced my decision, and then and there learned a fundamental truth — those who lost out thought that I was unfair and the man who was selected, feeling that he deserved the honor, was not really grateful. The trouble with the foundations was that I couldn't change them, although more than once we consulted counsel to see whether we could not use the income in a more satisfactory way. My own idea was to turn the money into a general fund and then make promotions step by step, instead of jumping an instructor from a salary of $5000 to one of $7000, with the news given publicity in all the newspapers. This would have avoided many heartaches and saved me a large amount of grief.

Naturally not all a headmaster's appointments turn out to be satisfactory. When I took over in 1933, one of my colleagues was obviously unsuited to his position and I was obliged to call him in and tell him so. When I gave him the sad news, he raised no objection, but merely asked, "Did you ever know how I happened to get this job?" "No," I replied, "I supposed that you applied for it." "Not at all," he explained. "Two years ago I was taking a trip to visit some of the private schools in New England and came to Andover. I thought it was polite to call on the headmaster and was ushered into his office. He asked me some questions about my teaching experience and finally said, 'Well, I have a vacancy in the Latin Department, and I can offer you $2500 a year, with board and room.' I was so much startled that I could hardly speak, for the salary was more than I was earning in public school, and I had never dreamed of getting into a place like Andover. But when I started to teach the next fall, I felt right away that I wasn't up to it. I just didn't know enough. I'll be glad to get out." I arranged with our trustees to give him $1000 to study in the Harvard Graduate School. He did well there and has since been a successful public school teacher. More than once he has thanked me for relieving him so gently from an embarrassing situation.

When I had been headmaster for ten years, a problem which had long been smoldering burst into flame. On the campus were the houses of eight secret societies, the oldest of which had been founded in 1874. They had been modeled in a general way upon the Yale senior societies, of which many Andover graduates were members. Although they held formal meetings on Saturday evenings, their chief function was social. Outside the regular recitation and study hours, the members could (quite legally) sit around in their comfortably furnished rooms, smoke and play pool, and by tacit agreement enjoy privileges denied to the undergraduate nonmembers. Undeniably these societies had long furnished pleasant diversion to those fortunate enough to belong, and many enduring friendships had been formed within their walls. To them many alumni had sentimental attachments of an agreeable nature.

By the 1930's, however, although many of their graduates did not realize it, the societies had become almost anachronistic. With the institution of Saturday night school movies a large proportion of the members preferred to see Ginger Rogers or Clark Gable rather than enjoy the traditional bull sessions. The groups were small, and the members would often develop disconcerting cases of snobbery and complacency. As for the unlucky ones who did not get elected, they and their parents often became embittered. I was never quite sure just what qualities were stressed for admission to a society, but the "smoothie" politician type predominated. With some rare exceptions the scholastic records of society members were lower than those of the "barbarian" undergraduates.

Sporadic efforts at reform produced occasional but temporary improvement. But the faculty, who knew the situation, were growing impatient with the abuses, and their protests could not be ignored. The evils were inherent in the system, which set aside certain groups as more deserving than others of special privilege and protected them in concessions which they did not earn. The situation had been well solved in colleges like Amherst by offering all the upper classmen the opportunity of joining a fraternity. Suggested steps to this end were not welcomed by the Andover societies, which blindly refused to recognize the handwriting on the wall.

Having been myself in college a member of a fraternity, Alpha Delta Phi, and later for two years its national president, I was not prejudiced in any way against secret organizations as such. As I watched them in Andover, however, I could find little to justify their continued existence. The initiations lasted a week and were often physically and psychologically cruel. When in the autumn of 1933 a candidate was killed in an automobile accident while he was being driven back in an ice storm from an initiation, the faculty took decisive action, limiting the time and nature of the initiatory procedures. This for a while improved matters; but two or three instances of flagrant violations of the school rules led me to consider whether the hour had not arrived for abolishing the societies. I had met with too many cases in which a fine boy had undergone emotional disturbances because of failure to make the right society. Furthermore I was told by the admissions office that the Academy was losing each year many promising lads whose parents refused to allow them to enter a school where such institutions were tolerated.

After discussing the matter with several leading members of the faculty, I finally presented the trustees at their meeting in April 1943, with a memorandum outlining the principal arguments against the societies. The discussion was very frank, and the trustees eventually passed, without a dissenting voice, a resolution to the effect that "the existence of secret societies at Andover is not to the best interest of the school." This was implemented by a formal vote that after the close of the current year no boys should be allowed to belong to or join any social organization not authorized by the faculty.

When the former Treasurer, Jim Sawyer, heard what had happened, he wrote me, "I know you have plenty of courage, but I hope you realize how much you're going to need!" I was soon to find out how great a matter a little fire kindleth. The undergraduate officers of the societies had met to tell me that they approved of the action of the trustees, and both faculty and student body were ready to stand behind it. Within a few hours, however, the news spread to the alumni, and then the storm broke. Telegrams and telephone calls urged the undergraduate members of the societies to "hold everything." At an alumni meeting of protest it was openly asserted that the rights of the faculty had been disregarded. Thereupon the faculty held a meeting on their own initiative — at which I was not present — and voted, with only two dissenters, that "the existence of societies with restricted membership is not to the best interests of Phillips Academy."

Meanwhile the alumni reaction, heated by a few agitators, had become in some quarters both vocal and violent. Having learned of the feeling of the faculty, they changed their tactics and now charged that even though my objectives may have been good, my methods had been wrong. It soon became apparent to me that I had made a mistake in judgment — not in urging the abolition of the societies but in not consulting certain alumni members before suggesting or taking action. On the fundamental issues I undoubtedly had a majority of the graduates with me, as a huge pile of letters and telegrams proved. Representatives of newspapers and national magazines called on me to say that they would support me in what they pleased to call my crusade. The faculty continued to be behind me almost to a man. But to me the welfare of the school was all-important, and I did not wish to alienate some very honest and loyal graduates who were disturbed by the action of the trustees. Accordingly I consented to what was frankly a temporizing policy and agreed to a rescinding of the original vote until more time could be given for a study of the situation by everyone involved. The situation was tense in the late spring of 1943. Two or three of the more irate alumni made a direct attack on me at an open meeting of the trustees, alleging that I had allowed the discipline to become soft and demanding a return to the inflexible punitive rules which "had made Phillips Academy what it was." The trustees, however, took my part and defended me and what had come to be called "my policies."

Encouraged as I was by newspaper and magazine editors and by a host of friends in the educational world, I might have decided to fight the issue out then and there to the bitter end. At that moment, however, my wife's chronic illness became critical, and she died, on July 26, 1943, in the Massachusetts General Hospital. With her on my mind I simply did not have the nervous strength to carry on the battle. Furthermore Colonel Stimson, to whom I was then very close, advised, "Jack, I'm sure you're right; but I don't think that it would be wise, merely to gain an immediate victory, to risk splitting the alumni at this moment. Why don't you drop the matter for the present and give the advocates of fraternities time to get educated?" It was sensible advice, and I am glad that I followed it, even though for the moment I seemed to be yielding to pressure. More than once during the next few years the trustees and the faculty reaffirmed their original conclusions, but the time never seemed ripe for taking the drastic steps necessary for the elimination of the societies. Almost by common consent the controversy was temporarily allowed to lapse, although the faculty put into effect much stiffer controls, and even the most resentful alumni behaved as if they were resigned to the eventual abandonment of the society system. The fact that the Phillips Exeter

Academy had meanwhile abolished somewhat similar organizations on its campus was being used cogently as a lever by those who realized how detrimental to Andover the continuance of the societies was turning out to be. Finally under my successor, Dr. Kemper, and after a continuing period of publicity and education, the societies were abolished. The number of those who opposed this action when it was taken was very small indeed.

While this dispute was going on, I was occupied almost without respite with the demands of the war and later with the reconstruction of the postwar period. The termination of World War II and the resumption of normal school operations made me feel that my contribution to Phillips Academy had probably been made. The fact that Principal Lewis Perry, of Exeter, had announced his retirement in June 1946, led me to think very seriously of following his example and returning to the biographical researches which meant so much to my career. I found myself, in the happiness of my second marriage, wishing for a life less restricted by routine. I must add that, as a very personal and sensitive matter, I had been growing gradually deaf, so much so that I often could not hear what was being said in faculty and trustee meetings. I was informed by a supposedly competent specialist that I had a progressive deterioration of the auditory nerve which could not possibly improve. I experimented, not altogether successfully, with hearing aids, and found myself very unhappy over my infirmity.

On January 10, 1947, Henry W. Hobson, the Bishop of Southern Ohio, was elected to succeed Colonel Stimson as President of the Board of Trustees — a very happy choice, for not only was he a religious leader with a national reputation but he also brought to the school a vigor and a vision which in the confused postwar era were tremendously important. Before the meeting of the trustees in April I had made up my mind that I ought shortly to retire; and luckily I could talk over matters with Bishop Hobson, my close personal friend, without embarrassment. Meanwhile, however, the trustees and alumni had made plans for a financial campaign, in which, of course, I would have to play a conspicuous part. It would have been unfortunate for me to leave until that project was on its way to success. Finally, on April 19, 1947, after talking with Bishop Hobson, I wrote him a formal letter, asking to be permitted to resign on and as of July 1, 1948, on which date I should have completed forty years of connection with the school and fifteen years as its administrative head. The trustees, in turn, accepted my resignation in a series of very flattering resolutions.

My final year was a busy one. The school was soon deep in the job of raising $3,500,000 for teachers' salaries, general endowment, and a new gymnasium. During the winter the campaign was launched with a coast-to-coast radio hookup, with Bishop Hobson, Dr. Stearns, and me speaking in Andover, Boston, and New York respectively, and alumni listening at dinners in many different cities. On December 17, 1947, Bishop Hobson was able to announce the name of my successor, Lieutenant Colonel John Mason Kemper, a graduate of the United States Military Academy in 1935, with a fine record behind him. Still under forty, he was a man of high intelligence, genuine culture, and tested administrative ability. I was proud to be allowed to propose the motion electing him and gratified to have the school carried on under a gentleman of his personality and character.

The commencement in 1948 was naturally for Lulie and me a very moving occasion. The school in my final year had opened with 740 students, the second highest enrollment in its history, and 75 full-time members of the faculty. Its reputation had not fallen off in the educational world. The Andover Fund was doing well. I had just published with Mr.

Emery S. Basford, Head of the English Department, an anthology of literature on education called *Unseen Harvests.* I could still, at sixty-three, do a full day's work; indeed my speaking program for the last week in May was almost staggering. I was glad to be able to leave the scene without many too obvious symptoms of decay.

As our departure drew near, the community was very kind to us. Gifts were made to fulfill our hearts' desire: Orvis fishing rods for both of us, with a magnificent assortment of tackle; a Smith-Corona typewriter; a silver platter from the KOA Society and a very beautiful cigarette box from my fellow trustees, with their names engraved on it; a swank leather golf bag and set of matched woods from the undergraduates; and from my fellow townsmen a painting of the headmaster's house together with a leather-bound book with the signatures of hundreds of our friends. I said my farewell to the alumni at the luncheon and then to the faculty the next morning at a final meeting. I left the faculty room as they all stood and applauded, and have never since returned to it.

Within a few weeks we had moved our furniture and my precious library out of the headmaster's house. Already I had new work to do. I had been commissioned to write the biography of a fellow Amherst man, Joseph B. Eastman, who had been Interstate Commerce Commissioner and Director of Defense Transportation during the Second World War. I had been asked by the selectmen to prepare a history of the town of Andover, and I had been urged by my publishers to write my reminiscences. I was also a trustee of several schools and colleges. So for me it was a transition from one satisfactory job to another. I was eager to resume my career, such as it was, as an author.

Before we settled down again, however, we wanted one more adventure. After an autumn spent in Washington, my wife and I started on a motor trip across the continent — to

Louisville, and from there to Memphis, Little Rock, Dallas, Tucson (where we had a wonderful two weeks at the Rancho de la Osa), Indio, Palm Springs, Pasadena, Santa Barbara, Monterey, San Francisco, and back by way of Bakersfield and Phoenix to San Antonio, Houston, and the Mardi Gras at New Orleans. From there we proceeded through central Florida to our always attractive Hobe Sound, and then motored leisurely back north by way of St. Augustine, Savannah, Charleston — with a week at Yeamans Hall — Baltimore, Princeton, and then to Chestnut Hill, near Boston, which was to be — and is — our permanent home. Alternating at the wheel about every two hours, Lulie and I covered more than ten thousand miles without mishap to either of us in our Buick. In two momentous days we drove the full 1006 miles from Dallas to Tucson — for us a record!

Meanwhile I had consulted another eminent aurist, who took a less gloomy view of my deafness. A combination of wise treatment and rest in sunny climates restored my hearing so that it was in better condition than it had been in twenty years. I was told that one important factor in my recovery was relief from nervous tension and the strain of unceasing responsibility.

It would be untrue, not to say ungrateful, to deny that it was a wrench to tear myself away from Andover after living there forty years. That school community as I saw it intimately was an almost ideal society. Although nobody had very much money, most families had enough to keep them contented. Social rivalry, jealousy, and malicious gossip were rare. The men and women enjoyed their pleasant minor vices, but they were high-minded and there were no private scandals. Children were well brought up, and the people were happy in their home lives. Furthermore everybody was ready to help everybody else. If anything, the community was too seductive, and it was perhaps easy to lose one's ambition in the solid comfort of day-by-day living. I know several exceptionally gifted teachers who preferred to stay in security at Andover rather than undertake a calculated risk in a college. For a man who liked intelligent companionship, good concerts and lectures, the solace of books and outdoor exercise, it was a perfect environment.

But even while recognizing all this, I was sure that the good of the school required that it be administered by men who had not passed the Grand Climacteric. In any institution comes the hour when a change is desirable — when one can almost hear the visiting alumni asking, "I wonder who'll take the Old Man's job when he leaves?" Following the war came a deluge of new problems which needed to be handled by a relatively young leader. I shall never regret that I "got out" while I was still able to walk off the scene. Fortunately I have since been so much occupied that I have had no idle hours in which to indulge in laments. But even though I do miss the school, I am still sure that my decision to leave when and how I did was sound. My work on Andover Hill was done, and I was ready for "fresh woods and pastures new."

XX

Progress or Retrogression?

IN his *Notes Toward the Definition of Culture,* T. S. Eliot, surveying the first half of the twentieth century in these United States, summarizes his conclusions as follows: "We can assert with some confidence that our own period is one of decline; that the standards of culture are lower than they were fifty years ago; and that the evidences of this decline are visible in every department of human activity." This is a dogmatic, comprehensive, and discouraging indictment, especially to those whose postadolescent careers, like mine, have covered almost exactly this allegedly decadent segment of time. It is a trifle difficult to see how Mr. Eliot can substantiate these obiter dicta so far as preventative medicine, surgery, sanitation, and communications are concerned except by maintaining that these are not departments of human activity. But education, on any level, is assuredly such a "department," and I am therefore compelled to consider, thoughtfully and candidly, whether with the best of intentions as a schoolmaster, I have been the ally, perhaps the unconscious agent, of deterioration and decay. Everybody knows that there have been changes since 1901, but has there been any real change? Has there been advance, or just ebb and flow, or possible retrogression?

The half century under discussion has been in the independent schools — and it is these alone that I am considering — unquestionably a period of experimentation, with little tendency, except on the part of a few isolated "die-hards," to cling like a leech to tradition or to emulate Walter de la Mare's Old Jim Jay, who "got stuck fast in yesterday." On the contrary, many educators have too readily accepted novel ideas before their worth was fully manifested. I tried recently to list the trends, some obviously good, others quite clearly bad, which to my mind have been particularly noticeable. Among them, capitalized for convenience, are the Liberation of the Curriculum; the Mania for Military Preparation; the Formations of Small Sections and of Fast and Slow Divisions; the Rediscovery of Interest as a Motive; the Apotheosis of the I.Q.; the Glorification of the Aptitude Test; the Popular Demand for Individual Attention; the Rise and Decline of Progressive Education; the Relaxation of Discipline; the Concessions to Student Government; the Cumulative Menace of the Movies, Radio, and Television; the Falling Off in Voluntary Reading; the Multiplication of Records; and finally the Training for Citizenship. Doubtless others will suggest themselves readily to my pedagogical contemporaries. I have merely joted down those which, as I look back over my career, seem most significant.

Thinking only of the curriculum, I have in my time seen the course of study dominated successively by the classics, by English, by the social studies, and by mathematics and science. Each in its golden prime enjoyed the perquisites of vested interests, and each in turn has yielded primacy because of circumstances beyond its control. Just which group is now in the saddle I am not quite sure; but if a large-scale fighting war develops, it will be the mathematicians and the scientists again — and a truly fine job they did in World War II!

Discussions over the curriculum will always be a perennially engrossing pastime for teachers. For my part, I am sure that the curricular diet has, over the past fifty years, been made more palatable and profitable. In one field especially, that of

English, the substance has been vastly enriched. The school requirements in 1901, when I was a candidate for admission to college, included for intensive study *Silas Marner* and "The Ancient Mariner" (the titles of which were invariably confused in the pupils' minds), *The Vicar of Wakefield* and *The Last of the Mohicans* (strange juxtaposition), Burke's speech "On Conciliation with the Colonies," Shakespeare's *Macbeth,* and Milton's minor poems. Much of this fare was ill-suited to adolescent tastes; and gradually some of us by sheer persistence managed to persuade college admissions officers and later the College Entrance Examination Board to permit a wider selection. Especially was there reluctance from conservatives to tolerate the use as texts of any literature less than a century old. The mere suggestion that any fine contemporary novel or play might be assigned for reading was disturbing to the Old Guard. But before I had done with teaching I was asking my classes in senior English to study Hardy and Galsworthy, Masefield and Frost, as well as Dickens and Thackeray, Tennyson and Browning. By 1932 the entire atmosphere and aim of English teaching had altered for the better. We had boldly challenged the assumption that the only good book was an old book. Furthermore the modified requirements of the colleges allowed teachers to select within broad limits the literature which they liked. Consequently English classes actually became rather exciting through the substitution of choices for fixtures. The material, without losing quality, has gained in freshness and vitality.

No instructor in his right mind would ever maintain that the English classics should be ignored in the schools. Shakespeare and Wordsworth are still timeless figures in drama and in poetry. But one of the chief purposes of an English teacher should be to convince his pupils of the durable satisfactions that come from reading. Radio and television have already done their sinful best to kill the love of books; and for the instructor, through inertia, to prescribe dull material when poems and novels which are both entertaining and stimulating are available is to misuse the tools of education. Furthermore for American boys Stevenson is surely a better model for prose writing than Sir Francis Bacon or even Joseph Addison.

If the teacher has the right qualities and is willing to exert himself, he can make any subject interesting. The decline of the Greek and Roman classics has been due largely to the fact that they have too often been regarded by pedestrian instructors as a medium for drill in "forms," which has about it nothing that is inspiring. It is still true that the pedagogical artist can make even Cicero's rhetorical orations glow with light and color. I do not, however, regret the gradual abandonment of Greek and Latin in our schools, nor do I regard the movement as evidence of deterioration. For selected groups of boys and girls these ancient languages are valuable, especially for those with a linguistic aptitude. But to compel every college candidate to take Latin always seemed to be psychologically unsound. I think I am aware of all the arguments on the other side. I have certainly heard them often enough, and they have been, in my judgment, effectively refuted. For me the present trend is not regrettable, provided that the student learns one foreign language well, whether it be Latin or French or German.

Since 1901, the teaching of nearly every subject has been improved by the informality which small classroom sections of twelve or fifteen permit. Many a parent has decided to send his son to Andover or Exeter because of the excessively large classes in the local public school. In a division of fifty the average student is likely to be called upon only once, and is seldom allowed to comment or ask questions. The so-called round-table system has made each pupil an active participant in the educational process. This is particularly the case in English and the foreign languages. I am not too young to recall the old-fashioned classroom with its fixed desks and drill-hall atmosphere, where each individual student "recited," usually from memory, and then settled back, his job for the day done. At Amherst, Professor Elwell, in Greek, followed each day a mathematical figure, a square or alternate rows or the letter X, and when the members had discovered the formula, each one knew when his turn would come and conducted himself accordingly. When I was a visitor at the United States Naval Academy, I was astonished to see that a similar rigid method was in operation even in that excellent institution. Nowadays in the reputable independent schools the recitation room has become a conference room, in which teacher and taught sit at ease with one another, like the directors of the First National Bank, and discuss freely the topic of the hour. The burden upon the instructor is heavier, but in practice he has been equal to it, and the results have been gratifying. The pupil, encouraged to think as well as to repeat from memory, develops self-reliance, and even finds it difficult to go to sleep.

All this is tied up with what I earlier called the Rediscovery of Interest, as an incentive to achievement. The traditional idea was to say to the victim, "You do this — or else!" Unfortunately it was often the "else" that had to be invoked — in the old days the rod or the ruler, in those somewhat more recent, various other types of compulsion. In my experience the prizes are usually won by interested students. This is true not only of the classroom but also of life. Once a human being anywhere acquires a strong motivation, he will work his head off. To create this desire, the teacher must employ every legitimate device, unashamed to become an actor or a salesman and not disdaining the arts of the Pied Piper or the Fuller Brush man. I will back in any intellectual competition the lad who is passionately interested against one who is there because of fear — even the fear of failure. This is one of the few positive convictions which I acquired during my years of teaching. Mr. Dooley, in his discussion with Mr. Hennessey on the education of the young, quoted Father Kelly as saying, "I don't care what ye larn thim so long as 'tis onpleasant to thim." To me this is just as shocking as the more familiar "spare the rod and spoil the child" — and just as out of date. Not without physical revulsion have I stood by while certain teachers of my acquaintance undertook to pound first-year Latin into the skulls of lads whose resistance was as instinctive as it was stubborn. All that was accomplished was the creation of a bitter, lifelong hatred of it.

The sorting out of people on the basic criterion of intellectual ability or native aptitude is relatively a modern conception. The theories originated by Binet and Simon were put into large-scale practical operation in this country during World War I, where I watched the first crude experiments. The army never went further than making a very superficial appraisal of a soldier's potentialities. Later, however, when the movement had spread into the schools, a tendency developed among teachers to accept the I.Q. as an almost absolute measure of a boy's mental endowment. When once the fatal score was recorded on a card, the poor fellow was labeled for the remainder of his course, if not for life. It has been like blood pressure, about which so much that is ridiculous has been said by half-baked physicians. Nowadays the specialist knows that blood pressure may be the consequence of various factors, some of them negligible, and that to condemn a patient to an early demise solely because of his record on the sphygmomanometer is often to commit a colossal blunder. Although aptitude tests are constantly improved, they are still far from infallible. Shrewd teachers learn to spot a moron in the offing; indeed one wise headmaster once remarked, "I don't need to give any examinations to prove I'm dealing with a damned fool!" Nevertheless aptitude tests have been useful as a means of ascertaining what may be expected of a candidate for admission to school or college. As a basis for predicting future success, they still have their shortcomings.

There are so many factors which as yet cannot be accurately measured. How is a researcher to determine the relative importance of interest, already mentioned? Physical deficiencies and emotional disturbances must be considered. The vagaries of the human will cannot be ignored. The whole question of motivation needs further exploration. At one period even a modest trial of practical psychiatry was viewed with suspicion by many otherwise reasonable men. I recall how Horace Taft, dear old conservative that he was, used to poke fun at the psychologists. Once at the Headmasters Association, a spokesman for Teachers' College, generally regarded in those days as a Home for Foolish Causes, read a paper which bristled with exotic nomenclature and technical jargon. When it was over, one of the muscular Christians in our midst rose, smote his chest, and orated, "Mr. President, this is one of the most erudite articles I have ever listened to, and I move you, sir, that it be published at the expense of this Association!" That body was in its habitual state of impecuniosity. Furthermore it was not its practice to authorize the printing of papers read before it. For these and other reasons, audible moans of protest came from the audience; and Uncle Horace, sitting by my side, leaned over and ejaculated, "Why is it, Jack, that when one damned fool reads the most absurd paper I ever heard, some other damned fool has to move that it be published?"

Psychiatrists would be the first to admit that theirs is not by any means an exact science. Nevertheless one of the outstanding achievements of the last half century has been the more thorough examination, in schools, of the individual student. The Phillips Academy to which I came in 1908 was rather proud of its ruthlessness. Although admission was deceptively easy, standards were intentionally kept high. If a boy failed in his studies, little effort was made to ascertain why he was flunking. The fact was enough — and out he went! The situation is, of course, very different now. While the mesmeric slogan "Individual Attention" is too glibly used today by certain schools trying to attract patrons and I am always a bit cynical when I come across it in italics in a catalogue, I am sure that it connotes an approach which is highly important.

Compare what happens now with what happened fifty years ago. Today, when a candidate is admitted to a good independent school, we secure the fullest possible information regarding his family background and inheritance; we insist on prompt and complete physical examinations; we detect at an early date signs of deafness, of poor eyesight, and of various bodily weaknesses; we are on the watch for emotional blocks, childish inhibitions and frustrations, and delayed adolescence; we know what harm can result from unhappy conditions at home. How can a boy of sixteen concentrate on his books when he knows that his mother is in Reno getting a divorce? How can he win A's when he cannot hear what the instructor is saying? The advent of the guidance officer, under whatever title he is called, is one of the striking phenomena of our times. The chapel and the infirmary have become adjuncts of the classroom.

Some skeptics feel that we have pushed a theory too far. But in spite of complaints in some quarters that education is growing "soft," I feel that we have not gone far enough. Having seen the miracles which can be accomplished in remedial courses, I know how rich the salvage can be. Many mysteries are still to be explained and dark corners of the human mind and heart must be illuminated. The more a physician knows of his patient's history and reactions, the more reliable will be his diagnosis and the more efficacious his drugs. The relation of teacher to pupil is analogous. It is the business of some expert to find out what kind of material is entering the school and give what prescriptions are needed. We have learned that by merely "firing" a troublesome customer, the problem is not solved. Somebody, somewhere, should or must do what the institution has failed to do.

Pampering must, of course, be avoided. On every campus will be found the lazy loafers, the show-offs, and the spoiled brats — usually the flabby inheritors of special privilege — who need a literal as well as a figurative kick in the pants. The psychiatrist who spends his time prowling about in quest of possible victims can be a menace, as I have some reason to know. But educational psychologists, though they have been criticized, have made their constructive contribution to pedagogy, and the schools are better administered because of them.

All this leads naturally to a weighing of the part played by the so-called "Progressives." In April 1933, I published in *Current History* an article entitled "The Promise of Progressive Education." This was just after I had become acting headmaster, but my investigations on the subject had been carried on during the preceding autumn, when I visited several "progressive schools" and read rather widely what the leaders had to say. The Lincoln School, probably the earliest organized protest against traditional practices in education, was established in 1917, by a subsidy from the General Education Board; and by 1933 the Progressive Education Association had more than 7000 members and had for a decade published its own magazine, called *Progressive Education*. I did not doubt then, nor do I now, that the movement was a badly needed and useful crusade, particularly when it advocated, in the words of Dean Henry W. Holmes, "a substitution as far as possible of interest, enjoyment in work, and a sense of the real value of study for all ulterior motives and rewards and punishments." The Progressives at their sanest only reaffirmed the creed of the great Edward Thring, Headmaster of Uppingham School in England, when he said, "The primary object of education is to call out thought, not to load the memory — to strengthen the mind and give it versatile power — not to crush it under an accumulation of undigested facts." They insisted that the educational process need not necessarily be repellent. Jacques Barzun recently pointed out that, at the close of a thoughtful life, William James believed he had found what philosophers most wanted — it was praise! And American boys — who are certainly not all philosophers — want the same thing, or at least the opportunity to earn and deserve it. All education today has profited by the evangelism of the pioneer Progressives. Because of them the techniques of teachers everywhere have changed, and usually for the better.

Progressive education, however, has been in my judgment more successful with preadolescents than with boys and girls beyond the age of fourteen. I suppose that everybody, no matter how young or how old, is the better in character for being obliged once in a while to carry through a task which he may not like, or may even loathe. Former pupils in progressive schools have explained to me rather apologetically that they were so much entertained that they made little effort to correlate, themselves, what they had learned. The Progressive Movement unquestionably attracted a group of fanatics who by their wild utterances threw the more intelligent leaders into disrepute, as if they were guilty by association. It has been responsible for much loose talk, some preposterous ideas, and not a little sheer quackery. But it must be granted that its philosophy has profoundly affected secondary education. Unconsciously, even unwillingly, the conservatives have accepted some of the fundamental principles of the progressive doctrine, just as the Republicans have accepted several of the fundamental principles of the once despised Populist party of the 1890's. The chief reason why progressive education is so silent today is because its critics have taken over the best it had to offer.

Progressive education has been very influential in its recognition of the fine arts. The Andover of 1908, like its rival schools, was scornful of "fads and frills," such as painting and music. Now nearly every independent school has its own departments of art and music, suited to its size and budget, and several of the art galleries, like the one at Andover, are of major importance. The annual group of singing sponsored each spring by several New England schools in Boston's Symphony Hall is almost professional in quality. I am sure that thousands of boys and girls find today the most satisfying outlet for their emotions and aspirations through the channels of the fine arts.

As a corollary, participation in these pleasing activities is no longer regarded as the prerogative of sissies. One may see a muscular discus thrower posing for his mates in the art studio or the captain of the wrestling team playing the violin in the orchestra. Undergraduates boast of their collections of phonograph records, read the "Recordings Section" of the *Saturday Review,* and obviously enjoy listening to a sonata or a symphony. I do not deny that much of the evidence as we see it in the Museum of Modern Art or listen to it from the juke boxes in Howard Johnson's restaurants rather justifies Mr. Eliot in his pessimism. But the American schoolboy should not be blamed for these aberrations.

Some laudators of the Good Old Days deplore what they describe as the current relaxation of discipline in the schools and maintain also that manners have deteriorated. I cannot myself honestly say that I have noticed any marked falling off. The eating habits of boys, except when they are under unremitting supervision, tend to lapse into the barbaric. When not compelled to appear properly dressed the average undergraduate prefers sloppy clothes, as he did when I was an undergraduate. In morals we have learned that an indiscretion is not necessarily a sin. Rules about smoking have been modified because they could not be enforced. When at Andover in 1913 the faculty decided by a close vote to permit the boys to play tennis on Sunday afternoon, one kindly old teacher warned his associates that the school was on the direct road to hell. He lived to tell me that he had been wrong. Even he perceived that the national mores had changed.

As for discipline, I gladly concede that it is less rigid than it was, but I personally feel that the trend towards a just flexibility is a step in progress. We still have with us advocates of clearly stated rules arbitrarily enforced, without regard for explanations or excuses, and I respect them for their consistency and sincerity. But when headmasters begin to consider the real function of a penalty like expulsion, they are confronted with paradoxes. After we began at Andover to consider each disciplinary case "on its merits" and therefore to use the extreme punishment less freely, the number of offenders actually dropped off. Much of campus misconduct is the consequence not of a sinful nature but of high spirits, and must not be confused with depravity. The headmaster of one of our most famous schools confided to me that on the night before his graduation from school he deliberately went out of his dormitory without permission — an offense for which "firing" was the recognized penalty — merely because he "felt good." Fortunately he was undetected, and went on his way rejoicing, with his diploma in his hand. If he had been expelled, he might never have gone to college, and the Headmasters Association would have lost one of its brightest luminaries.

Some of the worst undergraduate hellions that I ever knew have later turned into the most exacting of parents, just as some of the poorest scholars constantly harass their offspring for not making *cum laude*. Once when I was chatting informally with the Student Council in my library, a boy showed me a letter from his father, almost vicious in tone, castigating him unmercifully for his faults. "I taught your father," said I, "let's look up his record in his class yearbook." The young fellow began turning the pages and suddenly started to laugh. "What's funny?" I asked. "Look here, Mr. Fuess," he replied. "Dad had the largest vote for Biggest Bluffer in the Classroom. I've got him now!"

Student government, or student participation, is much more widespread than it was fifty years ago, and I wish I could be certain that this trend is for the better. The practice varies greatly, depending on the school. In one small academy with which I am acquainted, the Student Council sits in on all cases of discipline and has a voice in the final decision. In others, the council serves as an intermediary between the administration and the undergraduates, in a sense of interpreting one to the other. The dangers of granting students power over their own number are considerable. Boys between the ages of fourteen and eighteen are seldom qualified by experience or habits of thought to form judgments on such matters. The student code of morals and conduct is often different from that of the faculty, and the establishment of common ground is difficult. The success of student government is likely to depend on the quality of the undergraduate leaders for any one particular year, and also on the attitude of the faculty representatives, which may be narrow-minded and uncompromising.

In comparing yesterday with today, older teachers tell me mournfully that the reading of their pupils has fallen off. Instructors cannot count now even on a knowledge of the exploits of David and Samson, to say nothing of Ivanhoe and Robinson Crusoe and Jim Hawkins. The fascination of the movies and radio, and more recently of television, has lured boys and girls away from books. Even upper-class families no longer possess libraries, and the young peoples' periodicals are much inferior to *The Youth's Companion* and *St. Nicholas* and others of their type which flourished in my childhood. The normal grammar school boy, forced to stay indoors on a rainy day, used to seek solace in the printed page. If his rugged tastes disdained the Rollo stories and *Little Lord Fauntleroy,* he might pursue adventure with those thrilling individualists, Diamond Dick or Frank Merriwell or Nick Carter; but at least he was forming a good habit. Some of my friends see no great harm in our more modern diversions. However it is difficult to persuade a confirmed bibliophile that the old recreations were not, on the whole, more beneficial than the new. It was certainly better for a robust lad to get excited over *The Three Musketeers* or *The Master of Ballantrae* than to waste an evening watching female wrestlers or the slapstick comedy of the screen. My younger readers may charge this off to senile prejudice — and forget it!

The needs of military preparation have not operated steadily in recent years, but the schools have seldom been allowed to forget them. For boys who must expect to serve their country in the armed forces, mathematics and science seem indispensable. The ability to repeat the magical lines of the "Ode to a Nightingale," commendable though it may have been in the peaceful 1900's, is in wartime not so much needed as skill in mechanics or an understanding of atomic energy. This is the tragedy of our present younger generation — they must for their own preservation focus their minds on the instruments of destruction. This need did not exist fifty years ago, nor was it paramount until the Kaiser and Adolf Hitler started their mad careers and tore down the walls of our western culture. Here practical considerations, including the matter of personal and national safety, have effected a new arrangement of values.

One by-product of our more detailed study of the boy has been the multiplication of records, until a boy's dossier at eighteen may be almost a volume. Schools are top heavy with administrative officers, who unfortunately usually receive higher salaries than the teachers. English headmasters who visit us are astounded by the amount of paper work, the infinite number of memorandums, the thick files of directives, the rows of typists sitting at their desks, the throng of deans and assistant deans and secretaries. Things were simpler, and certainly less expensive, in the days when the teacher and his pupils had it out together, off the record. When I was a headmaster and rang for a student's file, it might be two inches thick, filled with one report after another, with comments from instructors and house masters and coaches. Then I realized that, with perfectly good intentions, I was responsible for this avalanche. I wanted to know all about the boy, and these people were telling me, each in a different way and from a different viewpoint. Was I wrong or right in helping to create such a mountainous weight of evidence about a youngster just escaping from his teens?

To turn once more to the credit side, perhaps the most significant and fruitful development of the last half century, in both public and independent schools, has been what might be called vaguely "training for citizenship." This begins naturally with sound instruction in American history and in the processes and purposes of government. This historical background is supplemented by frequent references to current problems, events, and personalities, with stress on debating and the discussion of live issues. Another aspect is the encouragement of community responsibility, granting as much self-government and freedom of decision as the maturity of the students will justify. The social conscience is aroused through charity drives, work in boys' clubs and camps, and active participation in philanthropic organizations. Through church and chapel and assembly as well as through talks by authorities in their respective fields the best schools try to bring their students into touch with the complicated society which they will soon join as workers, and it is to be hoped, as contributors.

Our newspapers, except for the always welcome *Christian Science Monitor,* assign large amounts of space to juvenile delinquency and teen-age gangsters, and "hot-rod" adolescents. But even these menaces existed at the turn of the century, although their weapons and their methods may have been different. Vandals desecrated graveyards, hoodlums broke into schoolhouses, and the Andover and Exeter undergraduates burst out into occasional riots. I am inclined to think that in this respect the times are really better. My predecessor, Dr. Stearns, once rashly remarked in morning chapel that the boys of that period (the 1920's) were tamer than those of his own childhood in the 1880's. They had, he complained, lost their initiative, their imagination, their vitality. His words were received at the moment with exquisite courtesy. But within the next twenty-four hours more hell was raised on Andover Hill than had taken place within the memory of the oldest inhabitant. Curbstones were shifted; signs were torn down; the skeleton was removed from the biological laboratory and suspended from a tree. The next morning Al, whose sense of humor never deserted him, stood up and said, "All right, boys, let's call it off! I take back my rash words. The present generation has vindicated itself—and now we'll go back to peace." There was prolonged applause, and the incident was closed.

It is charged intermittently by superpatriots that the faculties and undergraduate bodies of our independent schools are "shot full of communism," or "tinged with pink." I am not sure that I should recognize a Communist if I met one, although I have conversed with two or three who have been labeled as such by other people. We had on the Andover teaching staff several Democrats — which I know is very bad — even some who voted for F.D.R. — which apparently is worse. I have even heard of some headmasters who don't like Senator McCarthy. But as I have watched teachers through two world wars, as I have listened to their talks in chapel, as I have heard them on the public platform, I doubt whether we have, even in the Senate of the United States, a more genuinely loyal group.

In a school not very far from Boston a real-live Communist was invited by an undergraduate organization to come and speak to them. He delivered his address with a good deal of noisy eloquence. Then the boys bombarded him with questions. They refuted his arguments, proved that he had misquoted his authorities, and sent him back discomfited, with the remark, "Those damned kids are just like a swarm of mosquitoes." That's the best way to deal with communism, or indeed totalitarianism in any form. It cannot long stand up against the truth.

I am always troubled, on the other hand, when the undergraduates are too conservative, too much ruled by the politics of their middle-aged fathers. It is good for human beings to be liberal in their youth. I have never forgotten Robert Louis Stevenson's comment: "It is as natural and right for a young man to be imprudent and exaggerated, to live in swoops and circles, and beat about his cage like any other wild thing newly captured, as it is for old men to turn gray, or mothers to love their offspring, or heroes to die for something worthier than their lives." It would be no sign of progress if the boys of today were staid and hidebound and unrebellious. Mental ossification before twenty is a paralyzing disease which no antibiotic can eradicate.

We oldsters must beware of forming the habit of complaining about the Younger Generation. The recent revival of the books of the late F. Scott Fitzgerald has recalled memories of the 1920's and of what Gertrude Stein called the Lost Generation, symbolized by the obnoxious John Held "flapper" and the coonskin-coated "Joe College." At the time they were denounced by moralists as degenerates. Where are they now? They have recently been celebrating their twenty-fifth reunion and contributing liberally to the college till. The "Prom Girls" of *This Side of Paradise* are now plump matrons in middle life, sending their children off to summer camp, doing their own work in their kitchens, and often teaching in Sunday School; and the former raucous flask-toters are now cheery members of Rotary Clubs and pass the collection plate in the First Presbyterian Church.

Obviously we haven't reached the millennium yet, nor is it even visible beyond the horizon. I wish that the better independent schools could keep their tuition rates within the reach of professional people — the lawyers and doctors and clergymen and government officials who transmit such rich culture to their children. I wish that we could find a way to subsidize very promising boys and girls from poor families through preparatory school and college. I wish that parents would demonstrate by their own examples the manners and morals which they expect teachers to impress upon their offspring. I wish that all teachers were as self-sacrificing, and as stimulating, as some of them are. I wish, above all, that we could have a wider acceptance of the doctrine that the independent school is run primarily for the benefit of its pupils.

We shall reach these and other desirable objectives in due course, if we strive hard enough for them. Taking the long view, I just cannot be pessimistic. Many of my contemporaries in business or law or government have less hope than I do. They feel that one constructive era of human society may have reached its peak, and that we are entering with tragic inevitability and unawareness on another Dark Age. Having been so long surrounded by youthful minds and located in the midst of youthful vitality, I cannot share their gloom. Boys are, after all, impulsive, inexperienced animals, in need of guidance, although they may not admit it. It is the task of the teacher to find out what they are like, encourage their aspirations and implement their dreams, sympathize with their growing pains, and lead them on the slow path to maturity. The thoughtful teacher is bound to take a long-range view of man's gradual evolution from the brute.

Most "isms" are to be condemned, but there are two — altruism and optimism — for which I have a liking, and we could do with more of both. Even as we grope out of darkness, let us count our blessings. Gazing from my sexagenarian pinnacle, I can look back and perceive that, on the whole, American education is better than it was.

XXI

"There Is Hope!"

SOME danger is inherent in either judgment or prophecy, but most of all in prophecy. Writing in 1905 concerning John Hay's record as Secretary of State, Henry Adams said, "For the first time in fifteen hundred years a true Roman *pax* was in sight and would, if it succeeded, owe its virtues to him." In the closing sentences of his great *Education*, Adams expressed the desire that Clarence King, John Hay, and he might return to earth in 1938, their centenary year, and "perhaps then, for the first time since man began his education among the carnivores, they would find a world that sensitive and timid natures could regard without a shudder." Actually in 1939, when Adams had been dead only two decades, Adolf Hitler, already on his aggressive march, had absorbed Austria and carried out his Czechoslovakian coup, and a new global war, far more devastating than that of 1914–1918, was inescapable. Adams, if he could have stepped from eternity into time, would doubtless have resumed his philosophic pessimism as the only logical attitude towards the world and its future. No Golden Age could have been in sight.

In this example of mistaken prediction is a warning which any schoolmaster would do well to heed. Since Adams wrote his words, the Idea of Progress, so widespread among the Cheerful Victorians and so well expressed by Tennyson and Browning, has been discredited. It has been a long time since any Pippa has sung at dawn:

God's in his heaven,
All's right with the world.

Writers like Arnold Toynbee have made us feel that what has seemed like advancement has been only oscillation, and that newer civilizations will rise and fall like waves, as they have done in the past. It may literally be true of our own western culture that

The cloud-capp'd towers, the gorgeous palaces,
The solemn temples, the great globe itself,
Yes, all that it inherit, shall dissolve
And like this insubstantial pageant faded,
Leave not a rack behind.

With us, portents have not been lacking. The populace of Egypt and Babylon and Rome knew little of earlier centuries and probably went illusioned to their doom. We in the twentieth century, with our wealth of archeological knowledge and our acquaintance with recorded history, may be consciously watching our gradual disintegration, as the passengers on a launch might observe their drift towards some loud-heralded Niagara, partly in disbelief, partly in stupefaction, and partly in resignation to the inevitable.

It is the unwillingness to struggle which is so disturbing. It looks as if the ruin of two world wars had taken the heart out of humanity. Over the half century through which I have lived, many of the leaders of my generation have lost the racial will to survive. This gloomy mood has been expressed in much of our art, our music, and our poetry, to say nothing of our philosophy. Under these circumstances, what can one whose life has been spent in schoolmastering have on his mind?

H. G. Wells, in the closing chapter of his *Outline of History,* says in one of his characteristic obiter dicta, "Human history becomes more and more a race between education and catastrophe." This was written just after the First World

War, before Mussolini and Hitler and Stalin had shown the full horrors of totalitarianism. Now we know, if we did not before, that everything depends on the type of education and that education misused may be the prelude to tyranny. A regimented education, directed and employed by a dictator, is not only of no value in averting disaster, it may even create disaster. Only when education produces free citizens does it become a possible protection against the destruction of our civilization.

One of the perils in the United States today is a sinister form of chauvinism which would regiment our education in what it conceives to be the interests of the state, as Hitler did and Stalin is doing. "If I had my way," said a man in my presence at a club table in New York last winter, "every growing child would be taught the evils which FDR brought upon this country." Whatever we may think of the New Deal, it is easy to see what secondary education in America might become in the hands of a dogmatist like that. Even now, in small communities, loud-mouthed demagogues cause trouble. If the control were national in scope, the opportunity for rabble-rousing legislators in Washington would be unlimited.

I may as well say at once that after living for more than forty years in the midst of young Americans from all levels of society, I am not afraid to trust them with ideas. If good ideas cannot hold their own in open debate with allegedly bad ideas, the bad ones deserve to win. We shall never produce leaders by bringing up our youth ignorant of communism and fascism and nihilism and all the other pernicious doctrines which thrive on misery as buzzards grow fat on carrion. It is the completely cloistered boys and girls who succumb to vicious propaganda. The surest way to keep a young man straight is not to fence him in or wrap him in cotton wool but to teach him how to think. In this way he builds up a defense within himself. He may fumble, he may make foolish mistakes, but through his blunders he will gain strength. When I hear that communism is gaining ground in our schools, I do not believe it. Tell the pupils all the truth, and let Communists do their worst. Children who have been trained to weigh evidence are in little danger of corruption.

In a democracy like ours education can outrun catastrophe, if only we proceed on right principles. Clearly most of the work must be carried on in the public schools where such a large proportion of our children must be trained. In this field others can speak with far more authority than I. The public school system in the United States has been subjected to close scrutiny, and its weaknesses have frequently been exposed. I am more impressed, however, by its extraordinary accomplishment against many obvious handicaps. Generalizations over such a vast area can have little real validity. Some public schools, like those in Newton or Scarsdale or Winnetka, have high standards; others, in industrial centers, find it difficult to assimilate the heterogeneous population. I have, however, met a considerable number of high school principals and school superintendents and believe that as a group they deserve high praise. They are not, as a rule, too well paid; they are subject to a kind of community scrutiny which can be most annoying; they have in some cities too little personal freedom; and they have no choice in the selection of their pupils. Nevertheless each year they turn out a body of Americans who have at least an acceptable intellectual foundation on which, with the right motivation, they can build useful careers.

I feel much more at home in discussing the part which the private, or independent, schools can play in averting catastrophe. Here again, however, generalizations, though tempting, are hazardous, but I should like to indulge myself in a few observations based on experience. The independent schools are few numerically and take care of only a fraction of the population. It is disconcerting to a headmaster who thinks that his school is a great American institution to discover that it is completely unknown to citizens of Memphis or Des Moines. They do, however, vary widely in size and procedure, and there are enough to satisfy almost any taste or demand, even though it may be unusual. We have in the East the traditional democratic academy, the boarding school on the English model, the parochial school, the country-day school, the tutoring school, and others created for special requirements. The range in cost is extreme, from $700 at Mount Hermon to $2100 at Lawrenceville. Some are small, with a local or limited constituency; others are large and national in their outlook. Some draw their students almost entirely from the so-called upper classes; others gladly admit poor boys and offer them financial assistance. Some send virtually all their graduates to college; others prepare their students chiefly for business. A glance through Sargent's indispensable *Handbook of Private Schools* will leave the reader amazed at the lack of homogeneity and the almost infinite variety displayed. The institutions mentioned differ in their internal organization, in their codes of discipline, in their curriculums, in their religious affiliations, in the salaries they pay their teachers, and chiefly in their headmasters.

Nearly all of them were originally established from the worthiest of motives and are operated not for profit. Usually public-spirited benefactors furnished the necessary funds, and their only reward could come from the conviction that their schools were providing exceptional training for individual students and thus making a contribution to society. The private school developed in an atmosphere of *laissez-faire* which made its survival dependent on its ability to meet a need and allure customers. The analogy with storekeeping is not far-fetched. In any community there is bound to be competition among shops. Those which have a pleasing array of commodities, a tactful staff of salespeople, and a reputation for giving satisfaction are bound to do better than those which are sloppily managed. If the service is poor or the supply of goods inadequate, the store will ultimately give up the ghost. The independent school is in precisely the same situation. No matter how large its resources, it must have students. The school which draws nobody to its classrooms has no reason for existence.

The private schools through their individuality offer a healthy corrective to overmuch standardization and allow parents to choose deliberately the type of education which they wish for their children. One can never be quite sure what leads a father to select a school for his son. Obviously if a boy wishes to study Greek, he will seek out an institution where Greek is taught. If he is interested in the fine arts, he will examine catalogues to discover what instruction is provided in that field. Once at Andover a charming senior named Fred Hudson came to the headmaster's house for tea. My wife, to make conversation, inquired how he happened to come to Andover. Fred thought a minute and then replied, "I don't see why I shouldn't tell you. My father read an article in *Fortune* on famous American schools. Andover and two other schools were mentioned first, and my father thought, therefore, that they must be the best. Then he studied the photographs of Mr. Fuess and those of the other headmasters and finally turned to me and said, 'Son, you're going to Andover!' My curiosity was aroused, and I asked, 'That's all right with me, but why did you pick Andover over the others?' My Dad came right back, 'Because this man Fuss has a gentler face.' " It was indeed a strange reason for making a crucial decision, but it enabled me later to announce that although mine was not "the face that launched a thousand ships," it did bring at least one boy to Phillips

Academy. Hudson went to West Point, made a brilliant record as a soldier, and died fighting gallantly in Korea.

The private schools which are not equipped for competition have plenty of troubles. Many of the old New England academies, conceived in hope, had a few promising years and then perished of sheer inanition. Their abandoned buildings may still be seen, the shingles falling off, the grass and weeds growing tall around the porch, and the brick mottled by many a winter storm. Of the scores of independent schools in this country a considerable number are usually on the borderline financially between black and red, and are liable to be wiped out by any sudden drop in revenue. The old established ones, with adequate endowments and strong bodies of alumni, can sit tight, confident that they need no showy advertising. But there are many which, on August first, are never quite sure whether they will be full for the coming year.

While the headmaster is always an important factor, the larger schools like Andover and Exeter rely on efficient organization. In the smaller ones the personality of the head may make the difference between success and failure, and an autocracy, if it is reasonably benevolent, may be the most desirable form of government. Horace Taft used to tell with a chuckle the story about the old fellow who started a rural academy in Connecticut in the far-off days when the little red schoolhouse had no discipline and if the boys could thrash the teacher, it was regarded as a good joke. This new principal had his own conception of how a school should be run. On the first day a big bully started to make trouble and was promptly warned that if he did not subside he would be expelled. The next morning the boy repeated the offense and to his astonishment was told to go home and stay there. The irate father then appeared and protested. The principal never yielded an inch, and finally the exasperated parent burst out,

"As far as I can see you expect to do what you damned please with this school." The old pedagogue blinked and replied, "Your language is coarse and your manners offensive — but you have grasped the idea!" Legends of this kind indicate that individuality in a headmaster is regarded as a virtue.

From time to time somebody accuses the independent schools of being snobbish or complacent or provincial. It would be foolish to assert that these disagreeable characteristics do not exist, but I am sure that they are diminishing year by year. Even the most aristocratic schools cannot now afford to be socially exclusive. As for smugness, it carries with it its own penalty.

The independent schools can provide educational facilities for only a small proportion of the population. Considerations of space would in themselves prevent any such possibility. To some extent, then, and without intending to do so, they convey the impression of an aristocracy rather than a democracy. But any charge of special privilege can have little to sustain it. Even if they could afford the additional cost, many parents would not choose an independent school for their sons. Furthermore college admissions officers have made it clear that not all their preferred candidates come from private institutions.

The independent schools enjoy certain cherished privileges. They are relieved, like hospitals, from various forms of taxation, and they are exempt in most cases from community control. They can set and maintain their own standards without interference from any outsider. They can require attendance at religious exercises without any penalty except the withdrawal of pupils whose consciences are disturbed. It may well be asked by the general public whether these schools have deserved their immunities. Have they really, through the education which they provide for their pupils, been in any sense a bulwark against catastrophe?

Have they done as much for America as the famous public schools like Winchester, Harrow, and Rugby have done for England? Probably not — for the proportion of British statesmen trained at the public schools has been amazingly high. The tradition that Waterloo was won on "the playing fields of Eton," whether valid or not, illustrates the attitude of many intelligent Englishmen regarding the old school tie. No such myth has ever grown up in the United States.

On the other hand, the independent schools have no cause to be ashamed of their product. When a writer in *Fortune* magazine wrote categorically that our independent schools "have failed to arouse the admiration of the American people because the number of famous Americans who have sat in their classrooms is so small as to be embarrassing," he stirred up a nest of sensitive educational hornets. Andover retaliated with Samuel F. B. Morse, Oliver Wendell Holmes, and Henry L. Stimson; Exeter spoke proudly of Daniel Webster, Edward Everett, and Thomas W. Lamont; Groton, in existence only since 1884, mentioned Franklin D. Roosevelt, Dean Acheson, and Averill Harriman. An investigation of *Who's Who in America* for 1934–1935 showed that one Andover graduate out of thirty-five was listed in that publication while the ratio in the nation at large was one out of four thousand. The defenders of the independent schools on the basis of these statistics alone had a strong argument.

It is not essential for my thesis that I should prove that our private schools have turned out an exceptionally large number of cabinet members and Congressmen and judges. The list could be made impressive and perhaps astonishing. But the important fact is that the best of the independent schools, with their interest in the development of character, have been turning out good citizens. Among their graduates are drones — men who loaf through school and college, inherit wealth, and then spend their days in club windows or on Florida beaches, railing at the government and doing nothing to improve it. But the percentage is extraordinarily high across the continent of persons who in their communities are identified with good causes and are proud to serve the state. I think I know something of the heads and the faculties of these schools and what they are trying earnestly to do. In sincerity, perseverance, enthusiasm, and idealism they can hold their own with the representatives of any other profession.

In the long run the success of a school will be determined not by its buildings or its playing fields or even its library or chapel but by the quality of its teachers. It is axiomatic that we cannot expect in our somewhat sophisticated society the motivation which in the early nineteenth century led boys to walk a hundred miles to enter a school like Andover or which arose from the belief that a college degree necessarily means power. Nowadays teaching must be more than the presentation of ideas. It is the kindling by one glowing spirit of a flame in those who are under him. If the fire is already laid with kindling ready for lighting, so much the better. If it is not, the instructor must do the warming himself, and if he fails to try, he has not performed his duty.

A bored teacher will obviously have a bored class. On the other hand, vitality is infectious and acts like yeast to make dullards rise into animation. The young are quick to recognize and respond to any signs of essential humanity in a teacher. He can do little if his pupils do not perceive in him a person constructed like themselves, somewhat older and more scarred, but still struggling in the toils of half-truths and doubts, and still seizing every opportunity to learn. Cases may exist where austerity and studied aloofness make a teacher seem like a demigod, with the aura which comes from remoteness. But in the end he will accomplish more if he displays the attributes of a common man and not of a "very superior person."

Dr. Stearns was once conducting an opulent industrialist over the Andover campus and on the way introduced him to several of the masters. As his visitor was saying good-by at the Inn, Stearns asked a conventional question, "What impressed you most about the school?" The reply was entirely unconventional, "I was struck by the fact that several of your teachers looked as though they could earn a living in some other job." The answer was indicative of the businessman's attitude towards what he is sometimes pleased to call "starry-eyed idealists," and therefore is worth quoting. But there is no question that the average undergraduate likes a professor who could have been successful in journalism or banking or insurance, but who preferred to teach. An exceptionally gifted teacher once told me — in strict confidence — that if he could not get a salary for his services he would be glad to pay the school for letting him retain his position. This crusader would have set an example of which, as a former practitioner, I cannot publicly approve, but it must be admitted that such a glorious missionary spirit is as commendable as it is uncommon. No profession requires such consecration, such long-continued and unfaltering devotion. A teacher without this dedication is as uninspiring as a flat tire.

I once tried to paint a word portrait of the ideal teacher as I have seen him functioning in an independent school, and I venture to repeat it here because it sums up what I have to say on the subject:

> He should be intelligent but not pedantic, dignified but not pompous, firm but not intolerant. He should be young enough to remember his boyhood but old enough to have put aside childish things. With all his scholarship, he should be aware that it would be a one-sided world if all his pupils turned out teachers, like himself. He should not be ashamed to possess or disclose his ideals, but should temper them with practicality. He should be able, outside his own bailiwick, to mix with other people on even terms, without supercilious-

> ness, self-consciousness, or timidity. He should be able to maintain at all costs his patience, his sympathy, and his sense of humor, and be willing to laugh first of all at himself. If, in addition, he has energy and optimism, he should be able to secure and hold a position and leave behind him a place in the memories of the alumni. It will make little difference where such a man functions, whether in a gorgeous lecture hall or in an ancient classroom, with the desks carved by generations of undergraduates. He may never be awarded a medal or an honorary degree, but his spirit will remain alive long after his body rests in the local cemetery.

It will have been discerned that I have little faith in the efficacy of a "cloistered virtue." One of the objections to certain phases of modern education is that they have little relationship to life in the twentieth century. We should send our sons and grandsons out from school equipped to cope with the problems of the world of Eisenhower and Stalin and Winston Churchill and Nehru — not merely for those of some picturesque Utopia or imaginary Golden Age. There should be no course in the high school curriculum which cannot be fitted into a pattern for living.

But I am equally dubious about strictly vocational training. It is a truism that education should teach a boy not so much how to make a living as how to live. Einstein expressed this well when he said, "The school should have as its aim that the young man leave it as a harmonious personality, not as specialist." And added, "The development of general ability for independent thinking and judgment should always be placed foremost, not the acquisition of special knowledge." At a recent symposium at Kirkland House, at Harvard, a young Grotonian declared that his father had complained because Groton had taught his son nothing which would help him to become financially independent. "How can I answer him?" he inquired. I went through the appearance of solemn meditation and finally replied, "Remind him that life is still more than meat and the body more than raiment." "But he won't understand that," commented the young man. "Very well," I could only conclude, "he's the one that needs educating — not you!"

Most independent schools have openly and ardently stressed the development of character as their chief objective. The written constitutions of the two Phillips Academies at Andover and Exeter declare as a basic principle that "Knowledge without Goodness is dangerous," thus anticipating the great Dr. Arnold by many years. Furthermore these schools have always emphasized the importance of the social as well as the moral and ethical qualities in prospective citizens. The type of undergraduate in whom I used to put the most confidence was the one who had brains enough to secure A-plus grades if he devoted himself exclusively to the business of winning high marks, but who chose instead to spend some time in gregarious pursuits — athletics or journalism or debating — and therefore got only B's. If this seems heretical, the agreement of many of my contemporaries has made it almost orthodoxy. I do not believe that intelligence alone, unsupported by spiritual motivation, will enable education to outrun catastrophe.

Nevertheless it is also my conviction that the independent schools could do much more for the Bright Boy — the student who, under the right conditions, is capable of advancing faster than the average lad of his own age. We have done, and are doing, much to reclaim the mental outcasts and strengthen the weaker brethren. As a corollary of the democratic process, educational theory and practice, particularly in the public schools, have been adjusted to the needs of the so-called normal child; and no enlightened sociologist can doubt the importance of giving the future voter the foundation for forming his opinions. Unfortunately, however, the abler boys and girls are frequently held back, with serious danger to their morale. Psychologists have long been convinced that, allowing for the inevitable and dramatic exceptions, the child of high mentality is also likely to be the one with the most sensitive conscience and the best behavior. In spite of the antisocial character of an occasional Bright Boy, it is the more intelligent men and women who will save us — if we are destined to be saved. The independent schools, if they choose to do so, can do much through fast divisions and other devices to stimulate the student who wishes to go farther and faster than his fellows.

It is gratifying to find the Ford Foundation interested in reducing the waste of time in our American schools. President Lowell, of Harvard, always insisted that the Bright Boys were the young boys. Every teacher knows of countless cases where quick-witted lads of sixteen can answer glibly the questions over which the husky eighteen-year-old football players stumble. I certainly would not wish to see these slower pupils neglected, particularly because their steadiness and social maturity are so valuable in an undergraduate body. But any time saved in the period of formal education leaves the beneficiaries so much more opportunity for actual living.

Without laboring the point, let me suggest that a boy of superior ability graduating from Andover or Milton often finds himself repeating quite unnecessarily in his freshman year at Harvard or Yale the work of his senior year at school. Even with average boys and girls, a year could be saved by more careful dovetailing and an avoidance of repetition and duplication. Just a little co-operation between headmasters and freshmen deans is all that is required to enable physicians to start practice at twenty-eight instead of twenty-nine, without in any degree lowering the quality of preparation. Our schools could well install a high gear as well as a low one.

I have a deep-rooted respect for what the independent schools in the United States have done to protect and improve our civilization. I wish, however, that the privileges which they enjoy would lead them to more experimentation. The great virtue of our people in the early stages of their development was their pioneering spirit, their willingness to accept a calculated risk. The danger that we may now have reached a premature conservatism is greater than we realize. The American has always been at his best in blazing trails and broadening roads, not in standing firm and shouting:

Come weal, come woe,
My status *is* quo.

I am reminded also that education does not always have its source in schools and colleges, however excellent they may be. Books and lectures are important, of course, but so are travel and hardship and worship and love and all the diversified phenomena of our earthly pilgrimage. Some cynic has contributed the definition, "Education is that which remains after one has forgotten everything that he learned at school." But we are literally, I suspect, a part of all that we have met, although why one impact should be soul-shaking and another infinitesimal has never been fully explained. Towards the formation of a mature personality many elements may combine — not only the reminiscences of the classroom but also, perhaps, a movement in Beethoven's *Fifth Symphony,* a portrait by Velasquez in the Prado, a sermon by Bishop Oxnam on the text, "At midnight, Paul and Silas sang," a play like *Gentleman's Agreement,* a view from the Gorner Grat towards the Matterhorn, the Saint-Gaudens statue of Nirvana in Rock Creek Cemetery, a vesper service in King's College Chapel, the national anthem played at Arlington on Armistice Day, the smile on the face of a dying friend. Trifling items survive by some miracle when those which have been overemphasized are forgotten. Words uttered thoughtlessly have echoed down the ages. Whatever character we possess is a composite of experiences blended and unified by a power over which we have no control. And in the end we are what we are, and can only wish that we might have been better.

As I drew near to the close of my active professional career as a schoolmaster, I tried to sum up some of my conclusions, which were eventually published as "The Educational Creed of Phillips Academy." Because I am still prepared to stand by it, I shall beg nobody's pardon for quoting again from myself:

> Andover wants each boy in its charge to know the world around him, its history, its material structure, its problems. Andover tries to help him to carry on effectively his business affairs; to collect and weigh evidence, to think logically, to reach impartial conclusions, and to express them with some degree of clarity, precision, and force; to sympathize in more than a sentimental way with the poor, the sick and the oppressed of all lands; to comprehend the motives, the desires, and the hopes of men; to understand and practice the duties and responsibilities of good citizenship; to appreciate and love beauty in all its varied forms; to develop a sense of values so that he can distinguish the trivial from the important, the ephemeral from the durable; and finally to enter and explore the mysterious realm of the spirit, to move from the temporal to the things that are eternal.

For this statement I claim no especial originality. It does, however, represent the philosophy which, after many years of learning and teaching, I was attempting to carry out. If I were to amplify it at all, it would be to add that education must include religion. I do not mean necessarily creeds and dogmas, although I have for them much respect. I do mean, however, a faith in God and Man, such as that expressed in the Great Commandments, on which hang all the law and the prophets. I suppose that I was so filled with the Idea of Progress that I cannot abandon it. I believe, almost in spite of the evidence, that man is working upward from the brute and that this cannot be a meaningless universe. Perhaps Tennyson was right when he declared that the Golden Age of man's desiring lies neither in the past nor in the future, but that

> *Unto him who works and feels he works,*
> *This same grand year is ever at the doors.*

Nor does it weaken my faith to read the gruesome crimes publicized in our newspapers or to listen to the devil's advocate as he introduces the arguments for pessimism. As I type this, ninety cadets at West Point have been expelled for cribbing, and more scandals have been uncovered in the "basketball racket." Even a retired headmaster knows that many Americans are selfish and corrupt, and that the New York taxicab driver was right when he described our national motto as "Hurrah for me! To hell with you!" Teen-agers are performing as they always have performed since Cain and Rameses II and Augustus Caesar were adolescents. Sexual degeneracy is receiving wide publicity. Literature and art are said to have reached a new low in frankness and vulgarity. There is ample material for a satirist — as there was in the days of Aristophanes and Juvenal and Swift.

Of all this I am not unaware, but I am sure that in our discouragement we are merely repeating a perennial human mood. As a schoolmaster I saw another side of the picture. Here were young men who were not lewd or cynical or perverted; who honestly, if not too articulately, were trying to help their fellows; who enlisted in wars to save the civilization that they knew; who very humbly had resolved to devote themselves to some form of public service. It is no shallow optimism which leads me to believe that leaders trained as these and other young Americans have been may win ultimately the race between education and catastrophe. If they with their inherent fine qualities and training can't do it, I fear that we are lost indeed.

Index